Brewe...
Hertford...

Brewers in Hertfordshire

DR ALLAN WHITAKER

UNIVERSITY OF HERTFORDSHIRE PRESS

First published in Great Britain in 2006 by

Hertfordshire Publications
an imprint of the University of Hertfordshire Press
Learning and Information Services
University of Hertfordshire
College Lane
Hatfield
Hertfordshire AL10 9AB

Hertfordshire Publications
an imprint of the University of Hertfordshire Press
is published on behalf of the Hertfordshire Association for Local History

British Library Cataloguing in Publication Data
A catalogue record for this book is available from the British Library

ISBN 0-9542189-7-3

Design by Geoff Green Book Design, CB4 5RA
Cover design by John Robertshaw, AL5 2JB
Printed in Great Britain by Antony Rowe Ltd, SN14 6LH

Contents

* Taken over by Benskin's of Watford

List of figures

Hitchin

Hoddesdon

Kimpton

King's Langley

Redbourn

Rickmansworth

Royston

St Albans

Tring

Walkern

Watford

Wheathampstead

List of tables

Rickmansworth

Royston

St Albans

Tring

Walkern

Ware

Watford

Wheathampstead

Out-of-county

Amersham

Chesham

Ivinghoe

Abbreviations

These abbreviations are used in the tables of brewery tied estates.

FL   Full licence, enabling beer, wine and spirits to be sold to drink on or off the premises

BH   Beer house in which beer can be sold to drink on or off the premises

BW   Beer and wine house in which beer and wine can be sold to drink on or off the premises

OL   Off-licence where beer, wines and spirits may only be drunk off the premises

F.   Freehold, owned by the brewery

L.   Leased by the brewery

C.   Copyhold, pays an annual fee to the appropriate Lord of the Manor

Year The year when the brewery bought or disposed of the property

Key: When other abbreviations are used a key with the individual table explains the appropriate meaning

Acknowledgements

I would like to express my gratitude to:

The staff of the Hertfordshire Archives and Local Studies Office in Hertford for their help and access to many documents, tithe maps and Petty Sessions Licence Records and also for giving permission to publish plans of the White Horse Brewery and the Pale Ale Brewery of Baldock, the plans of the Peacock Brewery and the Harpenden Brewery in Harpenden, the plan of Pryor and Reid's Brewery in Hatfield and a photograph of a steam brewery lorry, the plan of the Lion Brewery in Kimpton, the plan of Groome's Brewery in King's Langley and the plan of the Kingsbury Brewery in St Albans.

The staff of Hitchin Museum for access to documents and also for giving permission to publish the plans of Marshall and Pierson's Brewery and the Sun Inn Brewery in Hitchin. The staff at the County Record Offices in Aylesbury, Bedford, Cambridge, Chelmsford and Greater London for access to documents and Petty Sessions Licence Records.

The staff at Friends House Library, Euston Road, London for access to books about Quaker bankers.

Nicholas Redman, the company archivist of Whitbread plc, for copies of documents from the company archives.

Reginald Carrington-Porter of the Estates Department, Allied-Tetley plc, for copies of documents from the company archives.

Ray Anderson and Mike Brown of the Brewery History Society for saving the Allied-Tetley plc brewery archive records in 2002 and 2003 and for ensuring that these documents have been deposited in the appropriate county Record Offices.

The help and encouragement that was given to me by members of the Brewery History Society. Ken Page provided detailed information about Page's of Ashwell, Rayment's of Furneux Pelham, Wright's of Walkern and Charles Wells of Bedford. Ian Stratford provided information about Hawkes' of Bishop's

Stortford and Taylor's of Saffron Walden and he has given me permission to publish a photograph of Hawkes' brewery yard. Bob Flood provided information about Meyer's of Orwell, Tooth's of Cambridge and other brewery properties in Cambridgeshire.

Michael Whitaker has given me permission to publish his drawings of the Kingsbury Brewery in St Albans and Wright's Victoria Brewery in Walkern.

I wish to express my thanks to Jane Housham and Kerry Gilliland at the University of Hertfordshire Press for their astute editorial comments and suggestions for improvements during the final stages of preparation of this book.

Finally I wish to express my thanks to Lorna Whitaker for her encouragement and patience during all stages in the research and preparation of this book.

Foreword

I was very excited when I was informed by Kerry Gilliland of the University of Hertfordshire Press that Dr Allan Whitaker had written a book on the history of brewers in Hertfordshire.

My family are still actively involved with the running of McMullen & Sons Limited and I was therefore fascinated to see what historical facts Dr Whitaker had found out about our brewery. I was not disappointed and it is obvious that he has done an enormous amount of thorough research into the subject. It is of course sad that many of the old brewing names of Hertfordshire have disappeared. However, I am pleased to say that we at McMullens have just completed building a new brewhouse on the same site (in Hertford) and intend to carry on brewing in Hertfordshire for many years to come.

I wish Dr Whitaker all the success he deserves for this fascinating publication.

FERGUS MCMULLEN
Production and Sales Director
McMullen & Sons Limited

CHAPTER ONE

Introduction

Brewing was an established activity in Hertfordshire by the sixteenth century. Ale and beer were essential beverages because most readily available supplies of water would have been unfit to drink. Until the early 1400s all beer was technically 'ale', in which water, malted barley and yeast were the only ingredients used to produce the fermented beverage. Hops are first mentioned in a monastery edict of AD 824 by Abbot Abelard of Covery (Hornsey, 1999). They were used on a small scale as an additive to ale brews, initially to act as a preservative, but also to give an aroma and a flavour. However they were not commercially grown in the UK until 1524 when Flemish weavers settled in Kent. This new type of brew using hops became known as 'beer', the result of combining malt, hops, yeast and water in the correct proportions and at the right temperatures. An alternative definition is an extract of malted barley, boiled with hops or hop extracts and fermented with yeast. Beer could be brewed to weaker strengths (4 to 5 per cent alcohol) instead of the ales which were often much stronger (7 to 10 per cent alcohol) to ensure longer shelf life. The Searancke family of Essendon, who were originally refugees from Flanders, are reputed to have introduced hops into beers in Hertfordshire when they started brewing in Hatfield during the 1500s.

At this time three types of licensed drinking establishments were legally recognised: 'inns' that sold ales, beers, wines, spirits, food and offered sleeping accommodation; 'taverns' that sold ales, beers and wines; and finally 'ale houses' that sold only ales and beers. These descriptive terms for licensed premises were later replaced by 'public houses' that sold beers, wines and spirits, 'beer houses' only selling beer and occasionally other licensed premises having licences to sell only beers and wines. There were also 'off licences' where beers, wines and spirits could be sold for consumption off the premises.

Historically in Hertfordshire, brewing would be carried out in small brewhouses that were attached to inns or taverns. These would have been found

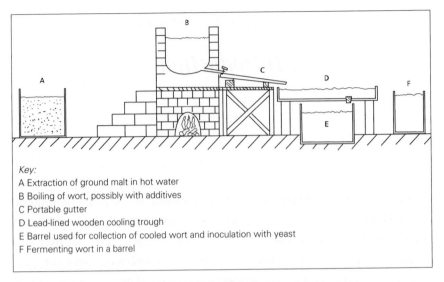

Key:
A Extraction of ground malt in hot water
B Boiling of wort, possibly with additives
C Portable gutter
D Lead-lined wooden cooling trough
E Barrel used for collection of cooled wort and inoculation with yeast
F Fermenting wort in a barrel

Figure 1.1 Stages of a medieval brewing process

at the *White Horse* in Baldock, the *George* in Bishop's Stortford, the *Old Bell* in Hemel Hempstead, the *Salisbury Arms* (*Bell*) in Hertford, the *Red Hart* in Hitchin, the *Bull* in Royston, the *Fleur de Lys* in St Albans, the *Saracen's Head* in Ware and the *One Bell* in Watford. Readers can no doubt think of other examples. These early brewhouses would have been very similar to the reconstruction at Lacock Abbey in Wiltshire (Davison, 1998) and Figure 1.1.

The malt was often ground at a local mill and sieved to remove some of the finer dust. Alternatively on a smaller scale it could be ground in a hand quern. Then the ground malt was put in a wooden mash tun and mixed with hot water to extract as much of the fermentable sugar as possible. The resulting liquid extract was strained through fabric to remove large particulate matter and boiled in a large copper vessel in a brick or stone surround that was heated from below with a wood fire. At this boiling stage herbs, spices or other materials might be added to improve the flavour, clarity and keeping qualities. Bog myrtle, wormwood, ground ivy, sage, juniper and rosemary have been used as well as spices such as nutmeg and cinnamon. This was before the use of hops. The wort would again be strained after boiling into another vessel and left to cool. At large establishments such as Lacock Abbey the hot wort would be run into a shallow lead-lined wooden trough via a portable wooden gutter and allowed to cool rapidly. Subsequently the cooled wort was drained into an open barrel where it was inoculated with yeast, stirred and transferred to an appropriate number of barrels to ferment. At small establishments the hot wort would be put directly into a fermentation barrel and left to cool before adding the yeast inoculum. Large estates, farms, schools such as the Blue Coat School off East Street in Ware, workhouses, and other large institutions also undertook their own private brewing and probably accounted for 50 per cent of the beer brewed in England in 1700 (Corran, 1975). All of these examples mentioned so far usually brewed batch volumes of beer that would be consumed on the premises within a week or fortnight. Unfortunately the quality of this type of beer was extremely variable. Beers were often brewed to produce a final 5 to 7 per cent alcohol concentration to give a longer shelf life. Second extracts from the malt might be made to prepare a much weaker 'small beer' or 'table beer'. It was probably this much weaker beer that a worker on a farm and elsewhere might be drinking when a gallon of beer per day was regarded as a normal habit.

By 1700 there were also people described as 'common brewers' establishing small breweries in Hertfordshire who would regularly brew beer of a more consistent quality and were ready to sell beer to owners of inns and taverns, the general public, the local nobility, etc. Their potential market was determined by the size of population within a few miles of their breweries. Beer can be considered as a relatively bulky low-value product to transport. Because approximately 95 per cent of the product is water, transport costs by horse and cart on poor quality roads would become a major component of the selling price, making it uneconomic to sell beer outside a radius of five to ten miles of the brewery in rural areas.

The more enterprising common brewers and brewing innkeepers began to buy local inns to give themselves a tied trade whereby only their beer could be sold in their own inns giving themselves more predictable volumes of beer to produce and sell. The Searancke family owned three inns in Hatfield before 1700 and bought another seventeen before 1800. Robert Thurgood of Baldock bought eleven inns between 1725 and 1763. In Hitchin the Lucas family owned nine inns before 1800. Elsewhere William Smith of Watford owned fifteen inns in 1790, Thomas Kinder of St Albans had a tied estate of twelve inns by 1800 and William Bedlam of Royston owned fifteen inns by 1805. These examples and others will be dealt with in more detail in the later chapters about the breweries in most of the towns and some of the villages in Hertfordshire.

In 1830 the Beer House Act was passed by Parliament and was to have a major influence on the licensed beer trade. This legislation allowed any householder to sell beer on their premises (a beer house) provided they paid rates and could afford the two guineas (£2.20) excise licence fee. Nationally

Table 1.1 Breweries in Hertfordshire

Town/village	Site name	Owner(s)	When in use	Maltings
Ashwell	Mill Street	Fordham	1839–1952	Yes
	Westbury	Christy, Page	1843–1921	Yes
Baldock	High Street	Thurgood, Pryor Simpson	1743–1965	Yes
	White Horse Street	Ind	c.1790–1815	Yes
	White Horse	Noy, Penn, Oliver, Parker	c.1735–1881	Yes
	Pale Ale	Oliver, Steed, Pickering, Morley	c.1820–90	Yes
Barkway	High Street	Gapes, Balding	1750–1908	No
Barnet	Wood Street	Various	1700–1909	No
Berkhamsted	Water Lane	Various, Locke & Smith	1811–c.1913	Yes
	Swan	Foster, Lane, Foster	1813–98	Yes
Bishop's Stortford	Water Lane	Hawkes & Co.	1780–1920s	Yes
	Fox	Various	1886–1915	No
Furneux Pelham	Barleycroft End	Rayment, King & Lake, Greene King	1855–1987	Yes
Hadley	Old Great North Road	Various, Harris Browne	1700s–1938	No
Harpenden	Harpenden Brewery	Curtis, Healey, Bennetts, Mardall	c.1837–93	Yes
	Peacock Brewery	House, Mardall, Glover	1837–1919	Yes
Hatfield	Hatfield Brewery	Searancke, Bigg, Field, Spurrell, Pryor, Reid & Co.	1764–1920	Yes
	Park Street Brewery	Pratchett, Complin	1700–1878	Yes
	Newtown Brewery	Bradshaw	c.1850–88	No
Hemel Hempstead	Anchor Brewery	Various	1841–91	Yes
	Star Brewery	Elliot	1850–1912	No
	Prince's Arms Brewery	Jeffery	1851–95	No
Hertford	Cross Keys Brewery	Various	1725–c.1860	No
	Fore Street	Young	1754–1893	Yes
	St Andrew's Brewery	Various	1774–1840s	Yes
	Mill Bridge Brewery	Ireland, Wickham	1826–1938	Yes
	Back Street, Mill Bridge, Hartham Lane	McMullen	1827–now	Yes
	Hope Brewery	Baker	1830–1920	No
	Back Street	Manser, Medcalf	1838–54	No
	West Street	Nicholls	1854–1966	Yes
	Crown Brewery	Medcalf, Hargreaves	1859–95	Yes

Town/village	Site name	Owner(s)	When in use	Maltings
Hitchin	Red Lion Brewery	Conquest, Lucas	1700–1800s	Yes
	Bridge Street Brewery	Draper, Lucas	c.1700–1923	Yes
	Sun Street Brewery	Crabb, Marshall & Co.	c.1760–1841	Yes
	Bucklersbury Brewery	Pierson	1842–52	No
	Sun Hotel Brewery	Various	1700s–1902	Yes
Hoddesdon	Hoddesdon Brewery	Briand, Whittingstall, Christie & Cathrow	1742–1928	Yes
Kimpton	Lion Brewery	Various	1835–1910	Yes
King's Langley	Saracen's Head	Cromack	1790–1849	Yes
	King's Langley Brewery	Goodwin, Groome	1720–1897	Yes
Little Hadham	Nag's Head	Various	1850s–1912	No
Markyate	Pickford Hill	Various, Griffith	1700s–1850s	No
	Lion Brewery	Rowley	1850–90	Yes
	11 High Street	Shemelds	1850s	Yes
Puckeridge	High Street	Fleming, Chapman	1880s–1907	No
Redbourn	Redbourn Brewery	Edwards, Bennett	1866–1900	Yes
Rickmansworth	Rickmansworth Brewery	Salter, Fellowes & Co.	c.1700–1924	Yes
	Mill End Brewery	Wild	c.1870–1900	No
Royston	Royston Brewery	Phillips	1725–1950	Yes
	Icknield Street	Bedlam	1776–1805	Yes
St Albans	Kingsbury Brewery	Carter, Niccoll, Searancke, Lloyd Bingham-Cox	1600s–1898	Yes
	St Albans Brewery	Kinder, Adey & White	1700s–1936	Yes
	St Peter's Brewery	Parsons, Adey & Co.	1832–1902	Yes
	Holywell Brewery	Kent	1826–1918	Yes
	Gentles Yard	Unknown	1800s	No
Sandridge	Not known	Parsons	1765–1832	Yes
Tring	Tring Brewery	Amsden, Field, Brown	1800–98	Yes
	Akeman Street Brewery	Olney, Batchelor, Rodwell	1839–1902	Yes
	Manor Brewery	Liddington	1839–95	No
Walkern	Victoria	Wright	1860s–1924	Yes
Ware	Cannon Brewery	Blake, Cox, McMullen	c.1850–91	No
	Star Brewery	Various	c.1860–1952	No

Town/village	Site name	Owner(s)	When in use	Maltings
Watford	Cannon Brewery	Pope, Dyson, Benskin	c.1715–1972	Yes
	Watford Brewery	Smith, Whittingstall, Sedgwick	1655–1923	Yes
	King Street Brewery	Healey	1851–98	No
	Lion Brewery	Thorp, Wells	1890–1952	No
Welwyn	Welwyn Brewery	Various	c.1830–97	No
Wheathampstead	Parrott Brewery	Wilkins	c.1780–1830	No
	Hope Brewery	Lattimore, Hill	c.1830–1904	Yes
Whitwell	High Street	Archer, Hill	c.1830–70	No

outlets to sell beer doubled by 1840. Because the majority of these beer house keepers did not do their own brewing on the premises, the common brewers were able to increase their brewing capacity and sell beer to the majority of beer houses at a competitive price. Later the local breweries bought many of the commercially viable beer houses to increase the size of their tied estates. However beer houses that still existed after 1945 had finally to obtain full licences from local magistrates' courts to be able to sell spirits and wine.

At least sixty-eight breweries were established in towns and many of the larger villages in the county (Table 1.1). This number was gradually reduced due to takeovers, closures and bankruptcies. By 1902 there were only thirty-two breweries. There was actually a thirty-third active brewery, Wells of Watford, but there was no tied estate in Hertfordshire until it opened an off-licence in Watford in 1932. Between 1918 and 1939, the number of active breweries was reduced by the takeovers and/or closures of Page of Ashwell, Glover's of Harpenden, Pryor, Reid & Co. of Hatfield, Wickham of Hertford, Baker of Hertford, Lucas of Hitchin, Salter's of Rickmansworth, Kent of St Albans, Adey & White of St Albans, Wright's of Walkern and Sedgwick of Watford. Post-1945 there were the takeovers and closures of Fordham's of Ashwell, Simpson's of Baldock, Rayment's of Ferneux Pelham, Nicholls' of Hertford, Phillips' of Royston, Wells of Watford and finally Benskin's of Watford. The sole survivor of the original list of 64 active breweries listed in Table 1.1 is McMullen's of Hertford. All these breweries will be discussed in more detail in the following chapters.

There were a few Hertfordshire maltsters that decided to buy breweries. Caleb Hitch who was a maltster in Ware, started the Star Brewery in Ware and built up a small local tied estate. He leased the brewery to Isaac Everitt in 1866 and to McMullen's in 1874 before finally selling it to William Wickham in 1879.

Table 1.2 Owners of licensed properties and the composition of their tied estates
in Hertfordshire in October 1902

Owner and location	Full Lic.	Beer H.	Off-Lic.	Total
a) Based in Hertfordshire				
Adey & White, St Albans	41	27	4	72
Bailey Bros, Bishop Stortford	0	0	1	1
Baker, Hertford	13	8	0	21
Balding, Barkway	1	1	0	2
Baldock Brewery Co., Baldock*	0	1	0	1
Barnet Brewery Co., Barnet	0	1	0	1
Bass and Abbott, Kimpton	0	1	0	1
Benskin, Watford	123	72	7	202
Chambers, Wheathampstead	1	5	0	6
Chapman, Hitchin	1	2	0	3
Christie & Cathrow, Hoddesdon	104	19	2	125
W.H. Drake, Little Hadham	0	1	0	1
Flinn & Co., Bishop Stortford	0	6	1	7
Fordham, Ashwell	20	33	0	53
Glover, Harpenden	11	18	1	30
Harris Brown, Hadley	1	1	1	3
Kent, St Albans	1	6	0	7
Lane & Co., Berkhamsted*	0	1	0	1
Locke & Smith, Berkhamsted	18	20	0	38
Lucas, Hitchin	31	9	0	40
McMullen, Hertford	55	69	7	131
Nicholls, Hertford	1	3	0	4
J.R. Page, Ashwell	6	11	1	18
Phillips, Royston	57	11	3	71
Pryor Reid, Hatfield	65	57	4	126
Rayment, Furneux Pelham	2	12	1	15
Rodwell, Tring	1	1	1	3
Salter, Rickmansworth	42	3	0	45
Sedgwick, Watford	41	23	4	68
Simpson, Baldock	73	32	0	105
Wickham, Hertford	2	2	0	4
Wilson, Baldock*	1	1	0	2
Wright, Walkern	6	6	2	14
Subtotal	718	463	40	1,221
b) Out-of-county				
Ashby, Staines	1	2	0	3
Aylesbury Brewing Co., Aylesbury	4	0	0	4
H.J. Barker, Aston Clinton	1	0	0	1
Bennetts, Dunstable	6	17	3	26
Brandon & Co., Putney	0	1	0	1
Cannon, London EC1	1	0	0	1
Chaplin, Harlow	2	5	0	7
Charrington, London E1	2	1	0	3
Chesham Brewery, Chesham	14	30	5	49
City of London Brewery, London EC4	1	0	0	1
Clutterbuck, Stanmore	36	19	0	55
Fuller, Smith and Turner, Chiswick	0	2	1	3
Greens, Luton	9	12	2	23
Harmen, Uxbridge	3	2	0	5

Owner and location	Full Lic.	Beer H.	Off-Lic.	Total
J.S. Holland, Wendover	0	1	0	1
Holt Marine Brewery, London E7	6	8	0	14
Hudson, Pampisford	1	0	0	1
Jarman, Meldreth	0	1	0	1
Mann & Crossman, London E1	2	0	0	2
Marshall Bros, Huntingdon	2	0	0	2
Meux, London WC1	4	0	0	4
Mitchill & Aldous, Hendon	0	4	0	4
Morris & Co., Ampthill	2	0	0	2
Roberts & Wilson, Ivinghoe	8	4	0	12
Rogers & Co., Stanstead	0	1	0	1
Savill Bros, Stratford	1	0	0	1
Truman, London E1	1	1	0	2
Watney, London SW1	5	1	0	6
Webb & Gibbons, Dunmow	0	1	0	1
Weller, Amersham	18	13	0	31
Wells, Bedford	2	1	1	4
Wells & Winch, Biggleswade	1	3	0	4
West & Co., Hackney	1	0	0	1
Wethered, Marlow	1	0	0	1
Whitbread, Finsbury	3	3	0	6
Williams, Woburn*	0	1	0	1
Subtotal	138	134	12	284
c) Free Houses in Hertfordshire	45	16	18	79
Grand Totals (a + b + c)	901	613	70	1,584

Key: * Non brewery owners

Members of the Page family were already established maltsters in Baldock when they decided to buy the Westbury Brewery in Ashwell in 1879. In 1921 the brewery was sold to Wells and Winch of Biggleswade with six tied properties and nineteen leasehold properties. Four of their maltings were sold separately to Paine & Co. of St Neots. More details can be found in the chapter about Ashwell. The Flinn family of Bishop's Stortford owned the Fox Brewery in Finchingfield in Essex between 1883 and 1886 and the small Fox Brewery in Bishop's Stortford between 1885 and 1902. They sold both breweries but retained the ownership of a few licensed properties. The Taylor family who also lived in Bishop's Stortford bought the Anchor Brewery in Saffron Walden in 1839. They owned the brewery with a tied estate of eighty licensed properties until 1897 when they sold the business to Watney of London. Further details about the Anchor Brewery can be found in the chapter on Saffron Walden.

The manufacture of malt

The major raw material used in the production of beer is malt obtained by the process of malting barley grains. Good quality malting barley requires light free draining soils and a relatively low rainfall. These conditions are found in eastern Hertfordshire and other parts of East Anglia. Mathias (1959a) described the region centring upon Ware, Hoddesdon and Stanstead Abbots as the oldest and most mature malting area in the country. Malting was established in medieval times as a major industry in Ware, Hertford, Hoddesdon, Stanstead Abbots and also in St Albans, Baldock, Ashwell and Royston. In 1339 a market was started in Ware to sell malt to London brewers and in 1571 malt was being transported from Ware to London by barge (Ware Museum). When the River Stort navigation was improved, many more maltings were built in Bishop's Stortford. In Victorian times other maltings were built elsewhere in Hertfordshire.

Aspects of the history of malt and its manufacture in Hertfordshire have been reviewed by Mathias (1959b), Branch Johnson (1966, 1970), Brown (1983), Clark (1998), Hornsey (1999) and Crosby (2001). In 1838 Robson's *Directory of Herts* listed seventy-eight maltsters. Some of them combined malting with brewing or another trade. Branch Johnson (1966) conducted a survey of the surviving sites; twenty-two in Ware, seventeen in Bishop's Stortford, ten in Hertford, seven in Baldock, four each in Stanstead Abbots and Ashwell, two each in St Albans, Sawbridgeworth, Tring, Watford and Wheathampstead and one each in Berkhamsted, Braughing, Furneux Pelham, Hatfield, Hitchin, Hoddesdon, King's Langley, Royston and Walkern. On each site there were between one and seven maltings. I am aware of two other converted maltings in Royston (Phillips Brewery) and one in Hitchin (not brewery linked). Since Branch Johnson conducted his survey some have been destroyed because of later developments or accidental fires.

At least forty-four of the county breweries also had their own maltings at some stage in their life history because of easy access to good malting barley. The brewer had better quality control because he or she would be using malts with known histories, and also would have a greater degree of autonomy over supplies of a major raw material. Some brewers from outside the county also owned maltings within Hertfordshire. Clutterbucks of Stanmore had a malting in St Albans, Paine's of St Neots had a number of maltings in Baldock, Bennett of Dunstable had a malting in Harpenden and another in Redbourn and the

Figure 1.2 Growing floor at Cannon Brewery malting, Watford in the 1890s (Barnard, Noted Breweries of Great Britain and Northern Ireland, Vol. 4, London, 1891, p. 47)

Chesham Brewery had a small malting in Berkhamsted. Extra malt also could be bought from local independent maltsters. Sometimes the brewer would buy the barley from known farmers to give the batch of grain to a particular maltster asking for malt with defined properties to ensure good quality control during brewing. A small minority of brewers owned their own farms to grow barley.

Malt is made by partially germinating barley grain under controlled conditions when enzymes modify the starch into soluble carbohydrates (mainly maltose) and proteins. When the conversion to malt has been judged to be completed any further growth and biochemical changes are halted by drying and heating the germinating grain at known temperatures in a kiln. The kilning process also makes the outer layers of the grain more friable and easier to mill in a crusher at the brewery. Historically this was a craft industry when the maltster had to rely on appearance, colour, taste and feel before analytical methods were established to give more reliable tests to monitor the process.

The traditional method was by floor malting. The smallest malting with a working floor space of about 20 feet by 120 feet (about 2,400 square feet) could be used to process a batch of ten to fifteen quarters of barley and could be operated by one man. A quarter of barley weighs 448 lbs and a bushel 56 lbs.

Although the weight loss during the malting process is only about 10 per cent, the recognised weight in the United Kingdom for a quarter of dried processed malt is 336 lbs and a malt bushel is 42 lbs.

Under ideal conditions barley germinates at between 50° and 60°F. Without any sophisticated temperature control within the building the working season was limited to October to May and led to an annual production of about 600 quarters of malt. This small size of older malting building can be seen, or would have been seen, at a number of the breweries in Ashwell, Baldock, Berkhamsted, Hertford, Kimpton, King's Langley, Royston, St Albans and Wheathampstead. During the 1850s maltings were being built for both brewers and independent maltsters that had batch capacities of 50 to 60 quarters on two or three floors. By 1900 large maltings were being built with a capacity for 250 quarters and smaller ones had a capacity of 100 quarters. These bigger maltings often had two working floors with a third floor for storage of barley or malt. The ground floor might be partially sunk below ground level to reduce the effect of higher ambient temperatures in the summer months and so extend the malting season. Malting floors were often between six feet and six feet six inches from the floor to the ceiling to help maintain a steadier temperature across the floor.

There are three recognised stages in the malting process. First steeping when the barley grains are soaked in water in a cistern to absorb water and start germination. The water is changed at defined intervals to prevent anaerobic conditions occurring. Between 1697 and 1880 when there was a Malt Tax in the United Kingdom there were regulations specifying the dimensions of a cistern and the way in which the grain was to be stacked and its depth (Mathias, 1959c; Clark, 1998). This process took two to three days. The soaked grain containing 45 per cent water was then placed in a wooden box known as a couch for twenty to thirty hours to allow it to swell and create some internal heat within the mass, as in a compost heap. This was also so that the excise man could check the volume of a batch of grain. After the abolition of the Malt Tax in 1880 couches were not required so the steeped grain could be heaped directly on the wooden, tiled or fine-surfaced concrete growing floors.

Germination took place on the growing floors that formed the major part of the building. The grain would be spread out to a depth of between three and twelve inches and left for up to two weeks. It was regularly turned manually with big wooden spades and rakes to ensure that the whole batch had uniform exposure to air, to remove pockets of carbon dioxide and to ensure the growing shoots did not become tangled up with one another. The temperature of 50° to

60°F and the humidity were controlled by opening and shutting the small louvred windows along the long walls, and by increasing or reducing the depth of grain spread on the floor. Water might be sprinkled on the grain at intervals to aid the process. Germination was considered to have reached a satisfactory stage when a growing shoot was approximately three quarters of the length of a grain.

The final stage was the drying and kilning of the grain to stop the germination process to give the appropriate sugar content and give flavour and colour to the malt (Brown, 1983; Clark, 1998; Hornsey, 1999). Grain was dried with hot air at 100°F from a furnace to reduce the moisture content of the grain to 5 per cent. The temperature was then increased to produce the type of malt required. Originally temperatures of 170°F were used to make pale malts and temperatures of over 200°F for darker malts. With better understanding of temperature treatments it was found possible to dry the grain uniformly at a low temperature of 120° to 155°F when the actual grain temperature was 70° to 85°F because of the cooling effect of moisture evaporation. The temperature was then raised to over 200°F even for pale malts. Longer drying periods and hotter air temperatures would produce much darker malts for stouts and porters. Dark brown malts for porter brewing were first manufactured in Ware in 1722 (Ware Museum).

The early furnace was a simple fire basket with a cast-iron sheet above it to disperse the heat. Hornbeam coppice wood was often used as a fuel in Hertfordshire as it produced an intense heat and was said to 'burn like a candle' (Sawford, 1990). Later good quality anthracite became the fuel of choice since it creates hardly any smoke. The drying floor was originally a horse-hair carpet but later wire mesh, perforated tiles or iron plates were used. This floor was approximately twelve feet above the furnace. The smallest kilning floors were about twenty feet square. In the Victoria Maltings in Ware in 1907 there were three kilning floors of sixty-five feet by twenty-two feet. After the appropriate kilning programme the malted grain was cooled, screened to remove remnants of the dried shoots and other debris and bagged and stored until dispatched to a buyer.

Very few brewers in London made their own malt because traditional floor malting needed a lot of floor space, labour costs were higher than in the country and barley was a bulkier product to transport and store than malt. If land were to be available next to a brewery then it normally would be used for expansion in brewing capacity. In Hertfordshire in the late 1800s usually land would have been available near a brewery at a much lower price than in London to build more maltings. However in many cases it was considered more important to invest spare capital in property and increase the size of the tied estates. There were a few breweries that invested in larger maltings such as Benskin's, Fordham's, Christie & Cathrow, Phillips' and McMullen's. Benskin's even converted Sedgwick's brewery building in Watford to maltings in 1927.

A few traditional floor maltings are still being used in the UK in 2005 but none has been operational in Hertfordshire since the 1970s. In the vast majority, mechanical handling and turning is now used on the floors using about one-third of the labour that was originally employed.

After 1900 the trend for the independent maltsters of Hertfordshire was to build larger maltings with more mechanical aids. Many of the older smaller maltings were no longer considered economic to use and were pulled down or put to other uses. In 1926 J.S. Taylor of Bishop's Stortford ceased trading. Associated British Maltsters bought H.A. & D. Taylor of Sawbridgeworth in 1958. In the same year Gripper & Wightman of Hertford ceased trading. J.R. Page of Bishop's Stortford amalgamated with J. Harrington of Hertford in 1962 to form Harrington Page. A year later Harrington Page bought Henry Ward & Sons of Ware. During 1965 Harrington Page became part of Pauls Malt Ltd of Ipswich (Clark, 1998). Finally, the Harrington Page maltings in Ware were closed in 1994. So there are now no operational maltings left in the county.

Within Hertfordshire, old maltings have been put to various uses, with or without conversion. New uses include village and church halls, boy scout or other social clubs, a night club, an agricultural merchant's store, a fish and chip shop, printers, a hair dresser, an estate agent, shops, motor repair businesses, light engineering workshops, flats and a housing complex for the elderly. The last malting kiln in Watford in the Lower High Street formed part of a petrol filling station in 1978.

Brewing

Brief reference has been made to early medieval breweries (Davison, 1998a). Most breweries in Hertfordshire follow or followed a fairly standard production process that is illustrated in Figure 1.3. The various stages will now be outlined before explaining in a little more detail. The malt is screened and crushed in a grist-mill and passes as a coarse powder to a mash tun where the soluble components of the malt are extracted with hot liquor (water). Then the liquid extract, technically known as wort, is heated in a copper with hops and possible

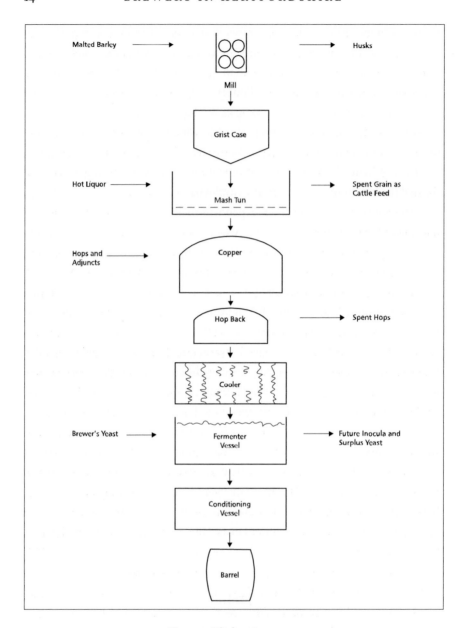

Figure 1.3 The brewing process

adjuncts. This hot liquid is passed through a hop back to filter off the spent hops and then cooled before being put in the fermentation vessels with a yeast inoculum. The brew is left for a few days while the yeast converts the soluble sugars to alcohol. Finally the beer is put into barrels to condition or further processed for kegging or bottling (Hornsey, 1999).

In the first stage of brewing a batch of beer (gyle), malt from a store is put in a hopper, normally placed above a grist mill which has two pairs of metal rollers. The uppermost pair are set sufficiently close together so that the grains are crushed without causing too much damage to the grain husks but to extrude the endosperm and embryos within the grains. The softer inner contents are then broken down by the second pair of rollers set closer together to produce coarse particles known as 'grits' and finer particles termed 'flour'. The main objective at this stage is to produce particles that will be rapidly attacked by the enzymes in the malt yielding a good conversion rate to soluble components at the next stage of mashing. At the same time the coarse husks are used to form a good filter at the base of the mash tun. Test runs may be necessary with the roller distances to establish optimum conditions. In 1890 Benskin's of Watford had two grist mills each with a capacity of fifteen quarters of malt per hour (Barnard, 1891).

The 'grist' from a grist hopper is fed at a steady rate by a rotating Archimedes screw into a pre-heated mash tun and mixed with hot water at 150° to 160° F and held at this temperature for about thirty minutes and stirred. Historically the stirring would have been manual but later it was mechanical when steam engines were installed in breweries. The initial mashing was followed by a 'sparging stage' using a rotating sprinkler arm to spread the water. During the mashing treatment at least ninety per cent of the starch is converted into soluble sugars. Nowadays because of the availability of analytical equipment the pH may be adjusted to approximately 5.5 for optimum enzyme activity. After the initial thirty minutes of mashing the temperature is then raised to boiling point for fifteen to forty five minutes depending on the type of beer that is required and once again the mash may be stirred. The precise procedure will vary at individual breweries. The mash may then be left for three to four hours to dissolve as much of the soluble sugars as possible. This procedure will also allow the husks and larger particles to settle out on a base plate of the mash tun and form a filter bed to take out as much of the finer suspended particles as possible. The base plate is perforated with small holes or slits. Modern base plates are covered with woven filter cloths. In the early 1890s the Pale Ale Brewery in Baldock was using a twelve quarter mash tun while Benskin's in Watford were using two twenty-five quarter mash tuns. Now modern mash tuns might be twenty feet to thirty feet diameter using a liquid to solids ratio of three to one.

Most of the breweries bored their own wells for their main source of water. The mineral salts content of the water obtained from this source would have an influence on the type of beer that could be produced. Nowadays salts may be added to change the character of the local water supply to make it possible to mimic the character of a beer from another area. For example the addition of calcium sulphate will enable beers similar to those from Burton on Trent to be brewed.

Some breweries, such as Fordham's of Ashwell, had problems with their water source because of contamination from farmyard effluent and had to run a pipe from a spring some distance from the brewery. A few other breweries were near to farmyards or had manure heaps fairly near to the brewery wells. These included the *Sun Hotel* in Hitchin, the White Horse Brewery in Baldock and the Lion Brewery in Kimpton. It is hoped that the top of a well was adequately protected to prevent any seepage into the borehole and any effluent from a manure heap was drained away from the borehole to prevent contamination.

Filtered malt wort is piped from the mash tun to a copper constructed from copper sheeting where it is boiled with hops to achieve the bitter flavours. The copper at the Pale Ale Brewery in Baldock had a working capacity of thirty-eight barrels of wort. Originally coppers were heated directly by fires underneath them but later indirect heating by steam pipes became the standard method. The wort is boiled for two hours to ensure it is sterilised and that essential oils and polyphenols are extracted from the hops. This procedure concentrates the wort during the boiling phase. Modern 'coppers' are now made from stainless steel mainly because of the cost and ease of cleaning.

Adjuncts such as cane sugar or small amounts of spices also might be added.

The very hot wort is passed through a filter called a 'hop back' to remove the spent hop remains and other debris and run through a cooler. The most primitive coolers were large open shallow trays. Christie & Cathrow of Hoddesdon used two cast-iron coolers twenty-seven feet long and twenty-four feet wide and two wooden coolers seventy-four feet long and twenty-four feet wide. Because this type of trough relied on air-cooling it was not very effective in hot weather and the large exposed surface area of wort might become infected with microbial contaminants and oxygen would slowly become dissolved in the wort. Faster cooling was achieved by passing the hot wort over metal plates or tubes containing circulating cold water. Once again, this procedure can lead to contamination and build-up of dissolved oxygen. Many breweries did use both these cooling methods. Plate filters are now more widely used. These are totally enclosed so there is less chance of contamination and much lower concentrations of dissolved oxygen. There is the added advantage that heat can be recovered from the hot wort to use elsewhere in the brewery.

Most fermentation vessels used in Hertfordshire were constructed from wood with a copper lining in the shape of a square box or cylinder up to seven foot in height and with an open top. McMullen's have used cylindrical fermenters and more recently have installed cylindro-conical vessels fabricated from stainless steel and completely enclosed.

Many of these breweries adopted the 'tower' principle of brewing during the 1800s when they were starting brewing in a new brewery or modifying older buildings if already established. The early stages of the process start on the top floor of the building and the brewing batch travels downwards by gravity through successive stages. If there were not many floors in the building the wort might be pumped back to a higher floor after it left the hop back.

Tied estates

The composition of tied estates and dates of ownership or leasing of properties by the Hertfordshire breweries are not always easy to establish. The earliest reliable sources are the terriers (a register of land and property) with the tithe maps *c*.1840 that indicate where all the licensed properties were located with a tithe reference number, the name, the owner or brewery, and the occupant. Fortunately most of these tithe maps of Hertfordshire have survived. Other earlier property deeds or sales deeds may not have survived.

Two types of ownership of licensed properties exist. Freehold properties are owned directly by a brewery. A brewery may also have use of leasehold properties that are rented by the brewery from the owners of those properties at agreed rents per year for an agreed number of years. Until Victorian times there were also copyhold properties. Copyhold was a tenure less than freehold of land in England that was recorded on a copy of the court roll of a Manor. This entailed paying an annual fee to the lord of the appropriate Manor. In the 1890s Phillips' Brewery in Royston had thirteen copyhold properties in Hertfordshire, twenty-five in Cambridgeshire and five in Essex. Fordham's of Ashwell had fifteen copyhold properties in 1897. Other copyhold examples were Healey's of Harpenden, the Hatfield Brewery in 1815, Young's of Hertford, the King's Langley Brewery, Bedlam's of Royston and Smith's of Watford.

After national legislation in 1869 all premises selling beer, wine and spirits had to be registered and obtain licences from the local magistrates. These details are still recorded in a standard form in Petty Sessions Licensing Records today.

Table 1.3 Estimated size of tied estates of some Hertfordshire breweries in 1902

Brewery	Estate in Herts	Elsewhere	Total
Benskin, Watford	202	c.150	c.350
McMullen, Hertford	131	c.35	c.165
Pryor, Reid, Hatfield	126	c.20	c.145
Christie & Co., Hoddesdon	125	c.40	c.165
Simpson, Baldock	105	c.50	c.155
Adey & White, St Albans	72	c.10	c.80
Phillips, Royston	71	c.150	c.220
Sedgwick, Watford	68	c.30	c.100
Fordham, Ashwell	53	c.50	c.100
Salter, Rickmansworth	45	c.20	c.65
Lucas, Hitchin	40	c.20	c.60

For the historian they provide a very good source of information about the brewery owner, the landlord, the type of licence and a record of any unlawful activities such as watering down of whisky, gambling, running a disorderly premises, etc. that had been brought to the notice of the magistrates. Unfortunately not all these early records have survived from some districts.

In 1902 there was a national census of licensed premises with a data return in January 1903. In Hertfordshire this was undertaken for each parish recording the owners of all public houses, beer houses and off-licences and indicating whether they were being leased to someone else. This makes it possible to give some grand totals for the county. In-county brewers had 718 full licences, 463 beer house licences and 40 off-licences giving a total of 1,221 properties (Table 1.2). Adey & White of St Albans, Benskin of Watford, Christie & Cathrow of Hoddesdon, Fordham of Ashwell, Lucas of Hitchin, McMullen of Hertford, Phillips of Royston, Pryor, Reid of Hatfield, Salter of Rickmansworth, Sedgwick of Watford and Simpson of Baldock all had at least forty properties in the county.

It is important to remember that most of the larger breweries had also bought or leased properties in neighbouring counties. By making use of estimated data for out-of-county properties and combining these figures with the 1902 Hertfordshire figures it is possible to make an estimate of the individual tied estates (Table 1.3). Benskin's still has the largest estate boosted by its takeovers of Hawkes' of Bishop's Stortford and Young's of Hertford but the pecking order of some of the remainder does change considerably. Phillips of Royston had a large estate in Cambridgeshire and bought Meyer's Brewery in Orwell plus Tooth's Brewery in Cambridge in the late 1890s. This made them the second biggest brewery in Hertfordshire rather than the seventh. McMullen's, Pryor, Reid & Co., Christie & Co. and Simpsons were probably of a comparable size. Adey & White did not have a big out-of-county estate and should come much lower at ninth position while Sedgwick's and Fordham's were larger businesses because of more properties outside Hertfordshire.

The 1902 census shows that out-of-county brewers had 138 full licences, 134 beer house licences and 12 off-licences making a total of 284 properties (Table 1.2). The breweries with the largest estates in Hertfordshire were Bennett's of Dunstable, Chesham Brewery, Clutterbuck's of Stanmore, Green's of Luton, Weller's of Amersham and Roberts & Wilson of Ivinghoe. Some such as Clutterbuck's and Bennett's had major parts of their tied estates in Hertfordshire. For a few years Bennett's had its registered offices in Hertfordshire before reverting to its original Dunstable base. Many of the big London breweries such as Cannon, Charringtons, City of London, Mann & Crossman, Meux, Truman, Watney and Whitbread had only bought a very small number of properties in Hertfordshire by 1902.

Later Roberts & Wilson, the Chesham Brewery and Weller's were taken over by Benskin's of Watford. This company also bought many of the other breweries in Hertfordshire between 1898 and 1952 when it had a tied estate of approximately 1,000 properties (Table 29.4). Benskin in turn was later to become part of the Carlsberg-Tetley Company. Green's of Luton bought Adey & White of St Albans in 1936, Phillips of Royston in 1949 and Fordham's of Ashwell in 1952. Green's later became part of the Whitbread Company. Greene King of Bury St Edmunds bought Simpsons of Baldock and closed the brewery in Baldock and Rayment's in Furneux Pelham which it already owned.

There was also a third category in the survey described as 'Free Houses' that were not directly owned by the breweries although some might be leased to them (Table 1.2). This group consisted of forty-five full licences, sixteen beer house licences and eighteen off-licences making a total of seventy-nine properties. The owners of some of these properties included the Lyttons of Knebworth Park (*Lytton Arms* in Old Knebworth, the *Chequers* in Stevenage), the Marquis of Salisbury of Hatfield House (*Red Lion* in Hatfield), Lord Brocket of Brocket Hall (*Brocket Arms* in Ayot St Lawrence), Earl Cowper (the *White Hart* at Hertingfordbury, the *Cowper Arms* and the *Rose & Crown* in Tewin), and the Bowes Lyon family of St Paul's Walden (the *Strathmore Arms* in St Paul's Walden). The Master and Fellows of Trinity Hall, Cambridge owned the *Sun* and *Angel Vaults* in Hitchin. Sometimes members of brewing families kept part of the tied estate after the sale of the brewery. Miss Young and Mrs M. Young of Hertford retained a number of licensed properties after Young's Brewery was sold to Pryor, Reid & Co. Each of them leased their properties to Pryor, Reid &

Co. Much earlier the Parsons family had leased the tied estate of St Peter's Brewery to Adey & White. The Kinder family also leased their tied estate to Adey & White in St Albans from 1868 until 1912. Leasing of 'free houses' was regarded as a good form of property investment.

At the same time as the 1902 survey was being undertaken, the populations (excluding schools and asylums) in the licensing divisions of the county were determined and compared with the licensed premises totals. The divisions of Odsey (Ashwell and Royston) and Welwyn both had one licensed property for every 85 residents and this total included women and children. At the other extreme Barnet had only one licensed property for every 272 residents. The results of this study were subsequently used by the magistrates as evidence to force the brewers to close some of their tied houses where it was considered that there was an excessive number in a town or village.

In the Cambridgeshire licensed-house survey landlords were asked the following question; Can you make any suggestions for the better conduct of the licensed trade in your District? Edward Millgate the landlord of the *Cock* at Swaffham Prior replied:

> Reducing the number of Licensed Houses in my opinion would give those still holding licences more control over their customers, trade would be better, and the licence holder would be able to refuse those who he thought had sufficient even though they were not the worst for drink, as now he is glad to sell all he can to try to make the business pay, if now refused they will tell you to keep your beer, we can get it somewhere else.

The Petty Sessions records from 1903 to the 1920s give details of the closures and the compensation given to the brewers or property owner for taking away the licences. It also became a policy of magistrates only to grant a new licence if another property licensed to a brewery was being closed.

Unfortunately the names of the various public houses, beer houses and off-licences were not included in this 1903 Hertfordshire county document except where there had been changes of tenant. Many of these public house and beer house names may be established by referring to the Petty Sessions licensing record books. The Inland Revenue records of 1910 comprising large-scale maps and associated records also give details of ownership, tenant, and the name and location of licensed properties.

Other sources of information about brewery tied estates are bills of sale, brewery record books, wills, old photographs and parish poor tax and water tax records. Branch Johnson's *Hertfordshire Inns*, Joliffe and Jones's *Hertfordshire*

Inns and Public Houses and local history books of towns and villages are also useful sources of information. Much of the information is in the county archives at Hertford. Many of the breweries also owned public houses and beer houses in adjoining counties so it is necessary to visit other county archives to help establish the full tied estate and the number of sales or closures of properties that occurred while a brewery was operational. In this way it is possible to see how many were public houses or beer houses, how many were in towns or rural locations and the distances from the brewery. Some breweries did not change the composition of their estates very much while others made many sales, disposals and closures during the time that they were operational. Fairly recently the archives of Whitbread in London and Carlsberg-Tetley in Burton on Trent have closed and much more valuable historical material has been deposited in county archives and become available as a research source.

Contents of breweries

Fairly detailed descriptions of the contents of the Victorian breweries of Youngs of Hertford, Christie & Cathrow of Hoddesdon and Sedgwick of Watford have been made (Hertfordshire County Record Offices a.). Also a comprehensive description of a large Victorian brewery was given by Barnard (1891) when he made a visit to Benskin's Cannon Brewery in Watford. Brief descriptions were also given in sales literature when a brewery was to be sold. Some of this information will be quoted when it is appropriate.

Brewery ownership and management by women

There are a number of instances in the history of Hertfordshire breweries where a woman became the owner or manager. This was often after her husband had died. Sarah Thurgood was in charge of the High Street Brewery in Baldock. Much later Evelyn Mary Penelope Shaw-Hellier was managing the same brewery when it was known as Simpson's. Elsewhere in Baldock, Margaret Steed managed the Pale Ale Brewery after both her husband and son died. In Harpenden Mrs Martha Mardall and Mrs Elizabeth Whittingstall-Healey were managing the two adjacent breweries at the same time in the late 1800s. Between 1851 and 1866 Mrs Mary Complin, Mrs C. Complin and Mrs Susan Complin managed the Park Street Brewery in Hatfield. In the mid 1700s, Mary Flower helped her husband Richard to manage the Cross Keys Brewery in

Table 1.4 Long-term ownership of some Hertfordshire breweries

Family	Town/village	Dates	Time in years
Searancke	Hatfield	1589–1815	226
Searancke	St Albans	1815–1868	53
Phillips	Royston	1725–1949	224
Lucas	Hitchin	1709–1923	214
McMullen*	Hertford	1827–2005	178
Goodwin/Groome	King's Langley	1720–1897	177
Pope/Dyson	Watford	1714–1867	153
Smith	Watford	1655–1790	135
Kinder	St Albans	1737–1868	131
Fordham	Ashwell	1836–1952	116
Young	Hertford	1777–1893	116
Simpson	Baldock	1853–1954	101
Hawkes	Bishop's Stortford	1780–1878	98

Key: * McMullen are the only still active brewers on this list

Hertford. Also in Hertford Emily Nicholls managed the family brewery from 1879 to 1896 when her sons William and George took over. At some time women managed three of Watford's larger breweries. Sarah Pope, Mary Dyson and Maria Benskin were involved at different times at the Cannon Brewery. Mrs Mary Ann Sedgwick managed the Watford Brewery when her son had mental health problems. At King Street Brewery Mrs Elizabeth Julie Healey was the owner or joint owner from 1863 to 1891 after her husband died when he was only forty-one.

Long-term brewery ownership

There are eleven good examples where ownership of Hertfordshire breweries remained with one family for at least eighty years through sons, cousins or nephews or when a son in law took over (Table 1.4). In a number of cases the brewery was sold because there was no son in the family to take over the ownership or because the son or sons had been killed, for example while on active service.

The Searancke family started with a small brewery attached to an inn at Hatfield in 1589. When John Searancke died in 1779, his nephews Francis and Joseph Niccoll changed their surname to Searancke so that they could inherit the brewery. When they sold the Hatfield Brewery in 1815 it had belonged to the family for 226 years. The brothers bought the Kingsbury Brewery in St Albans in 1815. Francis retired in 1868 with no apparent successor and leased the brewery to John Lloyd until 1889, when it was put up for sale. The Searancke and Niccoll families' involvement with brewing in Hertfordshire is by far the longest if the time in St Albans is included in the calculation.

Robert Phillips, a Quaker from Radwell near Baldock, established a brewery in Royston that was to belong to members of the Phillips family for the next 224 years. The family tree is complicated because five John Phillips became partners in the business. Nephews and cousins became involved in the management and ownership as well as sons. Cornell (1986) has made a study of members of this family involved with the Royston Brewery. A detailed investigation of the Phillips family becomes difficult because family members were also involved in the ownership of at least another twenty-five breweries in England and Wales (Luckett, 1986; Brown, 2003a and b). When the Royston Brewery was sold to Green's of Luton in 1949 there were still five members of the Phillips family serving as directors of the company. Why they took the final decision to sell is not known.

Another Quaker called William Lucas established a brewery in Hitchin in 1709 with his brother in law Isaac Gray. One of the family brewers William Lucas (1804–1861) wrote the following in his diary in 1841:

> I often feel such misgivings as to the holding of Public House property that I wish we were fairly out of the business; but then again it seems necessary to provide for the settlement of my six sons. By the return of malt consumed in the Irish distilleries it appears to have fallen in 1840 one-third. If high fed, paid and bred Protestant priests had as much influence and zeal as the voluntary supported Irish Catholics the days of English Brewing prosperity would soon see an end. John Whiting, who is the great advocate and support of teetotalism in Hitchin, has been frequently obliged by the doctor's orders to resume Beer, and today we hear he is again ill. Total abstinence is certainly irrational, unchristian and expedient, temperance is quite another thing.
>
> (Bryant and Parker, 1934)

In spite of William's personal feelings, successive generations of the Lucas family continued to own the brewery for 214 years until 1923 when it was sold to Green's of Luton.

Peter McMullen established a small brewery in Back Street in Hertford in 1827. He eventually moved to a site in Hartham Lane where the family business is still operational after 178 years. Successive generations of the family have been involved in the management of the company that has a tied estate of approximately 150 properties. This is the only Hertfordshire brewery still going strong, but it will be a good few years before it catches up with Lucas, Phillips or Searancke.

Mordecai and Henry Goodwin began brewing in 1720 in King's Langley.

Mordecai's daughter married Thomas Groome who inherited the business. It was their son, grandson and great grandson, amongst others, who made it possible for the brewery to be retained by the family for 177 years. When John Edward Groome retired there were no sons to take over so the brewery was sold to Benskin's in 1897.

A common brewer named John Pope began working in 1714 in a small brewery that was later known as Pope's Yard in New Street, Watford (Smith, 1988). When he died he left his business to Daniel, a son of his second wife. Unfortunately Daniel had a relatively short life (1708–1741) so the brewery was bequeathed to Daniel's nephew John Dyson, the son of his sister Sarah who had married William Dyson, a Watford maltster. John Dyson I's son, John Dyson II, and his grandson John Dyson III each owned the brewery in turn. John Dyson III never married so when he died in 1867 the family decided to sell the brewery and estate at auction. By that time the brewery had been owned by members of the Pope and Dyson families for 153 years (Smith, 1988).

William Smith is reputed to have started brewing at the *Swan* in Watford High Street in 1655. Successive generations of the family built up a small tied estate of fifteen properties. The long period of family ownership of 135 years ended when a descendant also called William Smith sold the business in 1790 to George Whittingstall. William Smith invested his proceeds from the sale into a farm of 199 acres at Nascot near Watford and died while living there in 1818.

The St Albans Brewery was started by Thomas Kinder while he was working as a common brewer and bought his first public house in 1737. Eventually a brewery was established in Chequer Street, St Albans and owned and managed by his descendants for 131 years. In 1868 the brewery was sold to Adey & White. However part of the tied estate was retained by the Kinder family as an investment and leased to Adey & White until 1910.

Edward King Fordham and his younger brother Oswald of Ashwell established their brewery in 1836 (Cornell, 1984). At a later stage Edward's son Wolverly Attwood Fordham became company chairman and was succeeded by his second cousin Edward Oswald Fordham. In 1939 Anthony Hill became a member of the board of directors when he was only twenty-five. He was the favourite nephew of Mrs Wolverly Fordham who was still a major shareholder in the company. Unfortunately Anthony Hill was killed on active service during World War II. After the war in 1952 the majority of the shareholders decided to accept an offer from Green's of Luton after 116 years of family ownership (Cornell, 1984).

The history of the High Street Brewery in Baldock while under the ownership of the Simpson family is well documented (Cornell, 1999). Details of the family history have been researched by Luckett (1986) and by Brown (2003a). Joseph and Thomas George Simpson bought the brewery from the Pryor family in 1853. They were the sons of Richard Simpson who had married Sophia Phillips, the sister of John Phillips IV who was one of the managing partners of the Royston Brewery. Before this brewery purchase Thomas Simpson was already married to his cousin Fanny Phillips, the daughter of Joseph Phillips II who was another managing partner of the Royston Brewery. When Joseph and Thomas Simpson died, the brewery was managed jointly by each of their sons, Evelyn and Francis Tom Simpson. Evelyn married his cousin Fanny Emily Agnes Phillips, the daughter of Joseph Phillips II of Stamford. In 1909 Evelyn changed his surname to Shaw-Hellier in order to inherit from an uncle. Tragically his son Arthur Joseph was killed in action during World War I. When Evelyn died in 1922, his investment in the brewery was inherited by his only daughter Evelyn Mary Penelope Shaw-Hellier. Francis Tom Simpson died in 1929 without any children of his own to inherit his share of the brewery. Much later Miss Shaw-Hellier was financially advised to sell the brewery because of the heavy death duties that would have to be paid because of her wealth. She wanted the Baldock brewery business to remain a viable unit and not split up and the brewery closed. Therefore Miss Shaw-Hellier and the other directors decided to sell the brewery in 1954 to Greene King of Bury St Edmunds, a brewery whose traditions and aims were similar to those of the Simpsons. Agreement for the sale was very rapid. Thus a family connection of 101 years with the brewery ended.

Quaker brewers

Mathias (1959d) stressed the historical significance of four Quaker families in the establishment of two large London porter breweries before 1830. These were the Buxton, Gurney and Hanbury families in Truman's brewery and the Barclay family in Barclay, Perkins & Co. (later Courage). Brewing in those times was not considered an improper occupation for Quakers (unlike the manufacture and selling of weapons or distilled spirits such as whisky or gin). Outside London Mathias mentions only Lucas of Hitchin as a Quaker brewer in Hertfordshire. Reference was also made to the Gibsons, another Quaker family who owned a brewery in Saffron Walden, Essex. In 1839 this brewery was sold to the Taylors.

Members of this second Quaker family were already established maltsters living in Bishop's Stortford.

Before examining the Quaker involvement in brewing and malting in Hertfordshire it is worth understanding how education, training and religious beliefs could influence their work and interaction with others in the 1700s and early 1800s. A short quotation from Clarkson (1806) serves as a good introduction:

> The Quakers generally bring up their children to some employment. They believe that these, having an occupation, may avoid evils into which they might otherwise fall, if they had upon their hands an undue proportion of vacant time. Friends of all degrees, says The Book of Extracts, are advised to take due care to breed up their children in some useful and necessary employment, that they may not spend their precious time in idleness, which is of evil example, and tends much to their hurt.

Raistrick (1968) quotes a number of examples of famous Quaker industrialists being sent by their fathers to serve apprenticeships with other Quakers before joining a family business. However he does not quote any examples of brewers or maltsters. Grubb (1930) writing about Quakerism and industry before 1800 made the following observation:

> As apprentices they were trained to Industry under careful supervision, they were frequently being cautioned against running into debt and warned to avoid trading beyond what they could afford. The love of accuracy, which was inoculated in them, made them cautious of dealing with those who would not pay them promptly, and their dislike of legal proceedings made them act in the same way.   (Raistrick, 1968)

In Quaker businesses where the majority or part of the work-force were Quakers, their literacy and habits of thought and study contrasted sharply with the majority of the working class at that time (Raistrick, 1968). This meant that many workers understood the need to improve work processes or introduce new ones. Good work practice was strongly encouraged to ensure the health and safety of workers.

Grubb (1930) comments that:

> Business affairs of the Society were democratic in their nature. Masters and servants, employers and employees met on a basis of equality. In such meetings the Quaker* employer may well have learnt to respect employees as men and not merely as hands.

---

*   Quakers were also known as members of the Society of Friends

Until 1837 all people wanting to get married except Quakers and Jews had to have a church wedding for it to be legally recognised. However a Quaker wedding is not an alternative form of marriage available to the general public. Until 1857 if a Quaker married a non-Quaker, he or she could be disowned by the Society of Friends. Quaker marriage certificates give details of the occupations of the bridegroom, his father, the bride's father and possibly the bride plus the signatures of witnesses, families and other guests present at the wedding ceremony. Thus it is relatively easy to identify Quaker brewers and maltsters and see how some of these families became related through marriages. Even abbreviated certificates give useful information.

Using Quaker archival evidence from a number of sources it is possible to establish how active Quakers were in the brewing and malting industries in Baldock, Hertford, Hitchin and Royston and to a lesser extent in Hatfield and Ware (Hertfordshire County Record Office a.). The archives show how a number of Quakers became related through marriage.

The Lucas family of Hitchin became Quakers in the late 1600s, established themselves as brewers and maltsters and owned a brewery until 1923. Before 1709, Samuel Lucas had formed a working partnership with his brother-in-law Isaac Gray I, another Quaker brewer who started brewing on a small scale. Much later in 1770 Mary Gray, the daughter of Isaac Gray II, another Hitchin Quaker brewer, married Ellington Wright, a maltster from Warboys in Huntingdonshire. It is very probable that Ellington Wright was a Quaker. However it is not recorded whether Isaac Gray II also worked at the Lucas Brewery.

During 1822 Richard Beck, a wine merchant of Token Place Yard, London, a son of Thomas Beck of Hitchin, married Rachel Lucas, a daughter of William Lucas a brewer in Hitchin. In the same year Richard's cousin Edward Beck, a maltster in Isleworth, London, the son of Benjamin Beck of Hitchin, married Jane Morris, a daughter of John Morris, a Quaker brewer in Ampthill, Bedfordshire.

The Pryor family who became Quakers in the 1600s were also well established as maltsters in Baldock. John Pryor (1741–1819) married Maria Fitzjohn the widow of another Baldock Quaker maltster in 1770 and obtained more maltings as result of this marriage. Soon afterwards he leased the High Street Brewery from the Thurgood family. John and Maria had four sons. John Izzard Pryor was eventually to take over the management of the brewery. Thomas and Robert leased a brewery in London and eventually became partners in Truman, Hanbury & Co. The fourth son managed the family maltings in Baldock.

When John Izzard Pryor married in 1798 it was recorded that John Morris, a Quaker brewer from Ampthill, was a witness at the marriage service. John Pryor's son Alfred also trained as a brewer and bought the Hatfield Brewery in 1837.

In 1853, because there was no experienced member of the Pryor family to take over the management of the Baldock High Street Brewery the decision was taken to sell it. The buyers were John and Thomas Simpson, nephews of the Phillips family, another Quaker family who owned the brewery in Royston (Brown, 2003a). It might be assumed that the Simpsons were Quakers. The Pryor family were also cousins to the Phillips family.

It is recorded that two Baldock maltsters, George and Thomas Wells Fitzjohn bought an interest in the St Andrew's Brewery in Hertford from Richard Flower, a Quaker Hertford brewer during 1803. George Fitzjohn had also been active as a brewer in Baldock c.1794 (Poole, 1984). The Fitzjohn family owned 3 and 3a Hitchin Street, Baldock, and also owned the malting directly opposite next door to the *White Hart*. This malting was later pulled down.

A little later in 1827, John Steed, the son of another John Steed, had a Quaker wedding. Both were brewers and owners of the Pale Ale Brewery in Norton Street, Baldock when the brewery was in an active phase.

Another town with strong Quaker links was Royston. Robert Brand, Michael Phillips and Robert Phillips were all established Quaker maltsters between 1717 and 1725. In 1725 Robert Phillips bought a plot of land in Baldock Street from a man named Hagar to build a brewery. It is evident from records that members of the Haggar or Hagar family were also Quakers. Members of the Phillips family including sons, cousins and nephews managed the brewery until 1949 when it was sold to Green's of Luton. This was another brewery that had been first owned by a Quaker.

There was also Quaker involvement in brewing and malting in Hertford. During the 1660s William Fairman was a brewer whose mother had owned the *King's Head* at the corner of Fore Street and Castle Street. His son Benjamin was also a brewer and maltster and an early occupant of the Young's brewery site. Another brewer at this time was Edward Byllinge. Maltsters included Nicholas Lucas, Richard Martin and Thomas Dowcra of nearby Ware (Rowe, 1970). William Fairman was found guilty of being at a conventicle at the house of Nicholas Lucas and sentenced in 1664 to be transported to Barbados; instead it is thought he was imprisoned for a short while in England. However Nicholas Lucas and Edward Byllinge shortly afterwards emigrated to the Quaker colony in West New Jersey in the United States. William Fairman's son Benjamin used a malting in Sow Lane (later South Lane) where the Young family were later to build their brewery (Hertfordshire County Record Office c.)

Another Quaker brewer, William Manser, had a small brewery in Back Street, Hertford, from 1822 to 1839 without any known tied estate (Rowe, 1987). He then leased the brewery to Thomas Medcalf. In 1862 William Manser's daughter Elizabeth married Samuel Lucas, a partner at the Hitchin Brewery. Also during the 1830s Thomas Gripper and his sons John and Joseph owned a successful family malting business. The Grippers later amalgamated with the Wightman family to form a malting company that was to remain in Hertford until it finally ceased trading in 1958. Mathias (1959d) made the following statement: Considering the large number of brewers in the country as a whole, the dozen or so known families of Quaker stock who were brewers would not appear to provide more than a very modest contribution to the industry. The evidence that has just been presented shows conclusively that Quaker families had a very significant role in establishing a number of brewing and malting businesses in towns in Hertfordshire. More details will be given when considering individual breweries. Further research will probably prove that many more Quaker brewers were active elsewhere in England.

Brewing and banks

Anyone who is interested in the financing of the English brewing industry in the eighteenth and early nineteenth centuries should read the classic discussion by Mathias (1959e). Mathias (1959f) stated that the initial capital for setting up a public brewhouse or 'common brewhouse' in the eighteenth century was not large if the building was rented. He thought that £200 would be sufficient for a copper and a furnace, a mash tun, a fermenting square, a cooler, a hop back, pumps, a few barrels and other implements.

Murison, a brewer in Edinburgh had an annual turnover of approximately £3,000 when he produced 400 barrels of strong ale at £5 a barrel and 200 barrels of table or small beer at £4 a barrel. In 1795 the production costs were £2,500. The main items of expenditure were malt, hops and coal (49 per cent), Excise duty (44 per cent) and wages (7 per cent) (Donnachie, 1979). As malting barley is the major materials cost, the market price would have a major influence on expenditure and the selling price of a barrel of beer.

Presnell (1956) made the observation that during the time of the industrial revolution, brewing was the only industry to produce many bankers other than those industries concerned with metals and textiles. Brewing required a lot of capital investment but the investment yielded good returns in an age in which a growing population habitually washed down its food with beer and when home brewing was gradually declining.

The impulse for a brewer to consider banking was provided by the accumulation of wealth but also supplemented by the existence of short-term credit in the industry. The transactions of brewers with suppliers of malt and hops and purchasers of beer were managed on the basis of credit. It was the brewers who were also maltsters who had the biggest advantage because of the way that excise duties on malt were paid. The duty was nominally payable every six weeks. However, if maltsters gave bond for the security of duties approved by the Commissioners of Excise, they acquired an extended credit of four to five months. This enabled the maltsters to trade on the capital derived from the duties. This may well explain why historically some of the Hertfordshire brewers also built their town maltings.

Mathias (1959g) has examined the development of some of the large porter breweries in London including Whitbread's, Truman and Hanbury & Co. and Barclay, Perkins & Co. Both Truman & Hanbury & Co. and Barclay, Perkins & Co. were owned by Quakers who had developed close ties with Quaker banks. There also was an intricate network of marriages that led to brewers marrying bankers' daughters or vice versa. Thomas Marlborough Pryor, a partner of Truman & Hanbury and a son of John Pryor, a Quaker brewer at Baldock, married Hannah Hoare whose father was either a brewer or banker in London (Brown, 2003a). As a result, strong ties were developed with the Barclay, Gurney, Bevan and Hoare banking families. Raistrick (1959) has written a good introduction to Quaker banking families. Because of these close relationships with major banks the Quaker breweries had adequate available resources to cope with financial problems that occurred during the Napoleonic Wars. In contrast, Samuel Whitbread had problems obtaining money he was owed or wanted to borrow and had to be financially rescued in 1797–9 and 1801 by his Whig friends and relatives (Mathias, 1959h).

Country Quaker banks

When the bank of Bassett, Grant & Co. was founded in Leighton Buzzard there were three young Quaker partners, John D. Bassett, Joseph Sharples and William Exton. In 1820 these three partners opened a bank in Hitchin trading as

Sharples, Bassett & Company's Hertfordshire Hitchin Bank. Sharples and Exton moved to Hitchin and married sisters of a Quaker family. They cut the business connections with Leighton Buzzard in 1827. This new company was based in Hitchin and took over Sharples and Exton's Hitchin, Ampthill and Luton branches. In 1836, Jeffrey Lucas, a son of Joseph Lucas (a partner in the Lucas Brewery) joined the bank as a partner when the business became known as Sharples, Exton & Lucas. On the death of William Exton in 1851, Jeffrey's brother Edward became a partner, as did James Hack Tuke (Matthews and Tuke, 1926). Jeffrey and Edward Lucas had married two daughters of a Quaker brewer named John Rickman who owned the Bear Brewery in Lewes, Sussex.

Jeffrey Lucas died in 1855 and Francis Lucas, a barrister and a son of William Lucas (of the Lucas Brewery) joined as a partner at the bank when it became known as Sharples, Tuke, Lucas & Lucas. When the Unity Joint Stock Bank failed in Hertford during 1858 the decision was taken to open a branch of Sharples & Co in Hertford three days later. One of William Exton's daughters had married Frederick Seebohm from York and in 1859 the Hitchin Bank partnership changed once more and became Sharples, Lucas, Tuke & Seebohm. William Exton's other daughter had married Joseph Gurney Barclay of 54, Lombard Street, City of London. The bank also opened sub-branches in Stevenage in 1873, in Hatfield in 1877 and New Barnet in 1885 (Foster, 1963).

Another Quaker bank was started over the county border in Saffron Walden. In 1824 Searle & Co were already established as the town bank. They envied the brewing and malting business of the Gibsons, who were a Quaker family, and decided to compete against the Gibsons by opening a malting in King Street, Saffron Walden. Gibson's brewery will be discussed later in this book. Gibson & Co. quickly took the decision to expand their range of business interests by opening the Saffron Walden and North West Essex Bank as an alternative bank in the town. Unfortunately Searle & Co failed soon afterwards in 1825. In 1863 George Stacey Gibson took into partnership his brother-in-law William Tuke, a tea merchant in London and a cousin Edmund Birch Gibson who was a miller. Tuke's brother was a partner in the Hitchin Bank.

In 1808 Edward King Fordham, John Fordham and Richard Flower formed a partnership and opened a bank in Royston as Fordham, Flower & Fordham. John Fordham and Richard Flower were brothers-in-law and had previously leased and later bought the St Andrews Brewery in Hertford from the Ireland family in 1785. Edward King Fordham was the great uncle of another Edward King Fordham who started Fordham's Brewery in Ashwell. All three of the partners were probably Quakers because their descendants were able to join a partnership with known Quakers. Later John E. Fordham of Melbourne Bury and John George Fordham joined the partnership and the bank became known as Fordham & Co in 1825. In 1880 the bank partnership changed when Henry Fordham and Francis John Fordham of Royston were joined by Edmund Birch Gibson and William Murray Tuke of the Saffron Walden and North West Essex Bank. The bank became known as Fordham, Gibson & Co. Subsequently Edmund's son Edmund Wyatt Gibson joined the partnership in 1885 when the partners opened a branch of the bank in Sawbridgeworth.

A major national bank merger of twelve principal banks took place in 1896 to form Barclay & Co Ltd. Three of these banks were Sharples & Co. of Hitchin, Fordham & Co. of Royston and Gibson & Co. of Saffron Walden. The comment was made that many of these banks were proud of their Quaker ancestors and values of frugality, prudence and trustworthiness in the Victorian world of banking though none of the managing partners of Barclay's Bank was still a practising Quaker (Ackrill and Hannah, 2001). The phrase 'the deliberated planning of marriages' was used as an observation about a very complex web of linkages between families both nationally and within Hertfordshire.

Other banks with brewery partners in Hertfordshire

In comparison, non-Quaker brewing/banking partnerships in Hertfordshire were limited. One of the earliest banks in Hertfordshire was started in Hitchin in 1789 by William Wilshere, an attorney who had been handling the business of writing legal money deeds for some years. There is a brief surviving reference that states:

> Capital advance in partnership with Joseph Margetts Pierson, John Crabb and Daniel Chapman to be employed in the business of banking in Hitchin at the joint and equal profit and risk of the four as pr. Articles dated 31 Augt. £500.

This bank was afterwards known as Chapman, Pierson, Crabb & Co. (Presnell, 1956). Wilshere himself was also a brewer (site unknown), a maltster (he later sold maltings to the Lucas Brewery) and owned the *Green Dragon* in Hitchin in 1795 (site unknown). John Crabb was also a brewer in Hitchin (see Hitchin chapter). Much later Pierson & Co. of Hitchin were acting as banking agents in 1838. However Marshall & Pierson's brewery failed in 1841 and the banking agency closed.

William Christie and George Cathrow, who owned the Hoddesdon Brewery, founded the Hertford Bank in Fore Street, Hertford in 1807 (Garside, 2002). The bank suffered a large loss by robbery in 1814 when a coach transporting £3,000 of the bank's money to London was held up and the money was stolen. Later that year the bank was taken over by Samuel Adams' Ware Bank. Adams was also a maltster in Ware (Pigot, 1827).

William Smith and Edward Whittingstall of the Watford Brewery established another bank in Hertfordshire in the 1860s. This bank opened branches in Watford and Hemel Hempstead.

In Bedfordshire, Samuel Wells established a brewery in Biggleswade in 1764. In 1830 his son Samuel Wells with sons-in-law Robert Lindsell and William Hogge established a bank known as Wells, Hogge & Co. Later the bank expanded and opened a branch in Baldock where it became known as the Biggleswade and Baldock Bank (Wilson, 1983; Poole, 1984). Later the bank opened another branch in Hitchin (Foster, 1963).

Merger mania

In 1954 there were 479 breweries operated by 305 companies in the UK. However during the 1950s and 1960s 'merger mania' took over, mergers and purchase of many regional brewery companies became very common, leading to the formation of what became known as 'the big six'. These companies were Allied Breweries Ltd, Bass Charrington Ltd, Courage Ltd, Scottish and Newcastle Breweries Ltd, Watney, Mann & Truman Holdings Ltd and Whitbread & Co. Ltd. The six companies owned about seventy-five per cent of the public houses in the United Kingdom and by 1972 brewed approximately eighty per cent of the beer and lager. In 1980 there were only 142 breweries operated by 81 companies (Gourvish and Wilson, 1994). Mergers and closures have continued so that there are now in 2005 in the United Kingdom approximately forty-five independent breweries with tied estates and about ten very large breweries operated by the remaining members of 'the big six' and the global brewers.

Nationally there were four surviving micro-breweries attached to public houses in the 1970s. These were the *All Nations* at Madeley, the *Blue Anchor* at Helston, the *Olde Swan* at Netherton and the *Three Tuns* at Bishop's Castle. Since then there has been a big revival in small-scale commercial brewing and there are now over 400 micro-breweries. Most of these new micro-breweries do not own any tied estates. Their main sources of sale are 'free houses' and beer festivals.

In Hertfordshire in 2005, McMullen's of Hertford is still operating as an independent brewery company. At present there are also seven micro-breweries. These are the Buntingford Brewery at Royston, the Green Tye Brewery at Green Tye, the Red Squirrel Brewery at Hertford, the Sawbridgeworth Brewery at Sawbridgeworth, the Tring Brewery at Tring and the Verulam Brewery at St Albans.

The UK government decided to introduce Beer Orders as a result of the Monopolies and Mergers Commission Report in the late 1980s. The Beer Orders gave tenants of these six national brewers the right to buy guest beers free from brewery ties. However the breweries decided to sell all or most of their tenanted tied estates to pub groups that did not own breweries. Some of these pub companies now own hundreds or thousands of public houses.

Meanwhile some of the national breweries have become part of international brewery complexes. Thus Watney at Mortlake is now part of Anheuser-Busch of the USA, Allied (Carlsberg-Tetley) is part of Carlsberg of Denmark and part of the former Bass brewing empire has been bought by Coors of the USA. Bass beers and Whitbread beers are owned by Interbrew of Belgium. The remaining two, Courage and Scottish Newcastle Breweries, have merged to form Scottish Courage and since bought Brasseries Kronenberg of France and Alken Maes of Belgium.

The scope of this book

In their historical gazetteer, *Hertfordshire Inns and Public Houses*, Jolliffe and Jones (1995) listed the last known brewery owner even if it was one of the 'Big Six' or owned by a pub group. However, when writing this book the aim was to identify a brewery tied estate as part of an active business when sold to a new owner or when closed. Another aim was to identify the individual public houses that had been sold separately, closed or returned to the owner at the end of a lease.

It is hoped that the town and village plans might encourage readers to visit some of the brewing and malting sites mentioned in the text. Unfortunately, developers are very active in Hertfordshire. Alteration or demolition may have occurred on a few of the sites while the book was being written.

In the chapters that follow each brewery is listed, with details of how long it was actively brewing, any plans, its capacity, the owners, the make-up of the tied estate and its geographical spread. The industrial archaeologist is also interested to know whether any of the brewery buildings still remain and whether there is a brewery house, a brewery tap, any brewery maltings, stables for horses, railway or canal links, wells or other sources of water. There may also still be traces of old brewery names on some of the buildings or public houses.

Historically the parishes of Chipping Barnet, East Barnet, New Barnet, Arkley, Hadley and Totteridge were all in Hertfordshire. Branch Johnson (1962–3) and Jolliffe and Jones (1995) included these parishes in their books on Hertfordshire inns and public houses. The same policy is being followed in this book even though these six parishes now form part of the London Borough of Barnet after boundary reorganisation.

The final part of the book will consider a few breweries in the counties of Buckinghamshire, Bedfordshire and Essex. These breweries are Weller's of Amersham, T. & J. Nash's Chesham Brewery, Roberts & Wilson of Ivinghoe, Bennett's of Dunstable, Green's of Luton, Wells of Bedford, the Anchor Brewery of Saffron Walden and Clutterbuck's of Stanmore. The reasons why these breweries were selected are explained on p.245.

References

Ackrill, M. and Hannah, L. *Barclays – The Business of Banking 1690–1996*, Cambridge University Press, 2001.

Barnard, A. Cannon Brewery, Watford. *Noted Breweries of Great Britain and Northern Ireland*, Vol. 4, London, 1891, pp.28–50.

Branch Johnson, W. *Hertfordshire Inns*, 2 vols. Hertfordshire Countryside, Carling Hitchin, 1962–3.

Branch Johnson, W. Hertfordshire Maltings, *Hertfordshire Past and Present*, Vol. 6, 1966, pp.19–47.

Branch Johnson, W. Brewing and Malting. *The Industrial Archaeology of Hertfordshire*, David and Charles, Newton Abbot, 1970, pp.28–47.

Brown, J. *Steeped in Tradition. The malting industry in England since the railway age.* Institute of Agricultural History, University of Reading, 1983.

Brown, M. On the Trail of the Phillips – Part 1, *Brewery History, The Journal of the Brewery History Society*, No. 111, 2003a, pp.38–64.

Brown, M. On the Trail of the Phillips – Part 2, *Brewery History, The Journal of the Brewery History Society*, No. 112, 2003b, pp.15–29.

Bryant, G.E. and Parker, G.P. (eds.) *Being the Diary and Reminiscences of William Lucas of Hitchin 1804–1861*, Hutchinson & Co., London, 1934, pp.238–9.

Clark, C. *The British Malting Industry since 1830.* Hambledon Press, London, 1998.

Clarkson, T. *Portraiture of Quakerism Vol. 2.* Longman, Hurst, Rees and Orme, London, 1806, pp.45–6.

Cornell, M. Fordhams of Ashwell, *The Brewery History Society Journal*, No. 39, 1984, pp.3–9.

Cornell, M. Phillips' Royston Brewery, *The Brewery History Journal*, No. 49, 1986, pp.6–12.

Cornell, M. Simpsons of Baldock. Two centuries of brewing in north Hertfordshire. *Hertfordshire's Past*, Vol. 46, 1999, pp.2–14.

Corran, H.S. *A History of Brewing*, David and Charles, Newton Abbot, 1975.

Crosby, T. Development of Malthouses around the Hertfordshire-Essex Border, *Brewery History, The Journal of the Brewery History Society*, No. 94, 2001, pp.4–29.

Davison, A.P. Ale fit for man's bodie. Brewing and malting in medieval England. Part 5. The brewhouse and its equipment. *Brewery History, The Journal of the Brewery History Society*, No. 93, 1998a, pp.38–45.

Davison, A.P. Ale fit for man's bodie. Brewing and malting in medieval England. Part 4. Medieval malting. *Brewery History, The Journal of the Brewery History Society*, No. 92, 1998b, pp.22–9.

Donnachie, I. *A History of the Brewing Industry in Scotland*, John Donald, Edinburgh, 1979.

Foster, A.M. A brief history of banking in Hitchin, *Hertfordshire Past and Present*, Vol. 3, 32–8, 1963.

Garside, S. *Hoddesdon. A History*, Phillimore, Chichester, 2002.

Gourvish, T.R. and Wilson, R.G. *The British Brewing Industry 1830–1980*, Cambridge University Press, 1994.

Grubb, I. *Quakerism and Industry before 1800*, Williams & Norgate, London, 1930, pp.174–5.

Hertfordshire Archives and Local Studies. a. Details of brewery contents. a. Christie's in 1886 (D/E Cb T1), b. Whittingstall's in 1862 (D/E Be T1), c. Young's in 1897 (D/E Le/B 11/3).

Hertfordshire Archives and Local Studies. b. Details of Quaker trustees of annuity from land in Ashwell. a. 1719–20 (53968-9), b. 1747–8 (53972–3), c. 1788 (53974). Details of Quaker marriages a. NQ1 5C/1, b. NC16 RG6.

Hertfordshire Archives and Local Studies. c. Details of deeds relating to land and property in Sow Lane Hertford, a. 1696 (74046), b. 1718 (74048).

Hornsey, I. *Brewing*, Royal Society of Chemistry, London, 1999, pp.58–84.

Jolliffe, G. and Jones, A. *Hertfordshire Inns: An Historical Gazetteer*, Hertfordshire Publications, Hatfield, 1995.

Luckett, F. Phillips' Breweries, *The Brewery History Journal*, 1986, No. 49, pp.3–5.

Mathias, P. *The Brewing Industry in England 1700–1830*, Cambridge University Press, 1959. a. p.437, b. Sections of chapters 11, 12, 13, c. p.355, d. p.287, e. pp.252–330, f. p.253, g. p.265, h. p.286, i. p.299.

Matthews, P.W. and Tuke, A.W. *A History of Barclays Bank Ltd.*, Blades, East & Blades, London, 1926.

Pigot, *Directory of Hertfordshire*, 1827.

Poole, H. *Here for the Beer*, Watford Museum, 1984.

Presnell, L. S. *County Banking in the Industrial Revolution*, Clarendon Press, Oxford, 1956.

Raistrick, A. *Quakers in Science and Industry*, David & Charles, Newton Abbot, 1968.

Rowe, V. *The First Hertford Friends* (published privately), 1970.

Rowe, V. The Quaker Presence in Hertford in the Nineteenth Century, *Journal of the Friends Historical Society*, 1987, Vol. 55, pp. 80–111.

Sawford, B. *Wild Flower Habitats of Hertfordshire. Past – Present – Future*, Castlemound Publications, Ware, 1990, p.38.

Smith, K.A. The Popes and the Dysons. Five generations of Watford brewers, *Hertfordshire's Past*, 1988, Vol. 25, pp.2–7.

Society of Friends. *London Yearly Meeting during 250 Years*, Devonshire House, London, 1919, pp.52–5.

Wilson, R.G. *Greene King. A Business and Family History*, Bodley Head & Jonathan Cape, London, 1983, p.233.

Hertfordshire towns and villages

CHAPTER TWO

Ashwell

Malting and brewing were established in Ashwell by the early 1800s. In 1746, Robert Thurgood, a brewer in Baldock bought the *Bay Tree* (later the *Three Tuns*) and a malting that were later sold to James Pryor of Baldock. James Ind, another brewer in Baldock purchased the *Rose and Crown* and a malting in June 1792. Many of the large houses and farms in the village had their own brewhouses. The rate returns of 1829 show that Thomas Chapman of Dixie's Farm, Mr C. Porter at Swan House, the Westropes at Bear House and Benjamin Christy at Westbury Farm all had their own brewhouses. Mr Lee at Jessamine House had a brewhouse, a malting and a barley barn.

Mr Porter was the first Ashwell resident to begin larger scale brewing on the corner of Mill Street, just off the High Street in 1830. This enterprise was not successful and in 1832 his brewing equipment, which included a fifty gallon vat, was sold to the Fordham family who had a small commercial brewery at Odsey Grange near Ashwell railway station. In 1793 the Fordham family had purchased Odsey Grange from the fifth Duke of Devonshire (McKinley, 1932). Elias Pym Fordham had originally founded a company in 1796 when he was described as a brewer, banker and wool-stapler. Elias had three brothers, George, John and Edward King and a sister called Elizabeth who married Richard Flower, a Quaker brewer from Hertford.

One night Elias's horse stumbled over a tipsy man who mumbled that "it was all along of Fordham's fine ale". This troubled Elias so much that he gave over the brewery to his brother George in exchange for some land in the parish of Sandon (Anon). Elias later became a Unitarian minister. John and Edward King Fordham became business partners with Richard Flower when they established the Royston Bank in 1806.

In 1843 Benjamin Christy and his neighbour John Sale also started commercial scale brewing on land beside Westbury House.

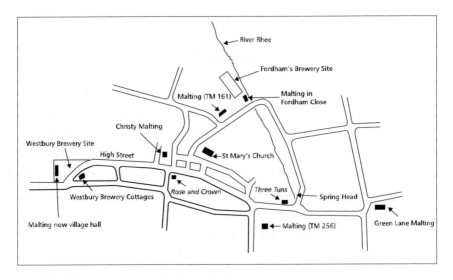

Figure 2.1 Brewing and malting sites in the village

Fordham's Brewery

George Fordham and his son Edward George began commercial scale brewing in 1836 at the northern end of Mill Street in Ashwell by the River Rhee. When George died in 1840 the brewery was left as a bequest to his son Edward George who evidently delegated the brewery management to his sons Edward King and Oswald. Successive generations of the family were to remain actively involved in the management of this brewery until 1952.

By 1846, Edward King Fordham and his brother Oswald were well known as brewers, maltsters, spirit merchants and farmers. Oswald died in 1862 and was replaced as a joint manager by his cousin Herbert Fordham. When Edward King Fordham died in 1889 his share of the brewery went to his second son Wolverly Attwood Fordham. Herbert Fordham died in 1891 and his brewery share was divided equally between his two sons Herbert George and Ernest Oswald. In 1897 the partnership became a limited company. Wolverly Attwood Fordham died in 1921 but his widow remained a major shareholder. Herbert George Fordham died in 1929 and his son William Herbert joined the company board. In 1939 Mrs Wolverly Fordham's nephew Anthony Hill became a director but was unfortunately killed on active service during World War II. Further details of the Fordham family history can be found in Cornell (1984).

The Fordham's brewery in Mill Street included a tun room, a cleansing room, a brewery office and a counting house. Some of the machinery came from

Odsey Grange or had been bought from Mr Porter. Power was obtained from a water wheel driven by water from a leat passing under part of the buildings. A local builder extended the brewery in 1856. Surplus equipment was sold off in 1860 and included coppers of thirty-four and twenty-three barrels' capacity, an iron mash tun, mashing machine, five square fermentation vessels and three round fermentation vessels.

In 1897 the estate of 131 licensed properties included 103 freehold, fifteen copyhold, six on long leases and seven on short leases. Annual profits were about £9,000. The beers being brewed in draught or bottled forms were XXXX, Double Stout, Oatmeal Stout, Milk Stout, Brown Ale, Pale Ale, Best Pale Ale, Light Ale, Light Bitter Ale, Old Ashwell Ale and Luncheon Ale.

At this time the brewery was still surrounded by farm buildings, stables, cowsheds, hay and straw stacks. A severe contamination problem in 1900 resulted in the production of very poor quality beers. A brewery consultant, Lawrence Briant thought that the major potential sources of contamination were the nearby farm yard and raw sewage in the River Rhee next to the brewery. He recommended that the farm buildings should be removed and an open wort cooler in the brewery should be scrapped. A reliable source of water was obtained by tapping the water spring at Springhead by the *Three Tuns* in the High Street and running a pipe to the brewery. Mr Briant returned in 1902 and described the best bitter as being "mawkish, rank and without character". The fermenting vessels used to brew best bitter were not fitted with attemperators (cooling coils) and therefore there was no control over the rate of fermentation. He thought that the mash tun and coolers were outdated and inefficient and should be replaced.

During the early 1900s the brewery was using at least sixteen shire horses to pull the drays for local beer deliveries. There were two beer wharves in the goods yard at Ashwell railway station to assist longer-distance transport by rail as there were a few tied properties in London. One free-trade outlet in Victorian times was the *Great East Hotel* in Great Yarmouth. Later in 1912 three Foden steam lorries were bought. A photograph taken in 1932 shows that two steam lorries were still being used as well as six conventional lorries.

The brewery always used its own maltings as a major source of malt. In 1828 John Edward Fordham bought from William Stanford a malting in Upper King Street, Royston that had previously belonged to Joseph Bedlam. The Fordham family also owned a malting in Kneesworth Street, Royston pre 1900. During 1893 a malting was built near the brewery. This building has now been converted

Figure 2.2 Fordham's Green Lane malting

into two houses and forms part of Fordham's Close. In Ashwell village the malting behind Mill Cottages (tithe map plot 161) was destroyed in a fire in 1892 together with 1,000 quarters of malt and 1,500 quarters of malting barley which caused £4,000 damage. The Fordham's had also lost another malting at Spring Head (tithe map plot 256) when the 1850 Ashwell fire destroyed a number of houses and other buildings. In 1902 a large malting was built in Green Lane opposite the war memorial (tithe map plot 151). At different times it has been used for housing prisoners of World War I, light industry, offices and has since been converted into flats.

Green's of Luton made an offer for the brewery in 1952, which was accepted by the majority of the share-holders. At this stage the tied estate of ninety-four licensed properties consisted of thirty-six in Hertfordshire, fifteen in Bedfordshire, twenty-six in Cambridgeshire, twelve in Essex, one in Suffolk and four in Greater London (Table 2.1). This included forty-five beer houses and three off-licences. Before this sale there were a number of other properties that Fordham's had closed, sold or had stopped leasing arrangements (Table 2.2).

Bottling of beers, which was already over 2,000,000 bottles in 1932, was continued after the merger of Greens with Flowers in 1956 and after the takeover by Whitbreads in 1962. This included Guinness, Worthington, Bass as well as Flowers and later Whitbread beers. Bottling was finally stopped in 1965. The brewery was demolished in 1973 and the site is now occupied by a small housing

Table 2.1 Fordham's tied estate sold to Green's in 1952

Herts

Ashwell	*Bushel and Strike* FL	Hitchin	*Woolpack* FL
	Engine FL	Hoddesdon	*Rose and Crown* BH
	Fox BH	Ickleford	*Plume of Feathers* FL
	Chalkman's Knoll BH	Knebworth	*Railway Hotel* FL, L. to FH.
Baldock	*Old White Horse* FL	Meesden	*Beehive* FL
Barkway	*Chaise and Pair* FL	Royston	*Jockey* (*Red Cow*) FL, C.
Bishop's Stortford	*King's Arms* BH		*Railway Tavern* FL
	Red Cow BH		*Red Lion* FL
	Red, White and Blue FL	Sawbridgeworth	*Gate* FL, C.
	Sawyers' Arms BH	Standon	*Fox and Hounds* FL, C.
Buckland	*Red Lion* FL	Stevenage	*Coach and Horses* FL
Buntingford	*Jolly Sailor* BH		*Dun Cow* BH, C.
	Railway Inn (*Shah*) FL		*Our Mutual Friend* FL, L.
Cromer	*Horse and Groom* FL		*Railway Inn* FL
Furneux Pelham	*Hoops* BH	Therfield	*Hoops* BH
Hitchin	*Black Horse* FL	Walkern	*Robin Hood* BH
	Leicester Inn FL	Wallington	*Derby Arms* BH
	Sailor Boy FL	Ware	*Bell* BH

Beds

Arlesey	*Fountain* FL	Sandy	*Lord Nelson* BH
Biggleswade	*Elephant and Castle* BH	Sharnbrook	*Railway Hotel* FL
	Peacock BH	Stopsley	*Brickmakers' Arms* FL
Clophill	*Stone Jug* BH	Stotfold	*Coach and Horses* BH, C.
Dunton	*Wheatsheaf* FL		*Peewit* BH
Gamlingay	*Spotted Cow* BH		*Queen's Head* FL, C.
Henlow	*Parachute* FL		*Stag* FL
Potton	*Horse and Jockey* FL, C.	Sundon	*Crown* FL

Cambs

Barrington	*Butcher's Arms* FL, C.	Melbourn	*Shant* BH
Bassingbourn	*Crown* BH		*Star* BH
	Pear Tree BH	Meldreth	*Deaf and Dumb Flea* BH
Bourn	*Duke of Wellington* BH, C.	Orwell	*Nag's Head* BH
Duxford	*Butcher's Arms* BH	St Neots	*Three Tuns* PH
Foxton	*White Horse* FL	Sawston	*Fox* BH
Great Shellford	*Peacock* BH	Stapleford	*Three Horseshoes* FL
Guilden Morden	*Chestnut Tree* BH, C.	Steeple Morden	*Jester* (*Railway Tavern*) FL
	King Edward VII BH		*Plough* BH
Linton	*Princess of Wales* FL	Toft	*Black Bull* FL
Litlington	*Beehive* BH	Whittlesey	*Plough* FL
March	*Royal Exchange* BH	Whittlesford	*Greyhound* FL
Melbourn	*Black Horse* BH		

Essex

Clavering	*Princess of Wales* BH, C.	Littlebury Green	*Rose* BH, C.
	White Horse FL	Lt. Hallingbury	*Hop Pole* BH
Debden	*Three Horseshoes* BH, C.	Manuden	*Yew Tree* BH
Great. Chesterford	*Elm Tree* BH, C.	Saffron Walden	*Old English Gentleman* BH

| Langley | *Robin Hood* BH, C. | Saffron Walden | *Queen Elizabeth* FL |
| Littlebury | *Carpenter's Arms* FL | Stanstead Mountfitchet | *Windmill* BH |

Greater London

| Harringay | *Cavendish Wine* OL | Highbury | OL Aubert Park N5 |
| | *Railway Hotel* FL | Tottenham | OL Seven Sisters Rd N11 |

Suffolk

| Bury St Edmunds | *St Edmund's Head* FL |

estate. There are still Fordham's signs on the front and on the roof of the *Nightingale* (ex *Leicester Inn*) in Hitchin.

Westbury Brewery

In 1843 Benjamin Christy and his neighbour John Sale began commercial brewing at Westbury Farm at the western end of the High Street (Figure 2.1). Soon afterwards they moved to a plot of land next door where a brewery, a malting, stables, a brewery house and other buildings were gradually constructed. By 1850 they were being described as brewers, maltsters and farmers. Shortly afterwards John Sale pulled out of the partnership and by 1861 Benjamin Christy's son, Benjamin Christy II, had become the brewer employing five men. At this stage there was a known tied estate of six licensed properties (Table 2.3). Another malting owned by the Christy family was in the High Street, behind shops near the entrance to Gardiner's Lane. This is now part of a private house but indications of the furnace chimney can still be seen in the tiled roof.

There were financial problems at the Westbury brewery in 1876 so it was mortgaged to Wells, Hogge and Lindsell's Bank in Baldock for two years. In 1879 the brewery was bought by Joshua Richmond Page who was already a large-scale maltster in Baldock and who may also have already owned or leased some licensed properties. The Page family had lived in Baldock since the early 1800s with their main residence at 10 Hitchin Street where there was a malting on the large plot at the rear of the property. Census records for 1881 indicate that Joshua Page a brewer, presumed to be J.R. Page's son age 20, was living at Dow house, West End, Ashwell.

Beer production was increased and the tied estate was added to (Tables 2.4 and 2.5). The ownership of the various inns and beer houses was spread among different members of the Page family. J.R. Page and G.E. Page bought thirteen

Figure 2.3 Westbury Brewery malting (now village hall)

Figure 2.4 Westbury Brewery brewer's house

licensed properties in Cambridge from brewers and other private owners during the 1880s. Most were later sold to other East Anglian brewers including Charles Wells of Bedford in 1893. The reason for these purchases and later sales in Cambridge is not known. After 1893 it would appear that the major part of the tied estate was held on short or long leases. There were nineteen leasehold properties when the brewery was sold to Wells & Winch of Biggleswade in 1921. At this stage only seven properties were owned by G.E. Page, Mrs J. Page and the executors of J.R. Page. Two others, the *Toll Bar* at Clothall and the *Cross* at Langford had previously been closed or sold.

Table 2.2 Fordham's tied estate disposed of before sale to Green's in 1952

Herts

Ashwell	*Australian Cow* BH	Hitchin	*Royal Oak* (*Boot*) FL
	Cuckoo FL		OL Walsworth Rd
	Swan BH	Reed	*Woolpack* BH, C.
	BH Back St	Royston	*Bushel and Strike* FL
	BH Blue Gates		*Woolpack* BH
	BH Mobs Hole	St Albans	*Jolly Malster* BH
	BH Odsey Lane		*Rising Sun* BH
Aspenden	*Carpenter's Arms* BH	Sandon	BH Roe Green
Barnet	*Platelayer's Arms* BH	Stapleford	*Three Horseshoes* BH
Barley	*King William* BH	Stevenage	*Lord Kitchener* BH
Bishop's Stortford	*Plough* BH		*North Star* BH
Codicote	*Rose and Crown* BH	Therfield	*Greyhound* BH
Hitchin	*Bushel and Strike* BH	Walkern	*Robin Hood* BH
	Curriers' Arms BH		

Beds

Arlesey	*Brickmakers' Arms* BH	Potton	*Eagle* BH
	Church House BH		*Horse and Jockey* BH
	Railway Tavern BH		*Railway Inn* BH
	Royal Oak BH	Shefford	BH Back Lane
Biggleswade	*Bushel and Strike* BH		*Gardener's Arms* BH
Dunton	*Wheatsheaf* BH, C.		*Saracen's Arms* BH
Henlow	*Gardener's Arms* BH	Shillington	*Edward VII* BH
Luton	*Brickmakers' Arms* FL		*Red Lion*
	Hare and Hounds BH	Stotfold	*Bell* (*New Inn*) FL
	Tiger OL		*Two Chimneys* BH
Northill	BH North Rd		*White Hart* BH
Potton	*Duke of Wellington*	Wilshamstead	*Elephant and Castle* BH
		Wrestlingworth	OL No name

Cambs

Bassingbourn	*White Horse* BH, C., L.	Melbourn	*Halfpenny House* BH
Guilden Morden	*Pig and Whistle* BH	St Neots	*Old Blue Ball*
Linton	*Princess of Wales* BH	Steeple Morden	*Pig and Whistle* BH
Meesden	*Beehive* BH, C.		

Greater London

Finsbury Park	*Station Hotel*	Hornsey	*Railway Hotel*

Suffolk

Lakenheath	*Brewery Tap*

Essex

Chrisshall	*Greyhound* BH

Wells & Winch were not interested in using the Westbury Brewery and the site was sold to the Fordham family. The old malting on this site was presented to the village to be used as a village hall and the stables were used by the local scout troop. Many of the other buildings were pulled down after World War II when building materials were rationed and re-cycled. This malting was still used as a village hall and by a pre-school play group in 2004. However its future is

Table 2.3 Christy's tied estate sold to the Page family in 1879

Herts				
Ashwell	*Cricketers* BH		Hitchin	*Shoulder of Mutton* BH
	Two Brewers BH		Royston	*Boar's Head* FL
Beds				
Arlesey	*Cock* BH *c.*1863		Potton	*Bushel and Strike* BH *c.*1841

Table 2.4 Page family sale of tied estate to Wells & Winch in 1921

a) Freehold			Vendor
Herts	Ashwell	*Cricketers* BH*	Excut. J.R. Page
	Baldock	*Black Eagle* BH*	G.E. Page
		White Lion FL*	Excut. J.R. Page
	Breachwood Green	*Fox* FL*	Mrs J. Page
	Pirton	*Red Lion* BH*	G.E. Page
	Royston	*Boar's Head* FL*	Excut. J.R. Page
Beds	Arlesey	*Lamb*	G.E. Page

b) Leasehold			Lease
Herts	Ashwell	*Six Bells**	Expired 1930
	Aston	*Fox**	Expired 1925
	Baldock	*White Horse* FL*	Expired 1937
	Buntingford	*Swan* BH*	Purchased 1962
	Hitchin	*Shoulder of Mutton* BH	Expired 1924
	Lilley	*Lilley Arms* FL*#	Purchased 1929
		*Red Lion**#	Purchased 1929
		*Silver Lion**#	Purchased 1929
	Mangrove Green	OL*#	Purchased 1929
	Sandon	*Two Brewers* BH*	Purchased 1962
	Weston	*Princess of Wales* BH*	Purchased 1921
Beds	Arlesey	*Cock* BH*	Expired 1926
	Potton	*Bushel and Strike* BH	Expired 1926
Cambs	Abingdon Piggotts	*Darby and Joan*	Expired 1927
	Cambridge	*Merton Arms*	
	Eyeworth	*Ongley Arms*	Purchased 1946
	Harlton	*Wheatsheaf*	Purchased 1921
	Steeple Morden	*Carriers' Arms**	Purchased 1932
	Thriplow	*Red Lion*	Purchased 1921

Key: *   Owned or leased by the Page family in the Quarterly Session Records for 1903
      #   The ownership of the properties in Lilley and Mangrove Green is as follows:
      1. 1907 Thomas George Sowerby to Clutterbuck's of Stanmore
      2. 1928 Clutterbuck's to Putteridge Estate Company
      3. Putteridge Estate Company sells leases to Wells & Winch

uncertain as developers would like to build houses on the site.

When the Page family sold the brewery and tied estate in 1921 they also decided to sell their maltings in Baldock. Four of these were bought by Paine & Co. Ltd of St Neots in 1921. Three of these maltings were still being used for malting barley in 1970. Some of them have since been demolished (Table 2.6).

Table 2.5 Page's disposals before 1921

Herts		Notes
Ashwell	*Stag's Head* BH	
	Two Brewers BH	Leased to J.R. Page in 1904
	BH Back St	
Baldock	*Pretty Lamp* BH	Leased to J.R. Page
	White Horse FL	Leased to J.R. Page in 1904
Clothall	*Toll Bar* BH	Leased by Joshua Page to J.R. Page in 1904
Hitchin	*Shoulder of Mutton* BH	Owned by J.R. Page in 1904
Kings Walden	*Fox* FL	Leased to J.R. Page in 1904 by Mrs A.F. Page
Layston	*Swan* BH	Leased to J.R. Page in 1904
Sandon	*Two Brewers* BH	Leased to J.R. Page in 1904
Weston	*Princess of Wales* BH	Leased to J.R. Page *c.*1918 by Pryor Reid
Beds		
Arlesey	*Cock* BH	
	Old Oak FL	Leased in 1891
Langford	*Cross* BH	Owned in 1903
Stotfold	*Pig and Whistle* BH	Sold in 1903 to Wrights of Walkern
Cambs		
Cambridge	*Ancient Druids* FL	B. Langton to Page to C. Wells in 1893
	Charles II FL	W. Buller to Page to Star Brewery Cambridge
	Claremount BH	P. Hudson to Page to Phillips
	Elm Tree FL	W. Apthorpe to Page to J. Nicoll
	Hearts of Oak FL	E. Bolton to Page to Bullards
	Hops, Beans and Barley Ears FL	Steward & Co. to Page to W. Edwards
	Horse and Groom FL	W. Edwards to Page to Reid Combe
	Little Rose FL	Meyer to Page to Lacon
	Prince of Wales FL	H. Daniel to Page to Lacon
	Red Cow FL	Burrell & Co. to Page to Star Brewery Cambridge
	Salisbury FL	G.E. Passment to Page to Lacon
	Ship FL	Pryor Reid to Page to C. Wells in 1893
	Volunteer FL	W. Apthorpe to Page to Lacon
Litlington	OL High St	
Melbourn	*Oak* BH	
Steeple Morden	*Hill House* BH	Leased in 1903, at Northbrook End

References

Cornell, M. Fordhams of Ashwell. *Brewery History Society Journal*, No. 39, pp.3–8, 1984.

Hertfordshire Archives and Local Studies. Acc. 3682, Box 11. a. Anon – an untitled manuscript giving details of early Fordham family history, b. Fordham family tree, c. Deed of appointment 1929, gives details of tied estate including copyholds and leaseholds, d. Box 10. Property register. D/E Wt B26, a. Photograph from Ashwell church showing malting that was burnt down in 1892, b. Draft of Fordham's tied estate at unknown date, c. Tithe Map for Ashwell, 1841, d. Tithe Map of Baldock 1850. This map shows the positions of five maltings owned by the Page family.

McKinley, M. A country brewery in rural surroundings. *Town and Country News*, 27 May 1932, pp.26–30.

Table 2.6 Page's maltings in Ashwell and Baldock

Location	Name	History of acquisition	Buyer	Current status
Ashwell				
On brewery site	Westbury Brewery	c.1870 to c.1920	Fordham family after 1921	Donated to be used as a village hall
Baldock				
Corner of High Street and Mansfield Road	Lion maltings	c.1850 from Pryors	Paines of St Neots 1921	In use until 1970. Now fish and chip shop and carpenter's workshop
Behind almshouses and *Angel Inn* in High Street	Seven Roes	c.1850 from Pryors	Paines of St Neots 1921	In use in 1970. Motor car repairs in 1995. Site cleared in 1999
Royston Road beside railway line	Bygrave maltings	Two maltings built in 1894 to 1898. Storage for 10,000 quarters	Paines of St Neots 1921	In use in 1970. c.1995 damaged by fire. Site cleared for industrial estate
Back of 31 Hitchin Street	Park Street	Parts c.1600's. Date acquired not known	Paines of St Neots 1921	Sold in 1936. Now a heath club
Back of 10 Hitchin Street	Hitchin Street I	c.1800 by Page family	In use 1852 but not in 1898	Pulled down
Corner of Hitchin Street and Cemetery Road	Hitchin Street II	c.1850 to after 1898	Not known	Pulled down before re-alignment of Hitchin Street
South side of Hitchin Street	Hitchin Street III	c.1800 to 1900	Not known	Pulled down c.1900
South side of White Horse Street	White Horse Street	Pre-1852 to ?	Not known	c.1850 to c.1920
White Lion	Park Street	c.1800	Paines of St Neots 1921	Pulled down

Page, K. Personal communication. Details of sales and lease transfers in 1921 by the Page family.

Petty Sessions Licensing Records for Hertfordshire, Bedfordshire, Cambridgeshire and West Essex.

Poole, H. *Here for the Beer*, Watford Museum, 1984, pp.2–5.

Richmond, L. and Turton, A. (eds.) *The Brewing Industry: A Guide to Historical Records*, Manchester University Press, 1990, p.145.

Sheldrick, A. *A Different World: Ashwell before 1939*, Ashwell, Courtney Publications, 1994.

Whitbread Archives, London. a. Outline plan of brewery pre-1900, b. Schedule of properties sold by Fordham's to Green's of Luton in 1952.

CHAPTER THREE

Baldock

Baldock is an old market town on the Great North Road at an important crossroads between Reading and Oxford to the west and Royston, Cambridge, Newmarket and Norwich to the east. Hence many mail coaches, stagecoaches and horses and wagons used Baldock as a staging place or for overnight stops.

Key:
Breweries
A High Street Brewery
B Ind's Brewery
C White Horse Street Brewery
D Pale Ale Brewery

Maltings
1 Thurgood and Pryor (now community centre)
2 Pryor and Simpsons (after Ind's Brewery)
3 Ind (behind Talbot)
4 Pale Ale Brewery Malting
5 Lion Malting – Page*, Paine
6 Seven Roes – Page*, Paine
7 Park Street – Page* to Paine
8 Hitchin Street I – Page*
9 Hitchin Street II – Page*
10 Hitchin Street III – Page*
11 Bygrave Maltings – Page*, Paine
12 White Horse Street – Page*
13 Pryor (now a private house)
14 White Lion – Pryor, Page*, Paine

* See Table 2.5 for full details

Figure 3.1 Brewery and malting sites

Figure 3.2 Thurgood and Pryor's malting in High Street

The town was also very near to some of the best malting barley-growing areas of East Anglia and on a direct road route to London. Some of the old inns such as the *Sun* (*Victoria*) and the *White Horse* already had their own brewhouses and maltings.

Brewing and malting were industries which began to increase in importance in Baldock in the eighteenth century providing a major source of employment for men from the town and nearby villages and continuing into the twentieth century. Four breweries can be identified plus a number of associated maltings. These were Simpson's brewery in the High Street (also Thurgood and Pryor), Ind's brewery and the White Horse Brewery in White Horse Street and the Pale Ale Brewery in Church Street (Figure 3.1).

Simpson's High Street Brewery

Robert Thurgood started the first commercial scale brewery in 1743 in the High Street on a plot of land where an active brewery was to remain for the next two hundred years. At the same time he acquired a part investment in the *Old Bull's Head* in Church Street. His father, John Thurgood was a maltster, who already had a mortgage for the *Cock* in the High Street. During the next thirty years

Table 3.1 Robert Thurgood's tied estate at the High Street Brewery

Herts					
Ashwell	*Three Tuns* L.	1746	Norton	*Three Horseshoes* F.	1763
Baldock	*Bull's Head* F.	1743	Stevenage	*Marquis of Granby* C.	1756
	Cock F.	1738	Willian	*Fox* (*Orange Tree,*	1725
	Eight Bells F.	1746		*Willian Arms*) F.	
Great Wymondley	*Green Man* F.	1750		*Three Horseshoes* F.	1763
Ickleford	*Old George* F.	1747			
Beds					
Stotfold	*White Horse*	*c.*1728			

Table 3.2 John Pryor's early additions to his tied estate at the High Street Brewery

Herts					
Ardeley	*Chequers*	1776	Little Wymondley	*Plume of Feathers*	1799
Baldock	*Chequers*	1778	Stevenage	*Fox*	1784
	George and Dragon	1777		*Red Lion*	1821
	Stag	1776		*Three Horseshoes*	1792
Barley	*Chequers*	1776		*Yorkshire Grey*	1786
Braughing	*Adam and Eve*	1786	Therfield	*Bell*	1801
Graveley	*George and Dragon*	1799	Wallington	*Plough*	1799
Hitchin	*Anchor*	1787	Weston	*George IV*	1806
	Three Moorhens	1777			
	White Lion				
Beds					
Stotfold	*Bell*	1795			
	White Horse	1783			
	White Swan	1798			

Robert Thurgood bought the freeholds of a number of public houses in Baldock and local villages plus the leasehold of the *Three Tuns* in Ashwell and the copyhold of the *Marquis of Granby* in Stevenage (Table 3.1). When Robert died in 1775, he bequeathed the brewery and tied estate to his daughter Sarah and her son Robert. She had married Thomas Clutterbuck who owned the brewery in Stanmore. Later in 1775 Sarah decided to lease the High Street Brewery and tied estate to John Pryor (1741–1819) a Quaker who was already established as a maltster in Baldock. He owned a number of maltings that he had bought, inherited from his father Robert Pryor, or obtained when he married Martha Fitzjohn, the widow of another maltster, most probably a Quaker.

During the next twenty-five years John Pryor bought a number of licensed properties (Table 3.2), built a substantial brewery house in the High Street and made additions to the leased brewery. However, it was not until 1800 that Robert Clutterbuck was able to obtain a private Act of Parliament so that he could change the very specific constraints of his grandfather's will and sell the

Figure 3.3 High Street Brewery house

Table 3.3 James Ind's tied estate sold to John Izard Pryor in 1815

Herts			
Ashwell	*Rose and Crown*	Sandon	*White Swan*
Buntingford	*Fox and Duck*	Stevenage	*Red Lion,* Shephall
Clothall	*Barley Mow*		*White Lion* L.
Great Munden	*White Lion*	Watton at Stone	*George*
Hinxworth	*Three Horseshoes*		
Beds			
Dunton	*Boot*	Red Hill	*Swan*
Langford	*Three Tuns*	Southill	*Red Lion*
Potton	*Green Man*	Stotfold	*Chequers*
	White Lion	Wrestlingworth	*Three Horseshoes*
Cambs			
Bassingbourn	*Hoops*	Melbourn	*Red Lion*

brewery and tied estate of eleven licensed properties to John Pryor. To make the application to Parliament successful, the brewery and maltings were described as 'very old and being in a ruinous and bad condition'. If this description had been true of a good operational brewery the motives of the buyer would have been suspect. Fortunately Parliament agreed to the changes proposed in the Private Act.

In 1815 John Pryor bought Ind's brewery on the corner of Clothall Road and

Figure 3.4 Pryor and Simpson's malting on Ind's Brewery site

White Horse Street with maltings plus a tied estate of approximately twenty properties (Table 3.3). After the purchase of this brewery it is thought that John Pryor had a tied estate of approximately fifty properties. When he died in 1819, his son John Izard Pryor took over the brewery and his younger brother managed the maltings. Two other brothers, Thomas and Robert owned a brewery in Shoreditch. Subsequently they amalgamated with Truman & Co. Each brother bought three shares for £47,350 out of forty-seven shares and became partners in Truman, Hanbury & Morris, a large brewery in London already managed by Quakers. In 1829 John Izard Pryor retired and leased the brewery to his sons John and Morris. Production at this stage was about 11,000 barrels per year. Production then rose steadily after the Beer House Act of 1831 when it was decided that anyone could open a beer house provided they paid two guineas. This created a big demand for wholesale beer from brewers such as the Pryors. In 1832 beer production had already increased to over 16,500 barrels and peaked at 19,000 barrels per year in 1840. At the same time John and Morris were increasing the size of the tied estate by purchases and by negotiating more leases and copyholds. This included a number of public houses bought at the auction of Marshall and Pierson's brewery in Hitchin in 1841.

John Pryor died in 1852 when his oldest son Morris was only seventeen. At this stage Thomas and Robert Pryor were probably still partners in Truman and Co. and a fifth younger brother Alfred was successfully managing the large

Table 3.4 Pryor's tied estate when sold to Simpson's in 1853

Herts

Ashwell	Rose and Crown i.	Little Wymondley	Plume of Feathers
	Three Tuns t.	Pirton	Shoulder of Mutton m.
Baldock	Bull's Head t.		White Horse m.
	Chequers 1778	Puckeridge	Woolpack
	Cock t.	Roe Green	Anchor
	Eight Bells	Rushden	Moon and Stars
	George		Rose and Crown
	George & Dragon 1777	Sacombe	Green Man
	Plume of Feathers	Sandon	Duke William
	Stag 1776		Six Bells
	Three Horseshoes		Swan i.
Barley	Chequers 1786	Standon	Star
Braughing	Adam and Eve 1786		Waggon and Horses
	Bear m.	Stevenage	George and Dragon
Buntingford	Fox and Duck i.		Marquis of Granby t.
Burnham Green	White Horse m.		Old Castle
Bygrave	Compasses		Red Lion
Clothall	Barley Mow i.		Red Lion, Shephall i.
Cottered	Bull		Three Horseshoes 1792
Cromer	Chequers		Unicorn
Furneux Pelham	Millwright's Arms		White Lion
Graveley	George & Dragon 1789		Windsor Castle
Great Hormead	Three Tuns		Yorkshire Grey
Great Munden	Chequers		BH No name
	White Lion i.	Therfield	Bell
Great Wymondley	Green Man t.	Thundridge	White Swan
Hertford	Green Dragon	Walkern	Three Horseshoes
Hexton	Plough (Raven)		White Lion m.
Hinxworth	Three Horseshoes i.	Wallington	Plough 1799
Hitchin	Anchor	Ware	Bell and Sun
	Cross Keys m.		White Horse
	Curriers' Arms	Waterford	Waterford Arms
	George	Watton on Stone	George i.
	Red Cow m.	Welwyn	Red Lion
	Red Hart		Wellington
	Robin Hood m.		White Hart
	Three Moorhens		BH
	Waggon and Horses	Weston	Crown and Anchor
	White Lion m.		Rising Sun, Halls Gr.
Holwell	White Hart m.	Willian	Fox (Orange Tree) t.
Ickleford	Old George t.		Three Horseshoes
Little Munden	Bell		

Beds

Barton in the Clay	Royal Oak	Northill	Barley Mow
	BH No name	Potton	Green Man i.
Bedford	Chequers		Queen's Head
	BH No name	Shefford	King's Arms
Biggleswade	Bear	Shillington	Marquis of Granby
	Ongley Arms		White Horse
Clifton	Golden Lion	Stanford	Red Lion
Dunstable	White Hart	Stotfold	Chequers i.
Dunton	Boot i.	Streatley	Chequers

Henlow	Beerhouse Inn	Wilhamstead	BH No name
Langford	Three Tuns i.	Wrestlingworth	Chequers
	Wrestlers	Wyboston	Sun

Cambs			
Abbotsley	Six Bells and Ringers	Melbourn	Dolphin
Bassingbourn	Hoops i.		Hoops
Eaton Socom	Bell		Red Lion i.
Eynesbury	Nag's Head	Meldreth	Bell
Gamlingay	Cock	St Neots	Blue Balls
Guilden Morden	Three Tuns		BH No name
Harston	Green Man	Steeple Morden	Horse and Groom
Litlington	Robin Hood	Yardley	Chequers

Essex			
Clavering	Axe and Compasses		

Key: t.   These were already owned by Thurgood
      i.   These were bought from Ind in 1815
      m.   These were bought at Marshall and Pierson's auction in Hitchin in 1841
           Dates refer to early estate acquired by Pryor family before 1800

Hatfield Brewery. Since production at Baldock had dropped to about 13,000 barrels per year and there was no other experienced member of the family willing or available to help manage the brewery effectively, Morris decided to sell the brewery which had a batch capacity of 200 barrels using forty quarters of malt. At this time the tied estate in Hertfordshire, Bedfordshire, Cambridgeshire and Essex, consisted of 122 owned or leased properties (Table 3.4). The biggest numbers were in Baldock, Hitchin and Stevenage. Most of the remainder were in the other small towns and villages mainly within a fifteen to twenty mile radius of the brewery but none were in Royston where their cousins, members of the Phillips family, owned a large brewery.

John and Thomas George Simpson, who were nephews of the Royston brewer John Phillips, bought the brewery, maltings and tied estate for £81,000 in 1853. They soon proved to be very successful brewery managers and increased annual production to 20,000 barrels per year by 1863. In 1867 they brewed over 22,000 barrels. They also steadily increased the size of their tied estate and bought a number of properties in Luton which at this time in the late nineteenth century was expanding very rapidly. However, in 1900 when the brewery had approximately 200 tied outlets only 16,000 barrels of beer were sold. The brewery was also still operating four of its own maltings in the town.

Figure 3.5 shows a ground floor level plan of the brewery in about 1900 when there was a major reorganisation on the four floors of the main brewery building. On the ground floor at the front a new steam boiler, a steam engine

Table 3.5 Simpson's tied estate taken over by Greene King in 1954

Herts

Place	Pub	Place	Pub
Ardeley	*Chequers*	Hitchin	*White Lion* p.
	Jolly Waggoners	Ickleford	*George* t.
Ashwell	*Rose and Crown* i.	Kimpton	*Boot*
	Three Tuns t.	Langley	*Farmer's Boy*
Aspenden	*Fox*	Lemsford	*Sun*
Baldock	*Boot*	Ley Green	*Plough*
	Bull's Head t.	Little Wymondley	*Plume of Feathers*
	Chequers p.	New Barnet	*Builder's Arms*
	Cock t.	Offley	*Gloucester Arms*
	Eight Bells t.	Pirton	*Live and Let Live*
	Engine	Rushden	*Moon and Stars* p.
	George and Dragon	Sacombe	*Green Man*
	Hen and Chickens	Sandon	*Six Bells* p.
	Stag	Standon	*Star* p.
	White Hart	Stevenage	*Chequers*
Barley	*Chequers* p.		*Crooked Billet* w.
Benington	*Bell* p.		*Marquis of Granby* t.
	White Horse w.		*Marquis of Lorne* w.
Braughing	*Adam and Eve* p.		*Red Lion* p.
	Brown Bear p.		*Red Lion* i. Shephall
Breachwood Green	*Red Lion* w.		*Rising Sun*
Buckland	*Red Lion*		*Three Horseshoes*, Pin.
Buntingford	*Fox and Duck* i.		*White Lion* p.
	White Hart		*Woodman's Arms*
Bygrave	*Compasses* p.		*Yorkshire Grey* p.
Clothall	*Barley Mow* i.	Therfield	*Bell* p.
Cottered	*Bull* p.	Titmore Green	*Hermit of Redcoats* w.
Dane End	*Boot*	Walkern	*Red Lion* w.
Datchworth	*Plough* w.		*White Lion* p.
Gosmore	*Bird in Hand*	Wallington	*Plough* p.
Graveley	*George and Dragon* p.	Ware	*Bell and Sun* p.
Great Hornmead	*Three Tuns* p.		*New Rose and Crown*
Great Wymondley	*Green Man* t.		*Punch House*
Hexton	*Raven (Plough)* p.		*White Horse* p.
Hinxworth	*Three Horseshoes* i.	Waterford	*Waterford Arms* p.
Hitchin	*Adam and Eve*	Watton at Stone	*George and Dragon* i.
	Anchor p.	Welwyn	*Rose and Crown*
	George p.		*Royal Oak*
	Gloucester Arms		*Wellington* p.
	New Found Out	Weston	*Crown and Anchor* p.
	Red Hart p.		*Red Lion*
	Three Moorhens p.	Willian	*Three Horseshoes* t.
	Waggon and Horses p.		

Beds

Place	Pub	Place	Pub
Arlesey	*Prince of Wales*	Luton	*Shepherd and Flock*
	White Horse		*Yorkshire Grey* w.
Barton in the Clay	*Royal Oak* p.	Meppershall	*Barley Mow*
Biggleswade	*Bear* p.	Northill	*Barley Mow* p.
Blunham	*Oak*	Pegsdon	*Live and Let Live*
Clifton	*Golden Lion* p.	Potton	*Green Man* i.
Dunstable	*Sugar Loaf*	Sandy	*Dick Turpin*
Dunton	*Bell*		*Prince of Wales*

Henlow	Brewhouse Inn p.		Royal Oak
	Five Bells	Shillington	Musgrave Arms
Langford	Wrestlers p.	Stotfold	Chequers i.
Luton	Butcher's Arms w.		Pig and Whistle w.
	Cooper's Arms		Two Brewers
	Gardener's Call		Two Chimneys
	George II		White Horse t.
	Hibbert Arms	Streatley	Chequers p.
	Mother Red Cap	Upper Caldecote	Royal Oak
	Princess Alexandra	Wrestlingworth	Chequers p.

Cambs

Bassingbourn	Hoops i.	Guilden Morden	Three Tuns p.
Gamlingay	Cock p.	Litlington	Horse and Groom
	Green Man	Melbourn	Dolphin p.

Key: t.   These were owned by Thurgood
      i.   These were bought from Ind in 1815
      m.   These were bought at Marshall and Pierson's auction in 1841
      p.   These were bought by the Pryor family
      w.   These were bought from Wrights of Walkern in 1924
      Pin. Pin Green

and an underback were installed. On the first floor there was a new twelve feet diameter mash tun and a malt screen. Moving on to the second floor there was a new eight feet by fourteen feet hot liquor tank and an eight feet by eight feet grist case and finally a new malt hopper on the third floor. At the same time, two fermentation vessels each twelve feet in diameter and one of ten feet diameter were scrapped on the ground floor and the floor space was converted for bottle washing and storage. The fermentation vessels were all put on the first floor. These consisted of two fourteen feet in diameter, one of twelve feet in diameter, one of nine feet diameter and two of eight feet diameter.

In 1900 transport still depended on horses and in the brewery yard there was stabling for about twenty-six horses, cart sheds, hay and straw stores plus workshops for a wheelwright and a blacksmith. The brewery drays were sometime pulled by as many as four horses working for up to twelve hours a day. The hours of employment were from 6 a.m. to 6 p.m. six days a week. The waggoners would start at 4 a.m. to feed and groom the horses and be ready to load at 6 a.m. The first steam lorry was bought in 1910 and one apparently was still used for local deliveries until 1952. Petrol driven lorries began to be used after World War I. Sometimes these were army surplus vehicles.

The brewery was using large numbers of barrels in a range of sizes, hence the need for coopers, carpenters and a timber store to make and repair them. There was a large cellar for storing beer that contained one oak vat of 1,500 barrels' capacity and two other oak ones that each held 1,000 barrels. These were

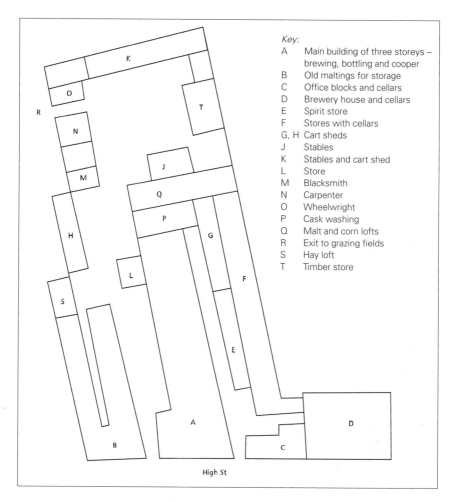

Key:
A — Main building of three storeys – brewing, bottling and cooper
B — Old maltings for storage
C — Office blocks and cellars
D — Brewery house and cellars
E — Spirit store
F — Stores with cellars
G, H — Cart sheds
J — Stables
K — Stables and cart shed
L — Store
M — Blacksmith
N — Carpenter
O — Wheelwright
P — Cask washing
Q — Malt and corn lofts
R — Exit to grazing fields
S — Hay loft
T — Timber store

High St

Figure 3.5 Plan of the High Street Brewery in early 1900s

demolished during World War I when heavy excise duties were placed on beer and this duty had to be paid monthly. This made it uneconomical to store beer to mature for months.

The licensing magistrates made a very important survey of Hertfordshire during October 1902, giving details of full licences, beer only and off-licences in each licensing division. Simpsons had seventy-one full licences plus thirty-two beer only licences. At this time the brewery also had full or beer only licences for at least fifty-five properties in Bedfordshire, eight in Cambridgeshire, possibly five in Huntingdonshire and one in Essex. This made a total of 170 tied properties. Later there was a transport policy to ensure that all properties were within twenty-eight miles of the brewery and the *Axe and Compasses* at Clavering

Table 3.6 Simpson's tied estate disposals before takeover by Greene King in 1954

Herts

Ashwell	*Stag's Head* w.	Little Munden	*Bell* FL
Aston	*Live and Let Live* BH	Norton	*Three Horseshoes* L.
Ayot St. L.	*Brocket Arms* w.LH	Pirton	*Shoulder of Mutton* m.
Baldock	*Bushel and Strike*		*White Horse* m.
	Falcon	Puckeridge	*Chequers*
	Saracen's Head		*Woolpack* p.
	Swan	Redbourn	*Lamb*
	Three Horseshoes	Rushden	*Rose and Crown* p.
Breachwood Gr.	*Sugar Loaf* w.	St Ippollytts	*Jolly Tailors* BH
Burnham Green	*White Horse*	Sandon	*Anchor, Roe Green* p.
Clothall	*Ram and Hurdles*		*Hoops*
Cromer	*Chequers* p.		*Old Swan*
Furneux Pelham	*Millwright's Arms* p.	Standon	*Waggon and Horses* p.
		Stevenage	*Falcon*
Great Munden	*Chequers* p.		*George*
	White Lion i.		*Old Castle*
Haultwick	*Bell*		*Unicorn (Fox)* p.
Hitchin	*Boot*		*White Horse*
	Cross Keys	Walkern	*Three Horseshoes* p.
	Curriers' Arms p.	Ware	*Harrow*
	Duke of Wellington		*King's Head* w.
	Queen's Head		*White Lion and*
	Red Cow		*Wheatsheaf*
	Robin Hood	Welwyn	*Queen's Head*
	Rose and Crown L.		*White Hart* p.
	Six Bells	Weston	*Live and Let Live*
	Sun L.		*Rose and Crown* p.
	White Hart		*White Horse*
Holwell	*White Hart* p.		

Beds

Ampthill	*Albion Arms* L.	Northill	*Sow and Pigs*
Arlesey	*White Horse*	Potton	*Bricklayer's Arms*
Astwick	*Greyhound*		*Queen's Head*
	Hod and Mortar	Pulloxhill	*Harrow*
	New Inn L.	Sandy	*Dun Cow*
Biggleswade	*Ongley Arms* p.		BH Tempsford Rd
Caddington	*Harrow*	Seddington	*Dun Cow*
Caldecote	*Royal Oak*		*Royal Oak*
Clophill	*Rising Sun*	Shefford	*Green Man* L.
Dunstable	*White Swan*		*King's Arms* p.
Dunton	*Boot* i.	Shillington	*Harrow*
Eaton Socon	*Bell*		*Live and Let Live*
	Queen's Head		*Marquis of Granby* p.
	Sun		*White Horse* p.
Langford	*Bay Horse*	Southill	*Red Lion*
	Boot	Stondon	*Three Horseshoes*
	Green Man L.	Stotfold	*Boot*
	Three Tuns		*Bull*
Luton	*Prince Albert*		*Jolly Butchers (Dust*
	Sportsman L.		*Hole)*
	Three Horseshoes		*White Swan*
	BH No name	Studham	*Sun*

| Maulden | *George* | Westoning | *Red Lion* L. |
| Northill | *Royal Oak* | Wilhamstead | *Chequers* |

Cambs

Abbotsley	*Ringers (Six Bells)* p.	Melbourn	*Red Lion*
Eynesbury	*Nag's Head* p.	St Neots	*Bell*
Gamlingay	*Cock* p.		*Bull*
	Green Man	Steeple Morden	*Horse and Groom* p.
Girtford	*Dun Cow* L.		BH Stingay Rd
Harston	*Green Man* p.	Wyboston	*Bell*
Litlington	*Red Lion*		*Sun*
	Robin Hood p.		

Essex

| Clavering | *Axe and Compasses* p. |

Key:	t.	These were bought by Pryors from Thurgood
	i.	These were bought by Pryors from Ind in 1815
	p.	These were bought by Simpsons from Pryors
	w.	These were bought by Simpsons from Wrights of Walkern in 1924
		Ayot St. L. Ayot St Lawrence

in Essex was therefore sold to an Essex brewery because it was in such a distant isolated position.

Unlike most other breweries there were no off-licences due a brewery policy of not bottling any beers. This situation was rectified soon afterwards when a hand-operated bottling plant was installed in the early 1900s. Demand for bottled beer steadily increased and an electrically driven plant was installed, buildings and yard space were modified to accommodate this development.

The only major tied estate purchase after 1902 was in 1924 when Simpsons bought twelve freehold public houses plus three leasehold properties from Wrights of Walkern when they closed their brewery and decided to concentrate on cider and lemonade manufacture. This enabled Simpsons to obtain a few more profitable outlets including two in Luton. During 1925 beer production increased significantly by an extra 2,000 barrels.

Evelyn and Francis Thomas Simpson succeeded their fathers as active partners owning the brewery. However in 1909, Evelyn Simpson changed his name to Evelyn Shaw-Hellier in anticipation of a major inheritance. Sadly his only son was killed during World War I. When he died in 1922, his partnership at the brewery was inherited by his eldest daughter Evelyn Mary Penelope Shaw-Hellier. In 1929 Francis Thomas Simpson died and Miss Evelyn Shaw-Hellier became the sole family partner. In 1935 the brewery was finally registered as a limited company with a share capital of £180,000. The other director was T.H.

Veasey, the family solicitor who became the company chairman. The brewery remained operational throughout World War II and in 1953 a new bottling plant was installed. Later in that year Miss Shaw-Hellier, who was still the major share holder, decided that future death duties on her estate would lead to the sale and possible closure of the brewery.

Exploratory talks were therefore held with a number of local regional brewers. Early in 1954 Greene King of Bury St Edmund decided to buy the brewery and a tied estate of 130 properties for £525,000 (Table 3.5). Soon afterwards the various maltings in Baldock were closed together with the *White Horse* at Benington, the *Compasses* at Bygrave, the *Red Lion* at Walkern and a few other public houses which had a low turnover of beer. It was agreed that the brewery would remain open. However in 1961 Greene King bought Wells and Winch of Biggleswade. Because of excess brewing capacity Greene King decided to use Furneux Pelham (Rayments), Biggleswade and Bury St Edmunds as their production sites, and the brewery in Baldock was finally closed in 1965. The brewery site was sold to Baldock Urban District Council in 1966. The major part of the site was cleared for development and now only a small part of the brewery maltings and the brewery house remain (Figures 3.2 and 3.3).

Ind's Brewery

This brewery was on the corner of White Horse Street and Clothall Road. There were also maltings (one or two) that may have been on the brewery site and/or on the opposite corner of the crossroads behind the *Talbot*. James Ind had established this brewery during the late 1700s. He is reputed to have first brewed behind the *Rose and Crown* also in White Horse Street and lived in a house on the site of Penfold's furniture shop. In 1792 he bought the *Rose and Crown* at Ashwell with a small malting in the yard. Besides brewing for the tied estate (Table 3.3), he also sold considerable quantities of beer directly to some private customers. His bill to the Reverend Sparhawke of Hinxworth for six months to May 1797 is an example of this type of business undertaken by many brewers at this time but not very well documented (Table 3.7). However, he died in 1810 and his son James who inherited the brewery died only a year later in 1811. Another son Edward decided to initially lease the tied estate to John Pryor as he already had a major interest in a brewery in Romford and did not wish to retain the brewery in Baldock. Soon afterwards he decided to sell all parts of this business to John Pryor with the proviso that his mother, Mary Ind, could live in the brewery

Table 3.7 James Ind's bill to Rev. and Mrs Sparhawke of Hinxworth

Date	Order	£ – s – d
22 Oct 1796	1 Barrel Best and 1/2 of Wh 71	2 – 3 – 6
14 Nov 1796	1 Kilderkin Best	19 – 6
23 Nov 1796	1 Barrel Best	1 – 19 – 0
28 Nov 1796	1/2 Wh 71	4 – 6
10 Jan 1797	1 Barrel Best	1 – 19 – 0
11 Jan 1797	1 Barrel Mid	1 – 13 – 0
9 Feb 1797	1 Barrel and 1 Barrel 0/1	2 – 5 – 0
1 Mar 1797	1 Barrel Table Beer	16 – 0
?	2 Barrels Best	3 – 18 – 0
?	2 Barrels Table Beer	1 – 12 – 0
5 May 1797	1 Barrel Best and 1 Barrel of Table Beer	2 – 13 – 0
	Total	20 – 2 – 6

house until she died, which she did in 1857. The Pryor family later demolished Ind's brewery and built a large malting complex on the site. This was converted into offices and private housing in the late twentieth century.

White Horse Brewery

The Noy family started a small brewery behind the *Victoria* (*Sun*) in White Horse Street before 1736 and also owned a small malting. William Penn bought the brewery in 1793 and was succeeded by William Oliver in 1841. Finally Josiah Parker bought the brewery in 1871 and operated it until its closure ten years later.

A 1871 plan shows a three-storey brick brewery building, stores and lofts, a cooper's shop, cask-cleaning shed, stabling and a substantial brewery house (Figures 3.6 and 3.7). There were also extensive cellars and there were reputed to have been passageways connecting to the *Victoria* and the *Eight Bells* in Church Street. Within the brewery complex there were also pigsties, a hen house, a barn and a straw yard. The old malting is no longer shown on the plan but there was building ground behind the brewery where a malting could be built. Originally there was another entrance to the brewery on the Church Street side of the *Victoria*.

The tied estate appears to have been always very small with never more than three or four outlets (Table 3.8). In 1828 the Noy family sold the *Victoria* to John Steed at the Pale Ale Brewery and shortly afterwards this public house was rebuilt. At the same time the *Bull* at Cottered was sold to the Pryor family at the High Street Brewery. In Baldock, George Oliver owned the *White Horse*, which was a large coaching inn, and an unnamed beer house in Church Street, and for

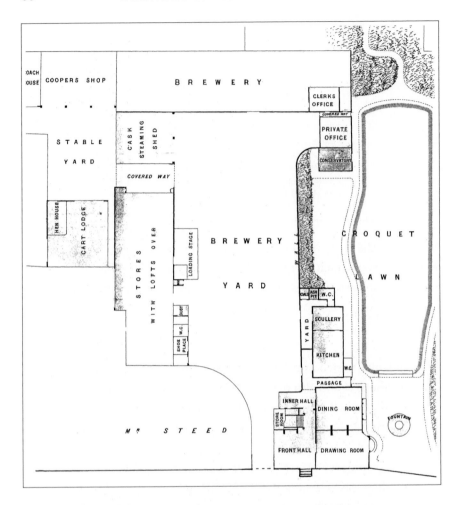

Figure 3.6 Plan of White Horse Brewery in 1871 (HALS)

a few years he leased the *Orange Tree* in Hitchin and the *Cricketers* in Ickleford. Most of the brewery was finally demolished in 1998 for a small housing development and now only the brewery house remains and is used for business purposes.

Pale Ale Brewery

William Oliver probably started the Pale Ale Brewery in Norton Street behind the *Star* in the early 1800s. In 1823 he leased the brewery to John Steed a Quaker who began to build up a tied estate. The Steed family bought the brewery in 1831

Figure 3.7 White Horse Brewery house

and began a major rebuilding programme in 1840. Meanwhile the Oliver family bought the White Horse Brewery. John Steed remained active as a brewer/owner until at least 1867 when he was succeeded by his son Oliver who was not of a robust constitution. Oliver died in 1888 after a long period of ill health.

In 1888, the brewery had a twelve quarter mash tun, a thirty barrel hop back, a twenty barrel under back, a copper for thirty-eight barrels of wort and four

Table 3.8 White Horse Brewery known tied estate 1736–1871

Herts		Notes
Baldock	*Victoria*	1736 owned by Noy, then Penn. Acquired by John Steed in 1828
	White Horse	*c.*1840 to *c.*1870 by William Oliver who lived there
	BH No name	Southern corner of Church Street on tithe plot 43
Cottered	*Bull*	1793 leased by William Penn, then leased by William Oliver
		and by Pryors in 1828
Hitchin	*Orange Tree*	Leased to George Oliver *c.*1840 to *c.*1870
	BH No name	Bancroft (Silver Street) 1847 George Oliver
Ickleford	*Cricketers*	1851–1864 leased by George Oliver

Table 3.9 Pale Ale Brewery tied estate in 1888

Herts				
Ardeley	*Old Bell* L.*	Hitchin		*William IV* C.
Baldock	*Beehive* C.	Ickleford		*Green Man* F.
	Hen and Chickens F.	Kimpton		*Bright Star* F.
	Rose and Crown F.*	Pirton		*Cat and Fiddle* F.
	Star F.*	St Albans		*King's Arms* F.
	Swan F.	Stevenage		*Fisherman* F.
	Victoria F.			*Prince of Wales* F.
Gosmore	*Red Cow* C.	Welwyn		*Baron of Beef* L.
Hitchin	*Albert* F.	Weston		*Thatched House* C.
	Bricklayer's Arms F.			*White Horse* F.

Beds				
Ampthill	*Compasses* L.	Flitton		*Jolly Coopers* L.*
	Engine and Tender L.*	Lower Stondon		*Thatched House* F.
Arlesey	*Church House* F.	Luton		*Bright Star* F.
	Rose and Crown F.			*Cardinal* L.*
	Steam Engine F.			*Jolly Topers* L.*
	True Britain L.			*Painter's Arms* F.
Bedford	*Boot* L.*			*Star and Garter* L.
	Harpur House F.	Maulden		*Commander in Chief* L.*
	Live and Let Live F.			*Compasses* F.
	Rose and Crown F.	Shillington		*Commander in Chief* L.*
	Royal Oak F.			*Engine* L.*
Biggleswade	*Fox* F.			*Noah's Ark* L.*
	Hole in the Wall F.	Stotfold		*Cricketers* F.*
	Running Stream F.			*Fox and Duck* L.**
Blunham	*Queen's Head* F.			*Sun* F.
Campton	*Wheatsheaf* L.	Upper Stondon		*Thatched House* F.
Clapham	*Vicar of Wakefield* F.	Wilstead		*White Horse* L.*
Clifton	*Admiral* L.*			

Cambs				
Barrington	*Fountain* L.*	Sawston		*Commander in Chief* L.
Girtford	*Swan* F.			*Flower Pot* F.*
Great Barford	*Beehive* F.			*Morning Star* L.
Melbourn	*White Horse* F.*			BH No name F.
Shepreth	*Green Man* C.*			

London				
Battersea Park Rd	*Champion* L.*	Tooley St		*Hop Pole* L.*
St George St	*Royal Crown* L.*			

Key: * These formed part of the 1903 sale
        ** Sold to Charles Wells of Bedford in 1895

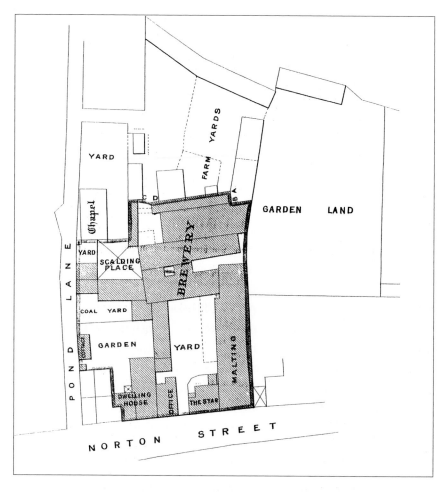

Figure 3.8 Plan of Pale Ale Brewery in 1888 (HALS)

fermenting vessels of 190 barrels total capacity plus a well and other ancillary plant. The plan shows the layout of the brewery, a twenty quarter malting, a farmyard, associated housing, the *Star* brewery tap and a chapel (Figure 3.8).

At this time the sixty-six tied houses were considered to be under-performing and only selling 4,000 barrels of beer per annum and selling a further 1,000 barrels to the free trade and private customers. This tied estate consisted of thirty-seven freehold, twenty-four leasehold and five copyhold properties with the main investments being in Baldock, Arlesey, Bedford, Luton and Sawston (Table 3.9). The brewery had only owned or leased a small number of other properties (Table 3.10).

Table 3.10 Other properties owned or leased by the Pale Ale Brewery not in 1888 or 1903 sales

Herts			
Ashwell	BH High Street	Baldock	White Horse
Baldock	Old Black Eagle	Royston	Rose and Crown
Beds			
Biggleswade	Sun	Luton	Prince of Wales
	BH No name		Saracen's Head
Langford	King's Cross	Sandy	Swan
	Red Cow	Shefford	Royal Oak

Oliver Steed's widow Margaret sold the brewery and tied estate in late 1888 or early in 1889 to William Pickering who soon sold the business to C. H. Morley. Brewing seems to have ceased at this stage. Part of the tied estate was sold in 1888–9 to a number of brewers including Charles Wells of Bedford, Pryor & Reid of Hatfield, Fordham's of Ashwell, Benskin's of Watford, J.W. Green of Luton and Lucas of Hitchin. In 1904 Wells and Winch paid £11,000 for the freeholds and leases of the remaining twenty-two properties of the tied estate plus the brewery. The brewery was closed and the buildings and land were used for storage. After the takeover of Wells & Winch, Greene King sold this brewery site to Baldock UDC in 1966 to use for house building. In 1980 Greene King decided to close the *Star*. One of the brewery directors commented that the toilets were archaic and there were no car parking facilities. Further investments in the property could not be justified. So a small pub dating from pre-1830 which was a genuine Brewery Tap and once claimed to have a beer pipe connecting it directly to the brewery was finally closed.

References

Burleigh, G. Last of the Baldock breweries, *Hertfordshire's Past*, Vol. 2, 1977, pp.20–1, 23 (White Horse Brewery).

Cornell, M. Simpson's of Baldock, *Hertfordshire's Past*, Vol. 146, 1999, pp.2–14.

Hertfordshire Archives and Local Studies. a. Tithe Map of Baldock 1850, b. Ind (D/Esb T153–5, 26635–6), c. Pryor (D/Esb T series 8, 22, 74, 144, 152, 155, 156 and D/ELB 52 Bundle 3), d. Simpson (D/Esb T series 144, 147, 150, 153, 171 and P 3, 4, 9), e. Thurgood (D/Esb T8, T22), f. Pale Ale Brewery (D/Ery B85), g. White Horse Brewery (37320), h. D/Ehx Z6 (Clutterbuck's private bill to parliament).

Madden, M. (ed.) *A Baldock Scrapbook*, Baldock, Egon Press, 1994.

Pedley, A.E. My memories of sixty years at Baldock brewery, *Hertfordshire Countryside*,

1965, Vol. 19, No. 76, pp.56–7.

Petty Sessions Licensing Records for Hertfordshire, Bedfordshire, Cambridgeshire and West Essex.

Poole, H. *Here for the Beer*, Watford Museum, 1984, pp.5–7.

Richmond, L. and Turton, A. (eds.) *The Brewing Industry: A Guide to Historical Records*, Manchester University Press, 1990, pp.300–1.

Wilson, R.G. *Greene King: A Business and Family History*, London, Bodley Head & Jonathan Cape, 1983, pp.220, 228–30, 245.

CHAPTER FOUR

Barkway

There was a small brewery in the yard behind the Brewery House at 71 High Street, Barkway. It was established in the 1750s and remained operational until 1908. The last two brewers were William Gapes (pre-1859–1861) and John Johnson Balding (1862–1908).

The brewery site was excavated in 1997. Findings indicated that the main building had been built in the late eighteenth century with an east-west alignment. It measured seventy feet long and twenty feet wide. There are no known surviving photographs or pictures but it is thought from the dimensions of the foundations to have been at least two storeys high.

In 1902 the identified tied estate consisted of the *Castle* FL in Anstey and the *Prince of Wales* BH in Royston. Both were later sold to Phillips of Royston. There had also been earlier ownership of an unnamed beer house in Ashwell High Street.

References

Petty Sessions Licensing Records for Hertfordshire.
Turner, C. and Hillelson, D. The Past Preserved – Archaeology at Brewery House, Barkway, *Hertfordshire's Past*, 2000, Vol.49, pp.9–17.

CHAPTER FIVE

Barnet

The Barnet Brewery in Wood Street is claimed to have started in 1700. John Buckthorpe was the brewer from 1822 until 1866. He was followed by Henry Earle & Co. (1870–86) and the Barnet Brewery Company (1890–1906).

There was an off-licence at the brewery and this may have been the main sales outlet when the brewery was active. There was also short-term ownership or leasing of the *Alexandra* in New Barnet in 1905 and the *Monken Holt* in Barnet High Street in 1907.

References

Petty Sessions Licensing Records in Hertfordshire.
Poole, H. *Here for the Beer*, Watford Museum, 1985, pp.7–8.

CHAPTER SIX

Berkhamsted

Brewing and malting are thought to have started in Berkhamsted during the sixteenth century. In the late 1700s, John Lane had a small brewhouse to supply the workmen at his nursery business. Later one of his descendants was leasing the brewhouse behind the *Swan* in the High Street. John Page was brewing his own beer at the *King's Arms* by 1800. Slightly later a brewery was built in Water Lane.

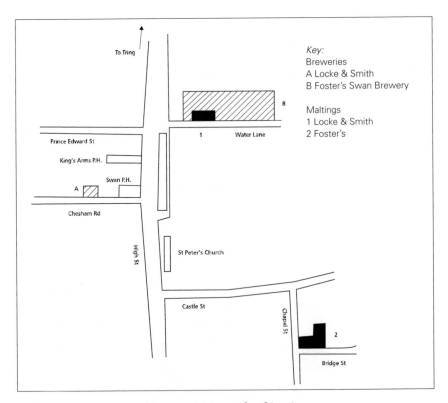

Figure 6.1 Brewery and malting sites

Table 6.1 Locke & Smith's tied estate at takeover by Benskin's in 1913

Herts

Aldbury	*Valiant Trooper* L.	Hemel Hempstead	*Star* BH
Berkhamsted	*Bell* C.		*Sun* FL
	Boot BH, C.	Long Marston	*Boot**
	Crooked Billet	Northchurch	*Boat*
	George and Dragon		*Crooked Billet*
	Goat		*George and Dragon*
	Lamb BH		*Stag*
	Plough FL	St Albans	*Painter's Arms*
	Royal Oak	Tring	*Britannia**
	Stag L.		*Castle**
	White Hart L.		*King's Arms* C. *
Bovingdon	*Three Horseshoes* C.		*Pheasant**
Chipperfield	*Two Brewers*		*Queen's Arms**
Great Gaddesden	*Cock and Bottle* BH		*Red Lion*
	Plough C.		*Royal Oak**
Hemel Hempstead	*Beehive* BH, C.	Wiggington	*Greyhound* FL *
	Grapes BH, L.		*Lamb* BH
	Hop Garland	Wilstone	*Buckingham Arms*
	Saracen's Head		

Bucks

Aston Clinton	*White Lion**	Chesham	*Portobello* FL, C.
Aylesbury	*Horse and Jockey*	Hawridge	*Rose and Crown*
	Plough and Harrow		

Key: * From Tring Brewery in 1898

Water Lane Brewery (Locke & Smith)

Thomas Archer started large-scale brewing in 1811 at the brewery in Water Lane off the High Street when Miss Elizabeth Billington was the owner of the property. He was followed by William Tomlin (1828–44), John Frost (1844–6), John Newman Frost (1846–55) and finally Alfred Healey (1855–68). The 1851 Poor Law tax records show that a malting was built on this site. At the same time John Newman Frost was the owner of an ale house and a beer house in the High Street.

Locke & Smith became the owners of the Water Lane brewery in 1868. They started a major expansion in the 1870s with the purchase or leasing of a number of inns or beer houses in West Hertfordshire plus a few just over the border into Bedfordshire and Buckinghamshire (Tables 6.1 and 6.2). Locke retired from the partnership in 1890. At this stage the brewery seems to have had financial problems which were solved by arranging another mortgage with Thomas Clutterbuck of Stanmore. In 1897 the brewery was registered as a limited company, Locke & Smith Ltd. In 1898 the brewery bought the Tring Brewery in Tring High Street from the Brown family for £30,050. The purchase also included nine tied houses, a large malting in Akeman Street, Tring which

Table 6.2 Locke & Smith's disposals before takeover in 1913

Herts			
Berkhamsted	*King Edward VI* BH 1876	St Albans	*Vine* FL, L.
Bovingdon	*Acorn*	Two Waters H.H.	*Bricklayer's Arms* 1876
Bury Mill End H.H.	*Bricklayer's Arms* 1876	Wiggington	*Lamb* BH
Northchurch	*Swan* 1876		

Beds			
Eaton Bray	*White Horse* FL 1903	Linslade	*Goat* BH 1872

Bucks			
Aston Clinton	*Green Man* BH 1872	Chesham	*Fishery Inn* BH 1872
Aylesbury	*Greyhound* FL 1878	Edlesborough	*Good Intent* L.1910
	Old Plough and Harrow	Hadsor	BH 1872
Buckland	*New Inn* FL, L. 1872	Marsworth	BH 1872

Key: Date indicates when part of tied estate
H.H. Hemel Hempstead

Table 6.3 Foster's tied estate

a) Sold to Chesham Brewery in 1898

Herts			
Berkhamsted	*Brownlow Arms*	Berkhamsted	OL Kittsbury
	OL Charles St		*Rose and Crown*
	George		*Swan*
	OL George St	Northchurch	*Pheasant*

Beds			
Leighton Buzzard	*Eagle*	Leighton Buzzard	OL No name

Bucks			
Aylesbury	OL No name	Buckland Common	*Rose and Crown*
Bierton	*Eagle*	Buckland Wharf	*Surprise*

b) Disposed before 1898

Herts			
Berkhamsted	*Crystal Palace*	Northchurch	*Red Lion* BH
	King's Arms		*Rose and Crown* BH
Bovingdon	*Stag's Head* BH		

originally had been owned by the Manor Brewery of Tring plus cottages, a shop and land. In 1910 the brewery was also leasing the *Good Intent* at Edlesborough and the malting at the Three Counties Brewery, Dagnall, from Fullers & Co, Ltd.

By 1911 there were severe financial problems and a receiver was appointed. A deed was issued in 1913 'charging' the brewery to the London County and Westminster Bank which decided that it should be put up for sale. Benskin's of Watford acquired the brewery and tied estate for £37,600. A few years later there was a recommendation to demolish the brewery and build a war memorial on the site. This proposal was not successful but most of the old buildings were

Figure 6.2 Foster's Chapel Street Malting

destroyed in a fire later in 1929. Finally the remnants were demolished and this area was converted into a car park.

Swan Brewery

George and Charles Foster took over the small brewery behind the *Swan,* at the corner of the High Street and Chesham Road in 1817, with the intention of supplying just this single outlet. There was originally also a small malting on this site that was demolished when the brewery expanded. James Foster was the owner from 1839 until 1850. J.E. Lane was there between 1853 and 1871 and he also bought the freeholds of the *Brownlow Arms* in Chapel Street and the *George* in the High Street. During 1871 Henry James Foster bought the brewery and the *Brownlow Arms* and the *George*. He bought or leased other properties including off-licences, and gradually increased the tied estate in Berkhamsted, Bovingdon, Northchurch and also in Bedfordshire and Buckinghamshire (Table 6.3). The Fosters also owned a fifteen quarter single storey malting in Chapel Street, which now belongs to the First Berkhamsted boy scout troop, and this building still has traces of the Foster's sign on an outside wall. The brewery and its tied estate were bought by Nash's Chesham Brewery in 1898. Henry Foster became a director of this company and remained there until 1914. Later the two-storey brewery building would appear to have been incorporated into the ancillary buildings behind the *Swan*.

References

Hastie, S. *Berkhamsted: An Illustrated History*, King's Langley, Alpine Press, 1999.

Hertfordshire County Records Office. a. Berkhamsted Tithe Map 1839, b. Locke and Smith (D/EB 965T1), c. Swan Brewery (D/Els B520).

Petty Sessions Licensing Records for Hertfordshire, Bedfordshire and Buckinghamshire.

Poole, H. *Here for the Beer*, Watford Museum, 1984, pp.8–9.

Richmond, L. and Turton, A. (eds.) *The Brewing Industry: A Guide to Historical Records*, Manchester University Press, 1990, p.213 (Locke and Smith).

CHAPTER SEVEN

Bishop's Stortford

In the 1700s the maltsters of Bishop's Stortford were prevented from competing successfully with the maltsters of Hertford and Ware to sell large quantities of malt to the London breweries because of the poor quality of transport by road or by river. The setting up of the River Stort Navigation Company in 1766 led to major improvements in the depth of the river and the building of sections of canal which enabled cargo-carrying boats to reach Bishop's Stortford by the improved River Stort. A rapid expansion of malt production began. There were at least forty maltings in the town in the early 1800s using barley from East Anglia.

Bishop's Stortford developed as a market town with many inns and taverns. Much of the beer drunk in the town was brewed at Hawkes' Brewery.

Hawkes' Brewery

Hawkes' Brewery was originally founded in 1780 on a site between Water Lane and Northgate End with the River Stort as the eastern boundary to the property (Figure 7.1). In 1793 William Woodham, William Hawkes and Thomas Bird were in partnership as the owners and were succeeded in 1820 by Hawkes, Nash, Johnstone & Co. Between 1832 and 1848 the partnership of Hawkes & Co. comprised Frederick John Nash, Elizabeth and William Robert Hawkes, William Johnstone and William and Thomas Bird. By 1846 Hawkes & Co. were describing themselves as brewers, maltsters, wine and spirit merchants. In 1876 James Wigan, his son James Lewis Wigan and one of his nephews, F.W. Blunt, bought the business and retained the name Hawkes and Co. until it was sold in 1898 to Benskin's of Watford. James Wigan had previously been in partnership with Charles John Phillips at the Elephant Brewery, Portnam Square, London and also owned three public houses in Mortlake and one in Dulwich.

By 1830 the brewery owned at least fifteen freehold and one leasehold

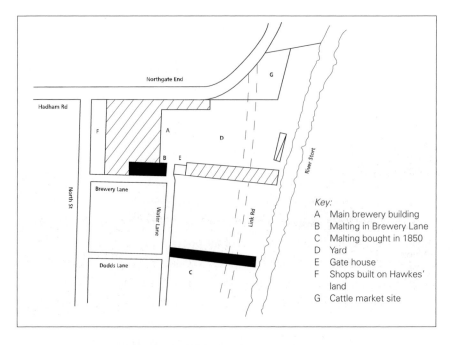

Figure 7.1 Simplified plan of Hawkes' Brewery site

licensed properties. These included the *Castle, Chequers, Currier's Arms, Dog's Head in a Pot, George, Half Moon, Star, White Horse* and *White Swan* in Bishop's Stortford plus the *Coach and Horses* and *Red Lion* in Hockerill. There was also a brewery house and a malting. In 1850 another malting in Water Lane was bought to increase capacity. Farmland was being leased, most probably for growing malting barley. The tied estate steadily increased to sixty-six properties in the 1870s. At this time the brewery building was expanded in the two main sections to four and six storeys plus a boiler house with a tall brick chimney (Figure 7.2).

The company bought William Hawkes' Black Lion Brewery in Braintree, Essex, as well as eight public houses and a malting in 1890 for £11,260. The two Hawkes families were not related. William Hawkes had previously purchased the *Black Lion*, Braintree, in 1869 and converted it into a brewery. By 1882 he was also described as a maltster with a malting in Black Notley and owned the *Duke's Head* in Bocking, the *Freemason's Arms, Nag's Head, Oak, Rose and Crown, Saracen's Head* and the *Swan* in Braintree plus the *Red Lion* in Stisted. This small brewery continued to operate until 1916 and was then used as a depot by Benskin's until 1933. Hawkes & Co. made a further purchase in 1898 of Mrs

Figure 7.2 Hawkes' Brewery yard in 1878 (Ian Stratford collection)

Smith's Great Bardfield Brewery, Essex, plus four more public houses which included the *Ship* (*Sparrow's Nest*) in Braintree, the *Crown* and the *Gate* in Great Bardfield and the *Swan* in Rayne. At this stage it is thought that Hawkes & Co. owned or leased nearly 200 tied properties with at least 100 in Essex, eighty-three in Hertfordshire, thirteen in Cambridgeshire, two in Kent, three in London and three off-licences.

Later in 1898 Benskin's bought the brewery and 161 public houses and beer houses for £263,000. Table 7.1 shows fifty-eight in Hertfordshire, twelve in Cambridgeshire, eighty-one in Essex, one in Kent, one in Suffolk and two in London. This makes a total of 157 including one off-licence. Before the sale in 1898 Hawkes & Co. already had sold or disposed of twenty licensed properties in Hertfordshire plus four in Cambridgeshire and at least seven in Essex (Table 7.2). It is recognised that Benskin's purchases of Hawkes' properties in Essex and the disposal list for Essex are incomplete and need further research. Brewing ceased in 1916 but the brewery buildings continued to be used as a depot and bottling plant. In 1910 Benskin's still had a malting at The Dell in Bishop's Stortford.

The majority of old brewery buildings have now been pulled down and the site has been redeveloped in the 1990s as a supermarket and car park. In Water Lane only a large malting, now used as a warehouse, and a house to the right of

Table 7.1 Hawkes' tied estate in 1898 sold to Benskin's

Herts

Albury	Catherine Wheel	High Wych	Hand and Crown
Barkway	Bull L. to F.	Hockerill	Coach and Horses
Bishop's Stortford	Anchor		Red Lion
	Barge	Knebworth	Lytton Arms L.
	Boar's Head	Little Hadham	Angel
	Bricklayer's Arms		Fox
	Bull's Head	Much Hadham	Bull
	Castle		Old Bell, Hadham Cross
	Chequers		White Horse, Green Tye
	Curriers' Arms	Sawbridgeworth	Bull
	Dog's Head in the Pot		Hand and Crown
	Falcon		King's Head
	Fox		Old Bell
	George	South Mimms	Black Horse
	Half Moon	Spellbrook	Greyhound
	Nag's Head	Standon	Windmill
	Railway Hotel	Stanstead Abbots	Bull
	Royal Oak		Five Horseshoes
	Star		Ryes (King's Arms)
	Swan		Pied Bull
	Waggon and Horses		Red Lion
	Weigh House	Stocking Pelham	Cock
	White Horse	Thorley	Green Man
	White Swan L.		OL, London Road
Braughing	Golden Fleece	Throcking	Adam and Eve
	Rose and Crown		White Horse
Cheshunt	Coach and Horses	Waltham Cross	Britannia
	Green Man, Goff's Oak	Ware	Chequers, Wareside
High Wych	Half Moon	Widford	Swan

Cambs

Cambridge	Castle	Great Shelford	Plough
	Live and Let Live	Horseheath	Montford Arms
	Mitre Tavern	Ickleton	Red Lion
	Sun	Linton	Swan
	Tailor's Arms	Sawston	Black Bull
	White Hart		Star

Essex

Ashdon	Rose and Crown	Hatfield Heath	Fox and Hounds
	White Horse	Helions Bumpstead	Marquis of Granby
Aythorp Roding	Axe and Compasses		Prince of Wales
Beauchamp Roding	Two Swans		Royal Oak
Bentfield End	Rose and Crown	Henham	Cock
Berden	Raven	Higher Laver	Chequers
Birchanger	Three Horseshoes	Langley	Bull
Bocking	Duke's Head*	Leaden Roding	King William IV
Braintree	Bell	Little Hallingbury	Sutton Arms
	Bird in Hand	Manuden	Cock
	Freemasons' Arms*		Jolly Waggoners
	Nag's Head*		Oak
	Oak*	Matching Green	Chequers
	Rose and Crown*	Matching Tye	Fox

	*Saracen's Head**	Mole Hill Green	*Three Horseshoes*
	*Ship***	Moreton	*White Hart*
	Sun	Netteswell	*Chequers*
	*Swan**	Newport	*Rose and Crown*
Chipping Ongar	*White Horse*		*Star and Garter*
Clavering	*Fox and Hounds*	North Weald	*Cross Keys*
Dunmow	*Chequers*	Old Sampford	BH
Elmdon	*Wilkes Arms*	Radwinter	*Plough*
Elsenham	*Robin Hood*	Rayne	*Swan***
Epping	*Black Lion*	Rickling	*Coach and Horses*
	Royal Oak	Rickling Green	*Cricketers*
Farnham	*Globe*	Saffron Walden	*Duke of York*
	Three Horseshoes	Sheering	*Cock*
Finchingfield	*Green Man*	Stanstead	*King's Arms* L.
Great Baddow	*New Found Out* L.		*Olde Bell*, Pine Hills
Great Bardfield	*Crown***		*Three Colts*
	*Gate***	Stebbing	*Red Lion*
	White Hart	Stisted	*Red Lion**
Great Easton	*Bell*	Takeley	*Four Ashes*
Great Hallingbury	*George*	Thaxted	*Cock*
	Hop Poles		*Sun*
Great Sampford	*White Horse*	Ugely	*Chequers*
Great Waltham	*Rose and Crown*		OL
Harlow	*Marquis of Granby*	Wendens Ambo	*Bell*
	Red Lion, Potter St	White Roding	*Whalebone*
	White Horse	Witham	*George and Dragon*
Hatfield Broad Oak	*Fox*		

Kent		*Suffolk*	
Dartford	*Freemasons' Arms*	Haverhill	*Old White Hart*

London			
Kew Bridge	*Express*	Whetstone	*Griffin*

Key: *   Ex Hawkes' Braintree Brewery
        **   Ex Mrs Smith's Great Bardfield Brewery

the old brewery entrance still remain (Figure 7.3). Virtually all the signs or emblems for Hawkes & Co.'s Entire Ales have now been destroyed. However the *Old Currier's Arms* in Bishop's Stortford, which is now a Wimpey Burger Restaurant, has a Hawkes & Co. badged drainpipe and the *Lytton Arms* in Old Knebworth still has a Hawkes & Co. pub sign frame in wrought iron.

Fox Brewery

There was also the very much smaller Fox Brewery situated at the corner of Hockerill Street and Warwick Road where they meet Dunmow Road and Haymeads Lane and opposite the *Nag's Head*. Between 1861 and 1915 it was owned by many people often for very short times. In 1861 John Baynes sold the

Figure 7.3 Corner of Brewery Lane and Water Lane showing part of Hawkes' Brewery
gate house and converted malting

brewery to John Evans who sold to William Cornwall in 1863. He sold to William Barnard in 1866, who in turn sold to J. R. Heath in 1877. For a short while J. Wolton was the temporary owner but ownership seems to have transferred back to Mr Heath. When Mr Heath finally advertised the brewery for sale, there was a two quarter brewery, cellar, yard, a four-stall stable, a beer house with an outdoor beer licence, hen house and piggeries on a half acre site. The brewing contents included a four-barrel copper, a mash tun, three coolers, two fermenting squares, a force pump and pipes, a washing copper, underback, two hand yeast gatherers, six barrels, thirty-six kilderkins, thirty firkins and thirty pins.

The brewery was sold to the Flinn (or Flynn) family in 1885, who were followed by William Redin Stanton in 1902 and the Bailey brothers between 1902 and 1915. Finally in 1915 the brewery was sold to Benskin's together with one off-licence. Among this group of owners until 1915 only the Flinn family, who were also maltsters in Bishop's Stortford, appear to have owned other beer houses or a brewery. Frank Flinn had previously been at the Fox Brewery at Finchingfield, Essex, between 1883 to 1886 when it was sold to Webb & Gibbons of Dunmow. Besides owning the *Fox* at Finchingfield, Flinns had also owned the *Rising Sun* FL at Isleham, Cambs in 1898. In Bishop's Stortford in 1903, the Flinns had the *Shades* BH, *Bridge House* BH, the *Rising Sun* BH and the *Robin Hood* BH

Table 7.2 Hawkes' disposals before takeover by Benskin's in 1898

Herts

Albury	*Fox*	Cheshunt	*Old Bull's Head*
Barnet	*Mitre*	Furneux Pelham	*White Lion*
	Old Red Lion	Great Hornmead	*Three Horseshoes*
Bishop's Stortford	*Bell*	Hertford	*Dimsdale Arms*
	Black Bull		*Unicorn*
	Peacock	Much Hadham	*Prince of Wales*
	Pewter Pot	Sawbridgeworth	*Bell and Feathers*
	Prince of Wales	Stanstead St M.	*Chequers*
	Six Bells	Turnford	*Bull*
Buntingford	*Adam and Eve*	Widford	*Royal Oak*

Cambs

Chesterton	*Admiral Vernon*	Swavesey	*Black Horse*
Over	*Black Lion*		*Green Man*

Essex

Beauchamp Roding	*Three Hurdles*	Radwinter	*Potash*
Braintree	*White Hart*	Stanstead	*Rose and Crown*
Hatfield Broad Oak	*Cock*	Wendens Ambo	*Neville Arms*
Little Laver	*Leather Bottle*		

Key: Stanstead St M. = Stamstead St Margaret

plus two off-licences in Bridge Street and Nursery Street. They also owned a beer house at Smith End in Barley which was finally closed in 1930. Presumably they bought beer from other breweries at those times when they did not own or lease a brewery.

At the present time the Fox Brewery site is occupied by a large car sales and garage business.

References

Hertfordshire County Records Office. a. D/E/Ic/T series, b. D/E/Be series, c. MiscVII, d. Acc.3883, Box 14. Volumes of *Pennant*, Box 24. Shelf 50–1. Property registers for Bishop's Stortford and Essex 1959–73 – details of ex-Hawkes, properties. Also tithe redemption certificates. D/Ebe T36 (purchase of malting in Water Lane).

Ind Coope Archives. Document giving details of Ind Coope tied estate in East Anglia in 1957.

Petty Sessions Licensing Records for Hertfordshire, Cambridgeshire and West Essex.

Poole, H. *Here for the Beer*, Watford Museum, 1984, pp.9–11 (Both Hawkes, and Fox Brewery).

Richmond, H. and Turton, A. (eds.) *The Brewing Industry: A Guide to Historical Records*, Manchester University Press, 1990, p.173.

Stratford, I. Personal communication about Hawkes' tied estate in Essex, Cambridgeshire, Kent and London.

CHAPTER EIGHT

Furneux Pelham

Historically the Calvert family brewed their own beer at the Hall in Furneux Pelham for the family and estate staff. They also had a financial interest in the City of London Brewery. William Rayment leased the Hall from the Calverts in the 1840s and by 1855 he was recorded in the county directory as a brewer as well as a farmer and was buying malting barley from local farms. In 1860 the lease for the Hall expired and William Rayment bought a piece of land at the crossroads

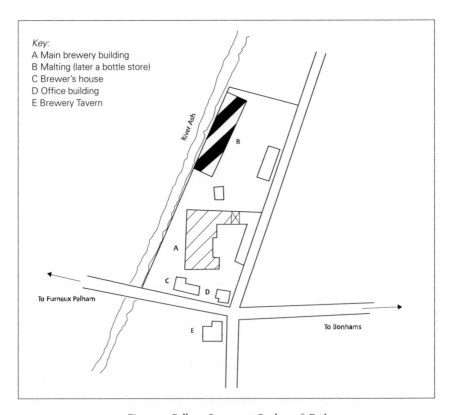

Figure 8.1 Pelham Brewery at Barleycroft End

Figure 8.2 Main brewery building and office building by gate

at Barleycroft End to build a brewery using bricks from his own brick yard. By this time he was described as a brewer, maltster, miller, farmer, brick maker and drainpipe maker.

Pelham Brewery

Although William Rayment died in the 1860s, the brewery was kept going by his executors on behalf of his wife and four sons. The brewer and manager was Stukely Abbot who employed between twelve and fourteen men, two in the brewhouse, two in the beer cellar, two in the office and six to eight as draymen. They brewed 150 gallons at each mash three to four times each week. The masher and mash tun were both situated on the ground floor of the brewhouse. This mash tun was installed by Briggs of Burton on Trent in 1870 and was still being used when brewing stopped over 100 years later. The louvred windows in the brewery building indicate that the wort cooler(s) must have been at first floor level. This was an unusual layout. At the same time a beer store with a thatched roof was constructed over a draught beer cellar. In 1913 the beer store burnt down and was replaced. The brewery obtained its power from a steam engine and later from a producer gas plant which also generated electricity for both the brewery and the village. In 1869 a malting was built beside the brewery

Figure 8.3 Malting converted to a bottle store

which was used until the 1950s. Mrs Elizabeth Rayment bought the *White Hart* in Buntingford in 1873 to start a tied estate. The last of William Rayment's sons died in 1888 and the brewery, trading as Rayment & Co. was put up for auction in December 1888.

The brewery with eighteen tied houses was bought for £18,200 plus £8,000 for rolling stock on 11 February 1889 by Frederick William King and Edward William Lake who were managing director and a director of Greene King & Sons' brewery of Bury St Edmunds. They did however run Rayment & Co. as a separate private partnership and gradually increased the size of the tied estate. In 1910 the brewery bought Newell's Brewery in Radwinter, Essex, plus the *Brewery Tavern*, and the Little Hadham Brewery. They acquired the *Nag's Head* in Little Hadham in 1912 as well as their first two lorries for beer deliveries. In the same year J.M. King retired and the remaining partners, Edward William King and Alan Henry Lake, sold the brewery to members of the Lake family for £29,980. At this stage there were twenty-six properties in the tied estate in Hertfordshire, Cambridgeshire and Essex (Table 8.1).

In 1931 the brewery and its thirty-six tied properties became a semi-independent subsidiary company of Greene King & Sons by issuing 15,000 ordinary shares to the vendors. The Lake family remained involved with the

Figure 8.4 The Brewery Tap *(or* Tavern*)*

management until 1967. Vice-Admiral W.J.C. Lake managed the brewery until
1937. Captain Neville Lake RN was appointed as the brewery manager until 1967.
However he did have a break while he was on active service during World War
II. It is claimed that he ran the brewery like a ship and even employed his ex-
coxswain. In his office he had a large scale map showing all Rayment's tied estate
which every summer indicated the progress of neighbouring county council
road men. When the steam rollers and tar boilers were approaching a Rayment's
pub he would drive in his car to meet the workmen and welcome them to a
generous supply of beer before concluding a bargain for the holes in the pub's
car park or yard.

The brewery began supplying working men's clubs and other social clubs.
There were sixty-seven clubs taking the brewery beers in 1937. Because of this
free trade this small brewery was the most profitable part of the Greene King
business at a time when most tied estates were producing low financial returns.
When Captain Lake became a Catholic, he converted an outbuilding at the
brewery into a chapel and started to entertain club chairmen and secretaries
(often with Catholic origins) to lunch. He steadily increased the club trade to 255
accounts by 1965. The brewery was ideally situated to supply the free trade in
north and east London with draught and bottled beers. By 1980 the free trade
accounted for 85 per cent of the brewery business.

Between 1860 and 1870, the 350-acre Lodge Farm in Furneux Pelham was

Table 8.1 Rayment's tied estate

		1912	1970	1984	Notes
Cambs					
Chatteris	BH No name				Petty Sessions 1893
Duxford	Wheatsheaf	*	*		Transferred to GK Bigg.1975
Guilden Morden	Pear Tree	*			Sold to Barclay Perkins 1920
Harston	Queen's Head	*	*	*	
Litlington	Crown	*			Sold to Barclay Perkins 1920
Essex					
Arkesden	Axe & Compasses	*	*	*	
Bardfield End Green	Butcher's Arms		*		
Birchanger	Three Willows	*	*	*	
Clavering	Waggon and Horses	*	*	*	Closed 1985
Debden	Plough	*	*	*	
Harlow	Willow Beauty		*	*	
Hatfield Heath	White Horse	*	*	*	
Newport	White Horse	*	*	*	
Radwinter	Brewery Tavern		*		Transferred to GK Bury. 1975
Saffron Walden	Axe and Compasses	*			Transferred to GK Bigg. 1975
	Five Bells				*c.*1920
	Gate	*	*		Transferred to GK Bigg. 1975
	Victory	*			Transferred to GK Bigg. 1975
Stanstead –	Ash	*	*		Transferred from GK Bigg. 1961
Mountfitchet	Cock	*	*	*	
	Dog and Duck	*	*		
Thaxted	Butcher's Arms		*	*	Transferred from GK Bigg. 1961
Wicken Bonhunt	Coach and Horses		*	*	
Herts					
Albury	Royal Oak	*	*	*	Closed 1985
	Yew Tree				pre-1912
Anstey	Windmill	*			Closed 1916
Barkway	Bull				pre-1912
	Tally Ho	*	*	*	
	Three Horseshoes	*			Closed 1952
Bishop's Stortford	Cellarman	*	*		
	Rose and Crown	*	*	*	
	Three Tuns	*	*	*	
	Wheatsheaf	*	*	*	
Braughing	Boar's Head	*			Closed 1923
Buntingford	White Hart				1875 to pre-1912
Furneux Pelham	Black Horse				pre-1881
	Brewery Tap	*	*	*	
	Star	*	*	*	Closed 1995
Great Munden	Plough	*			
Hertford	Bull				Sold to Pryor Reid *c.*1910
Hunsden	Turkey Cock		*	*	Before 1940 to 1988
Little Hadham	Nag's Head	*	*	*	
Meesden	Fox		*		After 1949 to *c.*1981
Sawbridgeworth	Prince of Wales	*			Closed about 1920
	White Lion	*	*	*	
Spellbrook	Three Horseshoes		*		
Tewin	Rose and Crown		*	*	From *c.*1958
Ware	White House				In 1920s

Wareside	Fox			c.1918 to 1924
	White Horse	*	*	From Pryor Reid c.1914
Total in tied estate		26	35	26

Key: Bigg. Biggleswade
      Bury. Bury St Edmunds

purchased by the brewery, most likely as a source of malting barley. It was not well managed by the Lake family who found it difficult to justify financial losses during the agricultural depression of the 1920s and 1930s as they were unable to sell it. The farm was finally sold in 1959 for £22,500 ending 100 years as a joint brewing and farming enterprise.

Greene King management reorganised part of Rayment's tied estate between 1961 and 1975. In 1961 the *Ash* at Stanstead Mountfitchet and the *Butcher's Arms* at Thaxted that had been part of the Biggleswade brewery estate (originally Wells & Winch) were transferred to Rayment's and the total number of properties increased to 35 in 1970. However, in 1975 Rayment's relinquished the *Wheatsheaf* at Duxford, and the *Axe and Compasses*, the *Gate* and the *Victory* (all three in Saffron Walden) to the Biggleswade brewery and the *Brewery Tavern* at Radwinter to the Bury St Edmunds brewery.

In 1970 the brewery had a capacity for about 12,000 barrels per year and was producing draught BBA, AK Pale Ale, XX Mild, Keg Dagger Bitter and Keg Mild. In bottled form there was also Pelham Ale, Super Ale, Brown Ale, Dagger Brown and Old Crony. At this time a much smaller beer range was being produced at both Bury St Edmunds and Biggleswade. The bottling plant, which had been originally installed during World War I and expanded in the 1920s when the bottling store labour force was increased to seven, was finally closed in 1973. The malting that had not been in use since the 1950s was converted into a two-level bottled beer store. A sixth fermenting vessel was added in 1976 to meet draught and keg beer demand from its own tied estate and the free trade outlets at clubs. A keg storage building was added in 1977. In 1987 brewing was stopped because of falling demand for draught beer and excess brewing capacity at the other breweries at Bury St Edmunds and Biggleswade. The Furneux Pelham site remained in use for a further ten years until 1997 as a depot for distribution to its public houses and free trade. In the meantime Rayment's BBA bitter was brewed at Bury St Edmunds. The site has since been sold and redeveloped for private housing.

References

Page, K. Personal Communication, 1998. Properties in 1912 and later transfers between Greene King breweries.

Petty Sessions Licensing Records for Hertfordshire, Cambridgeshire and west Essex.

Poole, H. *Here for the Beer*, Watford Museum, 1984, p.16.

Richmond, L. and Turton, A. (eds.) *The Brewing Industry: A Guide to Historical Records*, Manchester University Press, 1990, p.272.

Smith, K. and Crosby, T. Rayment & Company Ltd. *Journal of the Brewery History Society*, Vol. 104, 2001, pp.29–33.

Wilson, R.G. *Greene King: A Business & Family History*, London, Bodley Head & Jonathan Cape, 1983, pp.166, 188–9, 191, 203, 230, 245, 250.

Hadley

Hadley or Highstone Brewery

This brewery was on the old Great North Road at Hadley Green, Barnet and was originally established in the 1700s. Its known owners were Robert Thorp (1824), Robert and William Thorp (1826), William and Maria Thorp (1845), Anderson & Co. (1850), Henry John Salisbury (1855), W.T. Healey (1861), Hayward Edwards (to 1884), W.R. Dagnall (1884–7) and Harris Browne family (1887–1938). The brewery was rebuilt in 1911 as a three-storey building when only the cellars were retained from the original brewery.

Water was obtained from wells on the site to be used in the brewing of at least ten draught beers including XAK, AK, XBA, DDS and ten bottled beers including A1 Burton, XXX Burton, IPA Burton, BA Bitter, LB Bitter, XX Mild, DS Stout, Nourishing Stout, Oatmeal Stout and Porter. The brewery would also deliver half-pins (two and a quarter gallons) of draught beers to large houses and supply wines, spirits, ginger beer and mineral waters.

The brewery had a small tied estate of public houses, an hotel and off-licences and also sold alcoholic and non-alcoholic drinks to clubs that included the East Finchley British Legion Club (Table 9.1).

Harris Browne Ltd was taken over by Fremlins in 1938 and brewing stopped. The last brewer was Captain Dudley Mozley who later moved to Maidstone and joined Fremlins board of directors. Part of the site was used as an administrative and distribution depot by Fremlins and later by Whitbread Ltd. G.W. Smith & Co. (Radio Ltd) leased the remainder of the site. The three-storey brewery was finally demolished in 1970. Much later the site was cleared and three detached houses were built there.

Table 9.1 Hadley Brewery tied estate and club accounts

Herts			
Arkley	*Brickmakers' Arms*	Hadley	*Two Brewers*
Barnet	*Green Man* (to *c.*1905)		OL at brewery
Brookmans Park	*Brookmans Park Hotel*	New Barnet	*Green Man* BH
	OL	Potters Bar	*Bridge House*
North London			
Enfield	Brigadier Stores OL	Highgate	Holmesdale Stores OL
Highgate	*Victoria*, North Hill Rd	Southgate	*Brown Jug*
Club accounts in North London			
East Finchley	British Legion Club	New Barnet	Conservative Club
Friern Barnet	British Legion Club	St John's Wood	Club

References

Gelder, W.H. *Monken Hadley Church and Village*, Barnet, DeMandus Printers, 1986, pp.64–5.

Hertfordshire Archives and Local Studies. Acc. 3716. Box 13. Ledgers of Harris Browne Ltd.

Poole, H. *Here for the Beer*, Watford Museum, 1984, p.17.

Richmond, L. and Turton, A. (eds.) *The Brewing Industry: A Guide to Historical Records*, Manchester University Press, 1990, p.172.

CHAPTER TEN

Harpenden

Brewing started in Harpenden over 400 years ago. Thomas Hayward, a brewer and maltster was the owner of the *Black Bull* in Leyton Road. He sold the property to William Catlin, who was described as a brewer and beer house owner when he was fined in the local court in 1623 for keeping an unlicensed alehouse. By the early 1700s the brewhouse had a furnace, mashing vats, coolers, vats and tubs. In the 1870s this property was converted to a private house called the Sycamores. The *Dolphin* had its own malting in the 1780s and 1790s.

Larger scale brewing commenced in 1826 at a brewery owned by the Kingston family on the east side of the High Street and to the north of Vaughan Road (Figure 10.1). By 1893 a second independent brewery owned by the Curtis family was built on the adjoining plot of land (Figure 10.2). At this stage it is important to establish which brewery was on each site.

Unfortunately the name Harpenden Brewery has been used for both breweries at different times. On the 25 inches to the mile OS map of 1874 the southern brewery is labelled Harpenden Brewery (Peacock Brewery owned by Mardall's and Glover's) and the northern brewery is just labelled Brewery (Harpenden Brewery owned by Curtis and Healey). This indicates that even the mapmakers had been misinformed as to which was the Harpenden Brewery. The 1897 large scale OS map only shows one brewery to the north side of Vaughan Road labelled Harpenden Brewery. The two breweries will be identified by the names of the owners of each site to avoid confusion.

Peacock Brewery (Kingston, House, Mardall, Glover)

James Kingston, or possibly Jane Kingston, is reputed to have founded the Peacock Brewery in 1826. However neither of them has been recorded as being the owner of any local licensed property. Between 1839 and 1870 the brewery was managed by members of the House family of Wheathampstead. Initially this

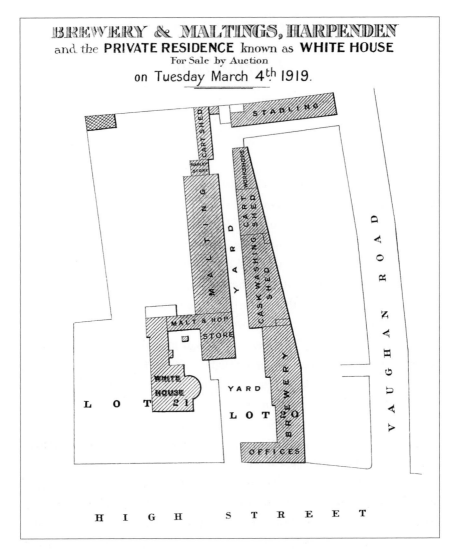

Figure 10.1 Plan of Harpenden Brewery in 1893 (HALS)

involved Jonathan and Thomas House followed by John Isaac House (1843), John P. House (1851), John House (1861), John and Thomas House (1866) and finally Mrs Elizabeth House (1870). In 1840 the family were leasing the malting behind the *Rose and Crown* in Sandridge from Edward Burr. Shortly afterwards the House family sold the brewery and tied estate to James Mardall. In 1871 the original Peacock House in the brewery grounds was pulled down and a new building with extensive cellars known as Brewery House replaced it (now 29A

Table 10.1 Peacock Brewery tied estate in 1919 sale

		Annual barrel sales		
		1911–12	*1912–13*	*1913–14*
Herts				
Abbots Langley	*Rose and Crown* FL	110	117	134
Friar's Wash	*Waggon and Horses* FL, L.	80	85	67
Frithsden	*Alford Arms* FL, L.			83
Hemel Hempstead	*Old Bell Gate* BH	85	91	90
	Waggon and Horses FL, L.	130	159	151
Beds				
Clifton	*Fox and Duck* FL	119	114	113
Dunstable	*Waggon and Horses* FL, L.			133
Houghton Regis	*Five Bells* FL	277	272	260
	White Horse FL, L.			287
Leagrave	*Three Horseshoes* FL	462	491	493
Luton	*Blue Lion* BH	169	209	150
	Four Horseshoes FL	183	258	244
	Hare and Hounds BH	87	101	87
	Queen's Arms FL	69	57	63
	Railway Inn FL	137	117	152
	Richard III FL	383	285	287
	Vine FL	227	187	191
	Worlds End BH	58	70	76
Shefford	*Woolpack* FL	84	83	97
Stopsley	*Sportsman* FL	227	269	371
Totternhoe	*Old Bell* FL, L.			98
	Total for year (barrels)	2,837	2,965	3,627

High Street). When James Mardall died in 1882, his widow Mrs Martha Mardall became the manager of the brewery.

The tied estate of this brewery was gradually increased in size by a number of individual acquisitions by the two families. The House family built the *Silver Cup* at Harpenden in 1838 and by 1840 they also owned the *Tin Pot* at Gustard Wood, the *Three Horseshoes* near Banville Wood Farm, Harpenden and the *Swan* at Wheathampstead. During the early 1870s James Mardall built the *Railway Hotel* at Harpenden and bought the *Richard III* at Luton and the *Sportsman* at Stopsley. His widow bought the *Oddfellows' Arms* (*Oak Tree*) at Harpenden from Sir John Lawes and the *Wicked Lady* (*Park Hotel*) at Wheathampstead.

Eventually the Mardall family trustees sold the brewery, a twelve quarter malting and the combined estates of the two Harpenden breweries to Richard Glover for £58,000. Soon afterwards he undertook a major rebuilding programme on the site and built a new tower brewery. In 1902, when he owned or leased forty public houses, he formed an amalgamation with Pryor Reid of Hatfield to form the Hatfield & Harpenden Brewery Ltd with a share capital of

Table 10.2 Peacock Brewery tied estate sales or closures before sale in 1919

		b.b.			b.b.
Herts					
Boreham Wood	*Wellington*	Be	Offley	*Cock* FL	WW
Friar's Wash	*Waggon and Horses* FL	Gr	St Albans	*Queen Adelaide*	Bn
Harpenden	*Fishmongers' Arms* BH			*Rule and Compasses*	
	Marquis of Granby FL	Be		*Verulam Arms*	Bn
	Oak Tree BH	Mc	Sandridge	*White Horse* BH	
	Old Cock FL	TH	Wheathampstead	*Cricketers* BH	PR
	Red Cow BH	PR		*Elephant & Castle*	PR
	Royal Oak BH			*Park Hotel* FL	PR
	Silver Cup BH	We		*Swan* FL	PR
	White Horse BH	Gr		*Three Horseshoes* FL	Gr
Leverstock Green	*Rose and Crown* FL	AW		*Walnut Tree* BH	Bn
London Colney	*Bull and Butcher* BH		Whitwell	*Fox* BH	
Beds					
Caddington	*Shepherd's Crook* BH		Houghton Regis	*White Swan*	

Key:	b.b. Brewery buyer	AW Adey & White	Be Bennett
	Bn Benskin	Gr J.W. Green	Mc McMullen
	PR Pryor Reid	TH Trust House	We Charles Wells
	WW Wells & Winch		

£163,000. However, both companies continued to brew under their own names.

The amalgamation finished in 1910 and subsequently the Harpenden Brewery was re-named Glover & Sons Ltd. A comparison of barrel sales was made between 1911 and 1914 for all the public houses. This analysis indicated wide differences between high volume beer selling to town public houses, such as the *Three Horseshoes* in Leagrave, the *Four Horseshoes* and the *Richard III* in Luton, and low volume beer selling to public houses such as the *Queen's Arms* and the *Worlds End* in Luton.

These figures show that Glover's brewed at least 2,837 barrels in 1911–12, 2,965 barrels in 1912–13 and 3,627 barrels in 1913–14 with four more outlets. Unfortunately in 1919 the company went into liquidation and J.W. Green of Luton bought the brewery and a few public houses. The remainder of the estate was sold to other local breweries. Before 1919 Glovers had already disposed of a considerable part of the estate. These earlier disposals and completion of leases are given in Table 10.2.

There is a plan of the brewery dating from 1919 which shows the brewery, a boiler house, an office and stores, a twelve quarter malting with a cellar underneath, a malt and a hop store and the brewery house (Figure 10.1).

The brewing machinery included a twelve quarter mash tun, a sixty-barrel copper, a 100 barrel hot liquor tank, a sixty-barrel wood hop back, a wooden

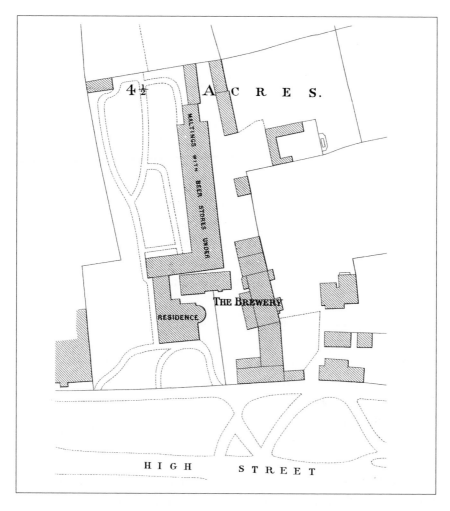

Figure 10.2 Plan of Peacock Brewery in 1919 (HALS)

wort cooler of sixty barrels' capacity, four sixty-barrel fermenting squares and three fifteen barrel fermenting squares.

After the closure of the brewery in 1919, it was bought and used by Waverly Sportswear Mills. The site was redeveloped in 1936 and the front part on the High Street is at the present time occupied by Boots and Argos. The Brewery House was occupied as a private dwelling until 1951 when the site was sold and is now occupied by W.H. Smith and Going Places. There are still extensive cellars under the building.

Harpenden Brewery (Curtis, Healey, Bennett)

Early details of the history of Curtis's brewery are extremely limited. In 1837, James Curtis leased the *Queen Victoria* at Redbourn. Later he also leased a beer house (tithe plot 842) at Hemel Hempstead in 1843, bought the *Greyhound* at St Ippollytts near Hitchin in 1845, obtained the copyhold of the *White Horse* at Hitchin in 1845 and bought the *Rose and Crown* at Abbot's Langley in 1852.

In 1853 the business was sold to George Healey of Watford who operated the brewery and a malting employing twelve men and a boy. His brother Charles Healey had established the King Street Brewery in Watford during 1851. He died prematurely in 1862, aged forty-two or forty-three, and his widow Elizabeth Whittingstall Healey continued to manage the business until 1874. She may have been a daughter of Edward F. Whittingstall who owned another Watford brewery. Subsequently the brewery was leased to Bennett's of Dunstable for nineteen years.

The brewhouse had a twelve quarter batch capacity, was a three-storey building which contained a malt store and malt mill, a steam boiler, an oak mash tun, a copper and a hop back. One fermenting room contained two square fermenting vessels of thirty-two and eleven barrels capacity. A second fermenting room contained three round vessels. Water was obtained from a 200 foot deep artesian well and stored in a one hundred barrel capacity cistern. There was also a granary with two floors and a malting with a fifteen quarter steeping cistern plus a germination floor of one hundred feet by thirty feet. Underneath there was an extensive cool beer store fitted with tram lines and a barrel hoist. On this large site there was also a substantial owner's or brewer's house, a counting house and a spirit store (Figure 10.2).

In 1893 the brewery and its tied estate were sold for £16,000 to Mrs Mardall, the owner of the other Harpenden brewery (Table 10.3). The *White Horse* at Hitchin and the *Greyhound* at St Ippollytts did not form part of this sale and were disposed of later. Other public houses owned or leased before 1893 are quoted in the second part of Table 10.3. The brewery was closed and brewing activities were concentrated on the other brewery site. A Methodist church was built on the site after the brewery buildings had been pulled down.

Red Cow Brewery

There was no active brewery in Harpenden until a micro-brewery was

Table 10.3 Harpenden Brewery tied estate

a) Healey's tied estate in 1893

Herts

Abbot's Langley	*Rose and Crown* C.*	London Colney	*Bull and Butcher* C.*
Batford	*Marquis of Granby* F.	Park Street	*Lamb* C.
Boreham Wood	*Wellington* F.	St Albans	*Peacock*
Friar's Wash	*Waggon and Horses* F.*		*Queen Adelaide* L.*
Harpenden	*Railway Hotel* F.		*Verulam Arms* F.*
	Three Horseshoes F.	St Ippollytts	*Greyhound* F.
Hemel Hempstead	*Old Bell Gate* C.*	Sandridge	*White Horse* F.*
Hitchin	*White Horse* C.	Whitwell	*Fox* BH

Beds

Dunstable	*Britannia* F.	Leagrave	*Three Horseshoes* F.*
Houghton Regis	*White Swan* F.	Luton	*Hare and Hounds* F.*

b) Brewery disposals before 1893

Herts

Flamstead	*Chequers* FL	Hemel Hempstead	*Lockhouse* BH
Hatfield	*Rising Sun* BH		*Plough* BH
Hemel Hempstead	*Brickmakers' Arms* OL		*White Lion* BH

Beds

Caddington	*Caddington Green* BH	Kensworth	*Farmer's Boy* FL
	Horse and Jockey BH		

Key: * Taken over by Peacock Brewery, Harpenden

established in the 1990s behind the *Red Cow* in Westfield Road. Unfortunately this only operated for a few years before the brewing equipment was transferred to the *Farmer's Boy* in St Albans.

References

Brandreth, E. *Harpenden*, Chalford Publishing Company, 1996, pp.34–6.

Hertfordshire Archives and Local Studies. a. D/Eby B.38, B89 (Glovers), b. D/Eby B219 (Healey's), c. Inland Revenue Map of Harpenden 1910, d. Tithe Map of Harpenden 1839.

Petty Sessions Licensing Records for Hertfordshire and Bedfordshire.

Poole, H. *Here for the Beer*, Watford Museum, 1984, pp.17–19.

Workers' Educational Association (Harpenden and St Albans Branches), *Wheathampstead and Harpenden IV: The Age of Independence*, Harpenden, The History Publishing Society, 1978.

CHAPTER ELEVEN

Hatfield

In the seventeenth century what is now known as Old Hatfield was situated at an important crossroads where a major road between Hertford and St Albans met the Great North Road from London to Edinburgh. The inns and beer houses provided drink, food and accommodation to a steadily increasing number of people travelling by coach and horses. Thus the Hatfield, Park Street and Newtown Breweries were eventually established to brew beer to satisfy the local demand.

Hatfield Brewery

The Searancke family, who were of Flemish origin, had settled in Essendon by 1545. They are reputed to have introduced hops to Hertfordshire. By 1589 John Searancke was a brewer at Woodside near Hatfield, possibly at the *Greyhound*. The family owned the *Chequers* in 1653 and the *Holly Bush* in 1666. Both of these were in Park Street in the centre of Hatfield. During the late 1700s the business which had been established as Hatfield Brewery in 1764 began to expand. The family owned eight licensed properties in Hatfield and possibly twenty others in the nearby towns and villages.

By 1801 four other inns in Hatfield had ceased to be part of the tied estate and the *Chequers* had been converted to the brewery house. The Searanckes also owned two maltings in Batterdale. One of these was given later in a marriage settlement to the Hare family.

During 1779 the Hatfield Brewery was left as a bequest to three Searancke sisters on the death of their brother John Searancke. One of the sisters, Ann, had married Francis Carter Niccoll of St Albans. Their son, another Francis, changed his surname to Searancke in 1781 to comply with stipulations within his uncle's will. In 1789 he became the owner of the brewery. Later he went into a partnership with his brother Joseph and a brewer from Stanstead Abbots,

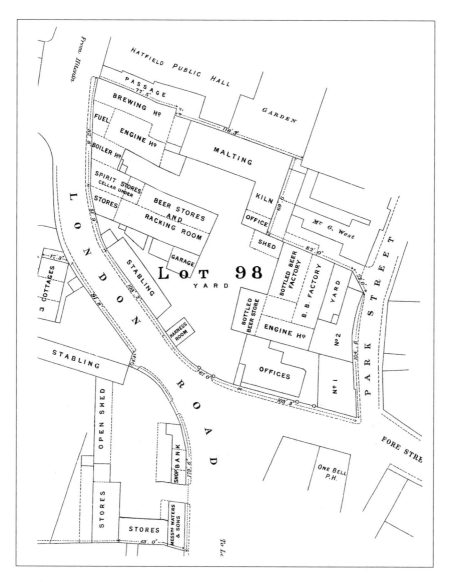

Figure 11.1 Plan of Hatfield Brewery in 1920 (HALS)

Joseph Bigg. They evidently built considerable storage capacity at the brewery. In 1805 there was a great surprise in Hatfield when a huge wooden barrel containing 525 barrels of beer stored at the brewery burst and its contents poured out into the street. In 1815, Francis Searancke, who also was well established in St Albans, decided to buy the Kingsbury Brewery in St Albans. Therefore he and his brother Joseph sold their shares of the Hatfield Brewery

Table 11.1 Hatfield Brewery tied estate (all in Hertfordshire) in 1815

a) In 1815 before sale to Joseph Bigg

Barnet	*Chequers*, Coopers Lane F.	Highwood Hill	*Three Crowns* L.
	White Lion, Dancers Hill C.	Lemsford	*Crooked Chimney* 1777
Bramfield	*Grandison Arms* 1787 C.	Mill Green, Hatfield	*Crooked Billet* 1773 C.
Brickendon	*Horns* F.	Newgate St	*Coach and Horses c.*1756 C.
Colney Heath	*Cock* 1771 C.	Northaw	*Sun* 1763
Colney Street	*Black Horse c.*1770	Redbourn	*George** 1800
Cromer Hyde	*Chequers* 1756		*Holly Bush** 1800
Harpenden	*Red Lion* C.	Roe Green	*Wrestlers* C.
Hatfield	*Eight Bells* pre-1815 F.	Shenley	*White Horse* 1800 C.
	Fiddle pre-1815	Sleapshyde	*Plough* 1776 C.
	Horse and Groom 1806 F.	Stanstead Abbots	*Three Wheatsheaves* F.
	One Bell 1746 F.	Totteridge	*Orange Tree* L.
	Two Brewers 1794 C.	Wadesmill	*Bull* F.
	White Horse pre-1788	Woolmer Green	*Red Lion* F.

b) Closed before 1815

Hatfield	*Bull's Head* 1767 – ?
	Chequers, 1 Park St 1653–1801, became brewery house
	Cock, 14–16 Fore St pre-1725
	Greyhound, Woodside, sold before 1679, leased *c.*1773–1780
	Holly Bush, Park St 1666

Key: * Not part of sale to Joseph Bigg

and its tied estate of twenty-six licensed properties to their partner Joseph Bigg for £11,154. The brewery property included a mash tun room (twenty-five feet long and thirty-five feet to the rafters), a store house for malt, hops and corn, a running store, a cooper's shop, a brewing office and a counting house. There was also an open shed for drays and carriages, stabling for twenty-eight horses, a thirty-five quarter malting, a brewery house and three cottages. Francis Searancke did however retain the *George* and the *Holly Bush* at Redbourn which were to become part of the tied estate of the Kingsbury Brewery of St Albans.

Joseph Bigg became bankrupt in 1819 and sold the brewery to Joseph Field. He made a number of changes to the brewery and slightly increased the size of the tied estate.

There were thirty-one full licences and eight beer only licences. The estate contained twenty-three freehold properties plus twelve copyholds and four leaseholds (Table 11.2). In 1835 the brewery had an annual production of 7,600 barrels (average of 1833–5).

A comprehensive sale document gives a detailed description of the brewery which included a recently built brick building containing a brewhouse, a wash house, a cooperage, a grist room, a mash tun room, a cooler room and a steam engine room. The equipment used in the brewery included a mash tun of twenty barrels' capacity, a brewing copper of thirty barrels' capacity, a cast-iron liquor

Table 11.2 Hatfield Brewery tied estate in the sale to Alfred Pryor in 1837

Herts

Barnet	*Boar's Head* FL, F.	Hatfield	BH French Horn Lane F.
	Sebright Arms FL, F.	Mill Green, Hatfield	*Crooked Billet* FL, C.
	White Lion FL, F.	Newgate Street	*Coach and Horses* FL, C.
Bramfield	*Grandison Arms* BH, C.	Potters Bar	*White Horse* FL, F.
Brickendon	*Horns* FL, F.		BH Coopers Lane F.
Colney Heath	*Cock* FL, C.	Roe Green, Hatfield	*Fiddle* BH, C.
Colney Street	*Black Horse* FL, C.		*Two Wrestlers* FL, C.
Cromer Hyde	*Chequers* FL, F.	St Albans	*Crab Tree* FL, F.
Harpenden	*George* FL, F.		*Farmer's Boy* BH, L.
	Red Lion FL, C.	Sandridge	*Dog and Badger* BH, L.
Hatfield	*Chequers* FL, F.	Shenley Hill	*White Horse* FL, C.
	Eight Bells FL, F.	Sleapshyde	*Plough* FL, C.
	Fiddle FL, F.	Totteridge	*Orange Tree* FL, L.
	Horse and Groom FL, F.	Wadesmill	*Bull* FL, F.
	One Bell FL, F.	Wheathampstead	BH no name, C.
	Two Brewers FL, C.	Woolmer Green	*Red Lion* FL, F.
	BH Fore St F.		

Beds

Caddington	*Bricklayer's Arms* FL, F.	Luton	*Swan* FL, L.
Luton	*George IV* FL, F.		*Vine* FL, F.

Greater London

Cockfosters	*Cock* FL, F.	Waltham Abbey	*Green Dragon* FL, F.

back of one hundred barrels' capacity, a fir hop-back of fifty barrels' capacity and an oak under-back of forty barrels' capacity. There were also three square fermentation vessels, one round fermentation vessel and thirteen storage vats of 1,829 barrels total capacity. The other buildings included malt, hop and barley stores, stabling for nine carthorses and a recently built malting. Further stabling for twenty more horses was provided in a nearby farmyard. A spacious family mansion plus various cottages also formed part of the proposed sale.

Field died in 1836, possibly bankrupt, and the brewery was sold at auction to James Spurrell for £24,350. Alfred Pryor of the Baldock Quaker brewing family had apparently wished to buy the brewery, but been unable to obtain sufficient financial backing from other members of his family. However, in March 1837 Spurrell sold the brewery to Alfred Pryor for £34,000 when he had managed to secure the necessary financial help from his brothers John and Morris Pryor. Eventually Alfred became the sole owner and managed it until his death in 1876. Soon afterwards his second son, Edward Vickris Pryor, bought the brewery for £29,442. Previously Edward had married Ethel Justina Reid, the second daughter of William Reid of The Node, Codicote in 1870. During 1881 his brother-in-law Percy Charles Reid became a joint partner in the business. The two of them decided to increase the capacity of the brewery and make additions

Table 11.3 Hatfield Brewery sale in 1920 – the tied estate

		B/Y			B/Y
Herts					
Aldenham	New Found Out OL	64	Hitchin	Sir John Barleycorn FL	299
	Round Bush BH	102	Kimpton	Boot FL	65
	Volunteer BH	95		Goat BH	86
Amwell, Great	Waggon and Horses FL	81	Lemsford	Sun FL	85
Barnet	White Lion FL	327	Lt. Berkhampsted	Five Horseshoes FL	218
Batford	Malta BH	145	Marford	Nelson FL	124
Bengeo	White Lion FL	115	Mill Green, Hat.	Green Man BH	110
Boreham Wood	Wellington FL	595		Old Crooked Billet FL	108
Bramfield	Grandison Arms FL	108	Newgate Street	Coach and Horses FL	267
Brickendon	Hart's Horns FL	261	Northaw	Sun FL	122
Burnham Green	White Horse FL	88	North Mymms	Woodman BH	83
Cheshunt	Horse and Groom BH	159	Nup End, Kneb.	Sheepshearer BH	86
	Old English Gentleman	311	Potters Bar	Chequers FL	222
Codicote	Goat FL, L.	78		White Horse FL	217
Colney Heath	Cock FL	85	Roe Green, Hat.	Old Fiddle BH	134
	Chalkdrawers' Arms BH	40	St Albans	Duke of Marlborough FL	166
Colney Street	Black Horse FL	120		Heath Stores OL	327
Cromer Hyde	Chequers FL	78		Lamb BH	147
Essendon	Rose and Crown FL, C.	152		Queen Adelaide FL	193
	Salisbury Crest FL	174		Swan BH	100
	Wheatsheaf BH	235		Verulam Arms FL	161
Gustard Wood	Cricketers BH	77		OL	66
	Royal Exchange BH	102	St Ippollytts	Greyhound BH	101
	Tin Pot BH	78	Sandridge	Green Man BH	243
Hadley	Queen's Head BH	60		Woodman BH	98
Harpenden	George FL	160	Shenley	White Horse FL	145
	Queen's Head BH	128	Sleapshyde	Angel BH	44
Hatfield	Baker's Arms BH	105		Plough FL	74
	Dray Horse BH	184	South Mimms	Black Horse FL	162
	East Indian Chief FL	129	Stanstead Abbots	Pied Bull FL	262
	Eight Bells FL	179		Rose and Crown FL	251
	Great Northern FL	494	Stevenage	Fisherman BH	60
	Gun FL	283	Ware	Waggon and Horses FL	186
	Horse and Groom FL	201		Windsor Castle BH	121
	New Fiddle FL	158	Watton at Stone	Bull FL	178
	One Bell FL	156	Welham Green	Hope and Anchor BH	167
	Platelayers' Arms FL	246	Welwyn	Rose and Crown FL	97
	Prince of Wales BH	117		Steamer FL	112
	Robin Hood BH	246		White Horse FL	111
	White Lion FL	134	Wheathampstead	Elephant and Castle BH	51
	Wrestlers FL	124		Railway FL	161
Hertford	Black Swan FL	144		Red Cow FL	110
	Blue Coat Boy FL	133		Red Lion BH	33
	Forester's Arms BH	204		Royal Oak BH	117
	Old Oak FL	175		Swan FL	111
	Warren House FL	70		Three Oaks BH	39
Hertford Heath	Havelock Arms BH	160		Traveller's Friend BH	67
	Two Brewer's Arms BH	246		Walnut Tree BH	119

Hertingfordbury	Prince of Wales FL	102		Wicked Lady FL	81
	Rainbow and Dove BH	97	Wild Hill	Woodman BH	137
Hitchin	Cricketers FL	218	Woolmer Green	Chequers FL	150
	George FL	177		Red Lion FL	174
Greater London					
Cockfosters	Cock FL	299	Waltham Abbey	Green Dragon FL	96
				New Inn FL	264

Key: B/Y Average number of barrels supplied for three years ending September 1914
              Hat. Hatfield
              Kneb. Knebworth

to the tied estate. The first acquisition in 1878 was the Park Street Brewery in Hatfield that they had previously leased from Arthur Sheriff. Then they bought the Newtown Brewery in Hatfield in 1888. This was followed by the purchase of Benjamin Young's brewery in Ware Road, Hertford in 1893 and it was closed five years later. During 1897 they leased seven public houses from the Lattimore family at the Hope Brewery in Wheathampstead eventually purchasing them in 1904. They merged with Glover's of Harpenden to form the Hatfield & Harpenden Breweries Ltd during 1902, but the two companies continued trading separately and eventually split once again into two individual companies by 1910.

In 1908 the mineral water factory on the main brewery site was destroyed in a big fire which fortunately did not damage the brewhouse (Figure 11.1). Later that year King Edward VII paid an unexpected visit to the brewery when the car he was travelling in broke down when passing through the town. He is reputed to have sat on a barrel and watched men rebuilding the mineral water factory while his car was repaired.

The details of barrels consumed per year (1912–14) at different outlets in the tied estate show some big variations in beer consumption between town and rural outlets (Table 11.3).

The tied houses selling at least 299 barrels per annum included the *White Lion* at Barnet, the *Wellington* at Boreham Wood, the *Old English Gentleman* at Cheshunt, the *Cock* at Cockfosters, the *Great Northern* in Hatfield, the *Sir John Barleycorn* in Hitchin and the Heath Stores off-licence in St Albans. All of these were in urban locations. They included full licences, a beer only licence and an off-licence. At the other extreme, the *Chalkdrawers' Arms* at Colney Heath, the *Queen's Head* at Hadley, the *Angel* at Sleapshyde, *the Fisherman* near Stevenage, and the *Elephant and Castle*, the *Red Lion* and the *Three Oaks* (all three in Wheathampstead) were serving fewer than 60 barrels per annum. These were in

Figure 11.2 Hatfield Brewery steam lorry in 1900 (HALS)

rural locations and all had beer only licences. Wine and spirit sales were given in the sales documents for those public houses with full licences.

The brewing equipment in a 1920 sales inventory included a nineteen quarter capacity mash tun, a pressure copper, a cold liquor (water) tank, a cast-iron cooling tank and a cast-iron hop back (all four being of eighty barrels' capacity). There was a cast-iron hot liquor tank and a cast-iron under-back (both of ninety barrels' capacity). There were also ten fir-wood fermenting squares fitted with parachutes and cooling squares giving a total brewing capacity of 804 barrels. Power was being obtained from steam and gas engines and electric dynamos. Further details of equipment can be found in the sales literature. The brewery still had its own stables and horses with drays for local deliveries but steam lorries were being used for the more distant deliveries *c.*1900 (Figure 11.2) and petrol driven drays were already in use by 1914.

Edward Pryor died in 1904 and Percy Reid continued to manage the business. Unfortunately his only son Geoffrey Reid was killed in 1915 during World War I. Since there was no other member of the Pryor or Reid family wishing to take over the ownership of the brewery it was decided in 1920 to sell

Table 11.4 Pryor, Reid & Co. licensed property closures, disposals or termination of leases before the 1920 sale

Herts

Barnet	BH Park Rd	Redbourn	Railway Inn
	Rising Sun	St Albans	Duke of St Albans
Codicote	Plough		Eagle and Child
East Barnet	Black Prince		Farmer's Boy
	British Flag		New Inn
	Prince of Wales		Trumpet
Hadley	Monken Heath Arms		OL Old London Road
Harpenden	Old Red Lion	South Mimms	Bull
	Red Cow	Stevenage	Black Horse
Hatfield	Butcher's Arms	Waltham Cross	Wheatsheaf
	Jacob's Well	Ware	Barge
Hertford	Black Horse		Bricklayer's Arms
	Bull		Clarendon (Vine)
	Prince Albert		Lion and Wheatsheaf
	Railway Tavern		Spread Eagle, Amwell
	Rose and Crown		White Horse, Wareside
Hitchin	White Horse	Welwyn	Black Horse
Much Hadham	Crown		George
	Hoops, Perry Green	Wheathampstead	Old Plough
Park Street	Lamb		Ship
Potters Bar	Pilot Engine	Whitwell	Swan
	Railway Inn	Wormley	Green Man

Beds

Caddington	Bricklayer's Arms	Luton	Mitre
Clifton	Exhibition		Prince of Wales
	Fox and Duck		Queen's Arms
	Woolpack		Railway Inn
Houghton Regis	Five Bells		Stag
Luton	Blue Lion		Vine
	Dudley Arms		Waggon and Horses
	Four Horseshoes	Shefford	Woolpack

Greater London

City Road	BH, York Rd	Ponders End	Beehive
Cockfosters	British Flag	Tottenham	Stag
Edmonton	Exhibition	Waltham Abbey	Queen's Head
Enfield	Black Horse		

at auction. Benskin's of Watford bought the business to add to their rapidly increasing tied estate. Shortly afterwards the brewery site was bought by Gray's of Hatfield to use as a garage for car sales and repairs. During the 1960s the site was cleared for the Salisbury Square development and any remaining traces of the old brewery were destroyed.

Table 11.5 Park Street Brewery tied estate

Herts		Notes
Colney Heath	*Crooked Billet*	Owned by Francis Complin in 1840
		St Albans–St Peters tithe map plot 538
		Bought by Henry Parsons of St Albans in 1854
Hatfield	*Traveller's Rest*	Leased in 1845, bought *c.*1865 by Complin's
		Leased by Sheriff in 1872 and then by
		Pryor, Reid & Co. Closed in 1906
Wild Hill	*Woodman*	Leased in 1851 to Complin's, then Sheriff,
		Pryor, Reid & Co. and Benskin's after 1920
Kimpton	*Black Horse*	Licensed to Sheriff in 1874. The only reference
South Mimms	*Bull* BH	Owned by Sheriff and sold to Pryor, Reid & Co.
Beds		
Luton	*Prince of Wales*	Leased by Sheriff in 1872 but owned by Pale Ale
		Brewery, Baldock in 1876

Park Street Brewery

The Park Street Brewery was the older of the other two small breweries established in Hatfield. It started in a malting *c.*1700 in the Arm and Sword Yard next to the *Horse and Groom* in Park Street. This site was owned by Richard Willetts, a maltster, during the 1780s. Richard Pratchett was probably the first brewer in 1829. Francis Denyer Complin leased the brewery in 1837 and had bought it before he died in 1851. In 1840 he owned an un-named public house on plot 538 of the St Albans–St Peters parish tithe map that seems to correspond with the *Crooked Billet,* Colney Heath. Joliffe and Jones (1995) do not name an owner in 1840 and claim that it was licensed as a beer house. Henry Parsons, a brewer in St Albans, bought the *Crooked Billet* in 1854. No other public houses or beer houses belonging to the Complin family have been identified on the tithe maps. Three more Complins, Mrs Mary Complin, Mrs C. Complin and Mrs Susan Complin continued to manage the business as brewers and maltsters. The executors of the Complin family leased the brewery to James Thatcher in 1866 and Arthur James Sheriff in 1872. He was a local man who was already a corn, seed and coal merchant who subsequently bought the brewery and sold it to the Pryors in 1878. The identifiable tied estate was always very small (Table 11.5).

The *Traveller's Rest* in Hatfield and the *Woodman* at Wild Hill were leased for the longest times. The *Black Horse* at Kimpton, the *Bull* at South Mimms and the *Prince of Wales* at Luton very briefly owned or leased by Arthur Sheriff.

Table 11.6 Newtown Brewery tied estate 1855–88

Herts		Notes
Hadley	*Bell* BH	Owned in 1873
	Monken Heath Arms	Sold to Pryor, Reid & Co. in 1888
	Queen's Head BH	Sold to Pryor, Reid & Co. in 1888
Hatfield	*Baker's Arms*	Sold to Pryor, Reid & Co. in 1888
	Rose and Crown,	Owned in 1855 and sold later to
	Tylers Causeway	Christie & Cathrow
	Rose and Crown,	Owned in 1855 and sold later in
	Wellfield Rd	1888 to Pryor, Reid & Co.
	White Lion	Sold to Pryor, Reid & Co. in 1888
Hertingfordbury	*Prince of Wales*	Sold to Pryor, Reid & Co. in 1888
North Mymms	*Woodman*	Sold to Pryor, Reid & Co. in 1888
Watford	*Greyhound*	Owned in 1852. Sold later to Benskin's
	Queen's Head,	Sold in 1860s to Sedgwick's of Watford
	Queen's Rd	

Newtown Brewery

The brothers Charles and George Bradshaw started the Newtown Brewery on a site behind the *White Lion* in Hatfield Newtown *c.*1850. In 1886 Charles was the sole owner and two years later he sold the brewery and tied estate to Pryor, Reid & Co Ltd. They bought seven of the public houses located in Hadley, Hatfield, Hertingfordbury, North Mymms and Watford. Three of the properties had been sold previously to three local large breweries.

The *White Lion* in Hatfield Newtown was the Newtown Brewery Tap and there was reputed to have been an underground tunnel between the two cellar complexes. The brewery later became a Salvation Army Mission Hall. Both the original *White Lion* and the brewery were pulled down before the new Hatfield town shopping centre was developed in the 1960s and 1970s.

References

Hatfield Workers' Educational Association. *Hatfield and its People*, Book 4, 1960, pp.6–9, 29–32 (Details of breweries, maltings and public houses).

Hertfordshire Archives and Local Studies. a. 70922, D/ELe B19/4 (Hatfield Brewery), D/Els B342 (Hatfield Brewery 1815).

Jolliffe, G. and Jones, A. *Hertfordshire Inns and Public Houses: An Historical Gazetteer*, Hatfield, Hertfordshire Publications, 1995, p.46.

Kirby, S. and Busby, R. *Hatfield: A Pictorial History*, Chichester, Phillimore, 1995.

Lawrence, B.G. The old brewery at Hatfield, *Hertfordshire Countryside*, Vol. 41, No. 321, 1986, pp.17–18.

Mid-Herts Citizen, 15 June 1983, p.11 (Newtown Brewery).

Petty Sessions Licensing Records for Hertfordshire and Bedfordshire.

Poole, H. *Here for the Beer*, Watford Museum, 1984, pp.19–20.

Richmond, L. and Turton, A. (eds.). *The Brewing Industry: A Guide to Historical Records*, Manchester University Press, 1990, p.295 (Sherriff).

CHAPTER TWELVE

Hemel Hempstead

Historically there were over twenty inns and beer houses in the High Street. Beer was either brewed on the premises, as it was at the *Rose and Crown*, or obtained from small local breweries or common brewers. The Anchor and Star breweries were established locally at Bury Mill End and John Jeffery had a small brewery in London Road. There were also a few other brewers in the town but these were only active for a short time.

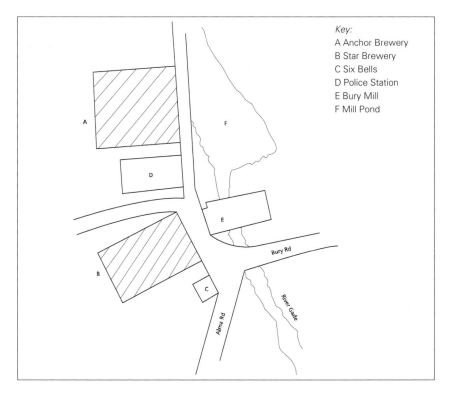

Key:
A Anchor Brewery
B Star Brewery
C Six Bells
D Police Station
E Bury Mill
F Mill Pond

Figure 12.1 Breweries and other buildings

Table 12.1 Anchor Brewery tied estate

a) Sold to T. & J. Nash of Chesham in 1891 or earlier

Herts

Berkhamsted	*Black Horse* BH	Hemel Hempstead	*Nag's Head* BH
Bovingdon	*Hope and Anchor* BH		*Oddfellows' Arms* BH
Bushey	*Royal Oak* BH*		*Post Office Arms* BH
Chipperfield	*Boot* BH		*Queen's Arms* BH
Great Gaddesden	*Fox* BH*		*Royal Oak* BH
Hemel Hempstead	OL at brewery		*Shah* BH
	Anchor BH		*Spotted Cow* BH*
	Artichoke BH		*Swan and Trout* BH*
	Bell FL		*Three Horseshoes* BH
	Brewer's Arms BH		*Whip and Collar* BH
	Drayman BH	King's Langley	*Jolly Miller* BH
	Fox and Hounds BH	Tring	*Black Horse* BH

Beds

Eaton Bray	*Rifleman* BH, L.

b) Disposed or closed before sale in 1891

Herts		*Beds*	
Hemel Hempstead	*Founder's Arms* BH	Caddington	*Star and Garter* BH

Key: * Bought by T. & J. Nash before 1891 sale

Anchor Brewery

Ownership of the brewery changed on numerous occasions. In 1841 the owners were William John Liddon, Thomas Elisha Deacon in 1851, Samuel Deacon in 1854, William Clement in 1859, Thomas Clement in 1862, Josiah Hales in 1871, Wyman & Hall in 1878 and Henry Wyman in 1885. Finally in 1891 T. & J. Nash of Chesham bought the brewery.

William Liddon initially built the small original Anchor Brewery and a malting near Bury Mill and the River Gade. He also owned one licensed house in Hemel Hempstead High Street on the edge of the church graveyard on tithe plot 771, possibly the *Brewer's Arms*. Josiah Hales was probably responsible for increasing the size of the brewery to cope with increasing demand from the tied estate of the *Bell* FL and twenty-two beer houses mainly within five miles of the brewery. Wyman & Hall bought the *Artichoke*, *Nag's Head* and *Royal Oak* in Hemel Hempstead, the *Jolly Miller* at King's Langley and the *Star and Garter* at Caddington. In 1891 T. & J. Nash of Chesham bought twenty-one of these properties to add to their own eventual tied estate of thirty-five licensed houses in Hertfordshire. They had previously bought four properties from Wyman before 1891. The remainder of the tied estate had been sold or closed. Henry

Wyman also independently owned the *Cricketer's Arms* BH at Watford Fields, Watford from the 1870s to the early 1900s and never sold it to T. & J. Nash.

Star Brewery

It is has been claimed that the Star Brewery was established in 1850 next to the *Six Bells*. James Elliot was there from 1859 to 1862 and William Spicer Elliot from 1882 to 1912. There is no evidence in Petty Sessions licensing records that either brewer ever owned any tied estate and both men may have been merely common brewers.

John Jeffery's Brewery

John Jeffery who was recognised as a brewer in 1851, began brewing behind the *Prince's Arms* in London Rd. By 1876 he had increased his tied estate and also include the *Greyhound* FL at Albury and the *Bell* FL, *Rose and Crown* FL and a beer house at Crouchfield (all in Hemel Hempstead). Shortly afterwards the *Bell* became part of the Anchor Brewery estate. John Jeffery was still recorded as a brewer in 1895.

References

Hertfordshire Archive and Local Studies. Tithe Map for Hemel Hempstead, 1843.
Petty Sessions Licensing Records for Hertfordshire and Bedfordshire.
Poole, H. *Here for the Beer*, Watford Museum, 1984, pp.20–22.

CHAPTER THIRTEEN

Hertford

Hertford developed as a major town for malting in the eighteenth and nineteenth centuries. The River Lea enabled malt to be easily transported by barge to London. In some years London brewers sent barley to Hertford to produce malt with defined properties because of the town maltsters' skills. Some of the old maltings still remain in the town but many of them have been converted for housing. Brewing was considered a less important industry. There have been more breweries in the town than anywhere else in the county but their brewing capacity probably was never as high as in Watford while Benskin's remained active. However McMullen's in Hartham Lane is now the only large brewery left in Hertfordshire. The brewing history is complicated and confusing because some breweries were owned or leased by a number of

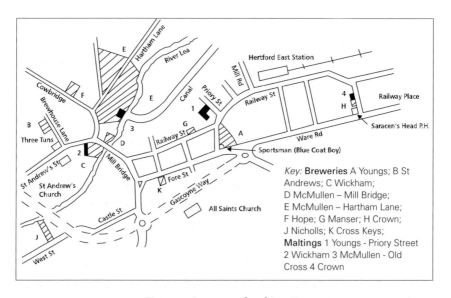

Key: **Breweries** A Youngs; B St Andrews; C Wickham; D McMullen – Mill Bridge; E McMullen – Hartham Lane; F Hope; G Manser; H Crown; J Nicholls; K Cross Keys; **Maltings** 1 Youngs - Priory Street 2 Wickham 3 McMullen - Old Cross 4 Crown

Figure 13.1 Brewery and malting sites

different families and occasionally these families owned or leased other breweries in the town at the same or different times.

At least nine breweries are known to have existed between 1702 and the present time. Chronologically these are: a brewery at the junction of South Lane and Fore Street (later Young's) in 1702, the *Cross Keys* Brewery in Fore Street started in 1725, St Andrew's Brewery in 1774, the Mill Bridge Brewery in 1826, McMullen's breweries in Back Street, Mill Bridge and Hartham Lane in 1827, the Hope Brewery at Old Cross in 1830, Manser's brewery in Back Street in 1838, Nicholls' West Street Brewery in 1853 and the Crown Brewery in Railway Place in 1859. The locations of these breweries are shown on a sketch map of the town.

Young's Brewery

In the 1660s William Fairman was a Quaker brewer who may have been brewing in the yard of the *King's Head,* an inn which was owned by his mother. His son Benjamin who also became a brewer had a malting in 1696 on the east side of Sow Lane (South Lane) off Fore Street. Deeds of 1702 record a new brewhouse on this plot. At this time the brewhouse and the malting were leased by Sir William Cowper to Joseph Catlyn (or Catlin). Joseph Catlin bought the property before he died in 1729. The next brewer, John Walter mentioned in his will that his heir should have the use of coppers, coolers, underbacks and other brewing equipment.

James Boor is the next known owner and/or brewer in 1770 who leased the property for twenty-one years to James Pycroft, a brewer from Greenwich. James's daughter Elizabeth Boor leased the brewery in 1777 for fourteen years to Robert Silversides and Robert Young. Robert Silversides also bought the *Red Lion* at Hertford, the *Two Brewers* at Enfield and the *Robin Hood and Little John* at Enfield between 1777 and 1782. This is the first written record of a member of the Young family on this site. In 1791 Elizabeth Boor negotiated a new lease for thirty-one years with Noah Young, who was Robert's eldest son. At the same time Robert's widow Deborah leased to Noah the *Old Barge* and the *Waggon and Horses* at Ware, the *White Lion* at Watton at Stone and the *Three Horseshoes* in the parish of Great Barrington, Cambridgeshire. This is the only reference to the *Three Horseshoes.*

Noah Young also bought the *Black Swan* (1791), the *Two Brewers* (1797) and the *Bull Inn* (1802) in Hertford. He also leased the *Blue Coat Boy* (now the *Sportsman*) in Hertford, the *Rose and Crown* at Welwyn and the *Three Tuns* at

Table 13.1 Benjamin and Charles Young's individual tied estates in 1857

a) Benjamin Young

Herts

Little Berkhamstead	*Five Horseshoes*	Stanstead Abbots	*Pied Bull*
Enfield (Gr Lond)	*Railway Inn*	Wadesmill	*Windmill* BH
Essendon	*Plough* BH	Ware	*Clarendon*
Fanhams Hall Green	*Wellington* L.		*Waggon and Horses*
Hatfield New Town	*Gun*	Watton at Stone	*Bull*

b) Charles Young

Herts

Bengeo	*White Lion*	South Mimms	*Black Horse*
Datchworth	*Chequers* BH	Standon	*Plough* BH
Hertford	*Black Swan*		*White Horse*
	Oak	Ware	*Bargeman* BH
	White Hart		

Essex

Pardon	*Horseshoes* BH		

Table 13.2 Young's Brewery tied estate in 1870

Herts

Amwell	*Waggon and Horses* L.	Hertford	*White Hart Tap* L.
Ayot Green	*Horse and Jockey* L.		BH, F. Cowbridge
Codicote	*Globe* BH, L.	Hertford Heath	*Havelock Arms* BH, F.
Digswell (Welwyn)	*Cowper Arms* L.		*Two Brewers* BH, L.
Essendon	*Rose and Crown* FL, C.	Hertingfordbury	*Rainbow and Dove* BH, F.
Fanham Hall	*Rabbits* BH, L.	Hitchin	*White Horse* F.
Great Amwell	*Waggon and Horses* FL, L.	Hoddesdon	*Rising Sun* BH, F.
Hatfield	*Green Man* BH, L.	Hunsdon	*Crown* BH, F.
	Jacob's Well FL, L.	Much Hadham	*Jolly Farmers* L.
Hertford	*Blue Coat Boy* L.	Northaw	*Sun Inn* FL, L.
	Bull FL, L.	St Albans	*New Inn* FL, F.
	Railway Tavern L.	Waltham Cross	*Wheatsheaf* BH, L.
	Ram FL, L.	Ware	*Barge* FL, L.
	Red Lion F.		*Red Lion* FL, F.
	Rose and Crown F.		*White Swan* BH, L.
	Warren House FL, F.	Welwyn	*Rose and Crown* FL, L.
		Wormley	*Green Man* BH, L.

Essex

Epping Green	BH, L.		
Roydon	*Temple Inn* BH, L.	Waltham Abbey	*Three Tuns* FL, L.

Greater London

Enfield	*Baker's Arms* BH, L.		

Waltham Cross. When he died in 1828 the brewery and estate was bequeathed to his son Noah Robert Young. When Noah Robert died in 1839 his only daughter Emily leased the brewery to Benjamin and Charles Young who were family relatives.

In 1857 Benjamin and Charles Young both owned separate tied estates. By

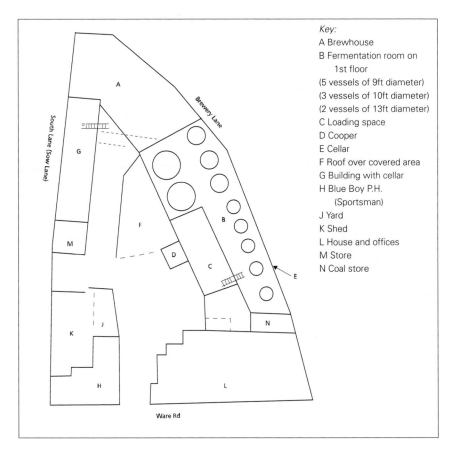

Key:
A Brewhouse
B Fermentation room on
    1st floor
(5 vessels of 9ft diameter)
(3 vessels of 10ft diameter)
(2 vessels of 13ft diameter)
C Loading space
D Cooper
E Cellar
F Roof over covered area
G Building with cellar
H Blue Boy P.H.
    (Sportsman)
J Yard
K Shed
L House and offices
M Store
N Coal store

Figure 13.2 Composite plan of Young's Brewery pre-1893

the time Charles died in 1869, Benjamin had bought a few more licensed properties and leased many more in East Hertfordshire (Tables 13.1 and 13.2).

This brewery in Hertford was gradually developed on a triangular plot surrounded by Fore Street (Ware Road), South Lane and Brewery Lane. A detailed inventory exists for 1870 when Charles had died. They had two mash tuns of eighty-two and twenty barrels' capacity. The brewing was being done using three fermenting squares of eighty-four, eighty-four and sixty-six barrels' capacity. Their own beers were X Mild, Farmers Beer, PA, XXX Mild, AK, Old X, Old XXX and Small Beer. The hop varieties at the brewery were Mannington from Sussex, Eynesford 1869, Knight Farnham 1868, Sussex 1869 and American 1868. The process monitoring equipment in the Brewer's Room was three thermometers to check temperatures and three saccharometers to measure the specific gravities of fermenting beers.

Figure 13.3 Young's Brewery house

The number of casks (gallons capacity) owned by the brewery was recorded as follows; 10 butts (108 gallons), 142 puncheons (70 gallons), 121 hogsheads (54 gallons), 702 barrels (36 gallons), 606 kilderkins (18 gallons), 244 firkins (9 gallons) and 29 pins (4 ½ gallons). This gives a total barrel capacity of approximately 56,000 gallons for a tied estate of fifty to sixty public houses. This would cover those being cleaned, filled and conditioned, being held by a public house and being returned to the brewery.

The brewery also had in stock from London brewers, Meux's Single Stout and Porter and Reid's Porter, DBS and Stout to cover a wider variety of preferences.

Plans for 1893 show that the brewery was built with three floors and cellars and also that it contained a hop loft, two corn lofts, six malt shops, two fermenting rooms, three tun rooms, an engine room, a coal store, a cellar with five vaults and a tramway plus a deep well. The plans indicate that in the fermenting rooms on the first floor there were now five vessels of nine feet diameter, three of ten feet diameter and two of thirteen feet diameter to give greater flexibility to the range of beers being brewed at the same time. There was also a large brewery house, offices and the *Blue Coat Boy* (Brewery Tap) at this location (Figure 13.2).

Charles sold the brewery and tied estate (Table 13.3) in 1893 to Pryor, Reid &

Table 13.3 Young's tied estate in 1893

a) Sold to Pryor, Reid & Co.

Herts

Amwell, Great	*Waggon and Horses*	Hertford	*White Hart Tap*
Ardeley	*Goose*	Hertford Heath	*Havelock Arms* BH
Ayot Green	*Horse and Jockey*		*Two Brewers* BH
Bengeo	*White Lion*	Hertingfordbury	*Rainbow and Dove* BH
Codicote	*Globe*	Hitchin	*White Horse*
Datchworth	*Chequers*	Hoddesdon	*Rising Sun* BH
Digswell	*Cowper Arms*	Litt. Berkhamsted	*Five Horseshoes*
Enfield (Gr Lond)	*Baker's Arms*	Much Hadham	*Jolly Farmers*
	Railway Inn	Northaw	*Sun Inn* FL
Essendon	*Plough* BH	St Albans	*New Inn* FL
	Rose and Crown BH	South Mimms	*Black Horse*
Fanhams Hall	*Rabbits* BH	Standon	*Plough* BH
Fanhams Hall Gr.	*Wellington*		*White Horse*
Hatfield	*Green Man* BH	Stanstead Abbots	*Pied Bull*
	Gun	Stanstead St Mar.	*Crown*
	Jacob's Well BH	Waltham Cross	*Three Tuns*
Hertford	*Black Swan*		*Wheatsheaf* FL
	Blue Coat Boy (Tap)	Wadesmill	*Windmill* BH
	Bull	Ware	*Barge*
	Great Eastern		*Bargeman* BH
	Oak		*Clarendon*
	Railway Tavern		*Red Lion*
	Ram		*Waggon and Horses*
	Red Lion		*White Swan* FL
	Rose and Crown	Watton at Stone	*Bull*
	Two Brewers	Welwyn	*Rose and Crown*
	Warren House BH	Woolmer Green	*Fox*
	White Hart	Wormley	BH

b) Closures or disposals before the sale

Herts

Hunsdon	*Crown* BH, F.		

Essex

Epping Green	BH	Roydon	*Temple Inn* BH
Parndon	*Horseshoes* BH	Waltham Abbey	*Three Tuns*

Key: Stanstead St Mar. Stanstead St Margarets
Litt. Little
Gr. Green

Co. of Hatfield. Miss Young continued leasing to Pryor, Reid & Co. Ltd the *Green Man* at Hatfield, the *Rainbow and Dove* at Hertingfordbury and the *Sun* at Northaw until 1904. At the same time Mrs M. Young was leasing to the same brewery the *Black Swan* and the *White Hart* in Hertford, the *Chequers* at Burnham Green and the *Plough* and the *White Horse* at Standon.

Today only the brewery house and the *Blue Coat Boy* (renamed the *Sportsman*) are evident. However the remains of the brewery are limited to traces

Figure 13.4 Young's Priory Street malting

of filled-in windows in the wall in South Lane. Brewery Lane has disappeared in the later development of Christ's Hospital.

Benjamin Young was also a maltster and owned maltings in Hertford and Ware. One was a sixty quarter malting in Crib Street in Ware with three cemented floors, two kilns, a screening house and a well house. In 1875 he built a large malt house in Priory Street in Hertford with four floors of 110 feet by 40 feet. Afterwards this was used as a depot by the Housing Department of Hertfordshire County Council and was later converted into a housing complex for the elderly.

Cross Keys Brewery

In 1725 Timothy Flower had a brewhouse in the yard of the Turk's Head coffee house at 42 Fore Street which later became known as the *Cross Keys* and Cross Keys Brewery. He was succeeded by Mary Flower, and Richard Flower, who later sold the business to Richard Alsager. John Gillman and John Gripper became the owners in 1785. A nephew, Benjamin Gillman was bequeathed the business in 1795 and bought the *Robin Hood* at Tonwell in 1800. His brother acquired the brewery in 1801 and although he bought the *Ram* at Hertford in 1810 he

Table 13.4 Robert Fitzjohn's tied estate sold to John Moses Carter in 1831

Herts			
Barnet	*Roebuck*	Hertford	*Rose and Crown*
Bengeo	*Green Man*	Standon	*Eagle*
	Reindeer	Wadesmill	*White Hind*
Benington	*George*	Ware	*Red Cow*
Hertford	*Coffee House*		*Star*
	Red Cow		*Three Harts,* Stoney Hills
Essex			
Harlow	*White Horse*	Stondon Massey	*Bell*
???	*Little Bell*		

Table 13.5 Carter's tied estate sold to Back and Hunt in 1842

Herts			
Barnet	*Roebuck*	Hertford	*Rose and Crown*
Bengeo	*Globe*		*Three Tuns*
	Green Man	Hertford Heath	*Green Man*
	Reindeer	Hoddesdon	*Queen's Head*
Benington	*George*	Little Berkhamsted	*Beehive* L.
Bishop's Stortford	*Cherry Tree*	Little Munden	*Harrow and Boot*
Buntingford	*Crown*	London Colney	*Bell*
	Windmill		*Bull*
Cheshunt	*Bargeman*	Standon	*Eagle*
	Coach and Horses	Wadesmill	*White Hind*
Hertford	*Black Horse*	Ware	*Red Cow*
	Bull's Head		*Star*
	Coffee House		*Three Harts,* Stoney Hills
	Cross Keys	Widford	*Victoria* BH
	Gardener's Arms	Wormley	*Queen's Head*
	Red Cow		
Essex			
Broadly Common	*Green Man*	North Weald Basset	*Horseshoes*
Harlow	*White Horse*	Roydon	*Green Man*
Hazelwood Common	*Rainbow and Dove*		*Plough*
Masely	*Rising Sun*	Stondon Massey	*Bell*
Nazeing	*Coach and Horses*		
???	*Little Bell*		

apparently ceased brewing. The brewery ownership is not known for the next thirty years. Between 1842 and 1845 John Moses Carter started brewing again at this brewery after selling the St Andrew's Brewery. William South bought the brewery in 1845 and it later was leased with the *Cross Keys* to McMullen's and afterwards to E.J. Wickham.

St Andrew's Brewery

Between 1774 and 1785 the Ireland family established the St Andrew's Brewery in

Figure 13.5 The Three Tuns in St Andrew's Street (Brewery Tap for St Andrew's Brewery)

Brewery Lane (Newsells Lane) off St Andrew's Street. John Ireland who was a common brewer initially bought a maltings complex in Brewery Lane in 1774. He died in 1779 and was succeeded by his son Timothy Ireland who also owned the *Ship*. He leased the business in 1785 to John Fordham and his brother-in-law Richard Flower which they later bought. In 1792 Fordham bought out Flower but then leased the brewhouse to him for thirty-one years. However in 1803, George and Thomas Wells Fitzjohn, who were maltsters in Baldock, bought the brewery. The Fitzjohns built up a small tied estate of fifteen properties which Robert Fitzjohn sold to John Moses Carter in 1831 together with the brewery (Table 13.4).

Carter was ambitious and built up the tied estate to forty-two properties (Table 13.5). In 1842 he bought the Hoddesdon Brewery from Christie & Cathrow. Later in the same year he sold his brewery interests in both Hertford and Hoddesdon to John Back and Robert Hunt who later closed the St Andrew's Brewery and only brewed at the Hoddesdon Brewery. Shortly afterwards John Carter became active as a small-scale brewer in Hertford. A small housing estate has recently been built on the site in Newsells Lane.

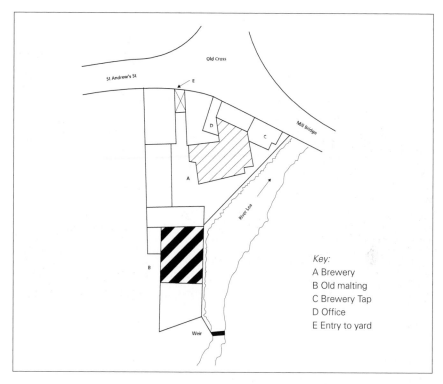

Figure 13.6 Plan of Wickham's Mill Bridge Brewery

Table 13.6 Mill Bridge Brewery tied estate

a) Sold to Wells & Winch in 1938			
Herts			
Bengeo	*Woodman* BH	Hertford	*Duncombe Arms* FL
Hertford	*Black Horse* FL	Ware	*Star Brewery Tap* L.
	Brewery Tap BH	Wareside	*Railway Tavern* BH
	Cranbourne Arms BH, L.		
b) Previous disposals or leases			
Hertford	*Cross Keys* FH, L. from McMullen		

Mill Bridge Brewery

In 1826 the small Mill Bridge Brewery by the River Lea at 7 Mill Bridge was owned by John W. Ireland and leased to Edward Wickham. Edward bought the business in 1829 and it then belonged to the Wickham family until 1938. Edward's son, Edward John Wickham became the owner of the brewery in 1874. His sons Edward and Harold, still trading as E.J. Wickham, finally sold the brewery to Wells & Winch of Biggleswade on 25 March 1938 for £20,000.

This small brewery produced approximately 1,000 barrels per year. On the

Table 13.7 McMullen's current tied estate

Herts

Aston	Rose and Crown		
Barnet	Green Man	Hoddesdon	Sun
	King's Head	Hooks Cross	Three Horseshoes
	Lord Kitchener	Ickleford	Green Man
	Old Red Lion	Kimpton	White Horse
	Queen's Arms	Lemsford	Long Arm and Short Arm
	Sebright Arms	Mardley Heath	North Star
	White Hart	Much Hadham	Jolly Waggoners
Bayford	Baker's Arms	Nomansland Common	Three Oaks
Bell Bar	Cock o' the North	Peters Green	Bright Star
Bishop's Stortford	Tanners' Arms	Potters Bar	Builders' Arms
Boreham Wood	Mops and Brooms	Puckeridge	White Hart
Botany Bay	Robin Hood	Rabley Heath	Robin Hood and Little John
Bourne End	White Horse	Redbourn	Bull
Broxbourne	Bull	St Albans	Blue Anchor
Buntingford	Black Bull		Camp
Cheshunt	Crocodile		Farrier's Arms
	Maltsters' Arms		Peahen
	Old Anchor	St Margaret's	Jolly Fisherman
Chorleywood	Stag	Sawbridgeworth	Three Horseshoes
Codicote	Globe	South Mimms	White Hart
Coleman Green	John Bunyan	Stevenage	Almond Tree
Colliers End	Lamb and Flag		Prince of Wales
Cuffley	Plough		Royal Oak
Digswell (Welwyn)	Cowper Arms		Two Diamonds
Eastwick	Lion	Turnford	Bull's Head
Elstree	Fishery Inn	Walkern	Yew Tree
Essendon	Candlestick	Waltham Cross	Vine
Flamstead End	Plough		Wheatsheaf
Gilston	Dusty Miller	Ware	Cannon Tavern
Goffs Oak	Prince of Wales		French Horn
	Wheelwrights		John Gilpin
Hatfield	Harrier		Jolly Bargeman
	Hopfields		Millstream
	Red Lion		Rose and Crown
Haultwick	Rest and Welcome		Saracen's Head
Hertford	Golden Griffin		Spread Eagle
	Great Eastern Tavern		Victoria
	Greyhound, Bengeo		Wine Lodge
	Lord Haig	Welham Green	Sibthorpe Arms
	Mill Stream	Welwyn	Steamer
	Ram Inn		Tavern plus OL
	Salisbury Arms	Welwyn Garden City	Chieftain (Woodman)
	Sele Arms	Weston	Rising Sun, Halls Green
	White Hart		Thatched House
	Woolpack	Whitwell	Maidenhead
Hitchin	Angel's Reply	Widford	Green Man
	Coopers' Arms	Woolmer Green	Fox L & F.
	Mill Stream (Ship)	Wormley	Old Star
	Orange Tree	Wormley West End	Woodman

Essex

Eastwick	Lion	Theydon Bois	*Sixteen String Jack*
Epping Green	*Traveller's Friend*	Thornwood Common	*Carpenters' Arms*
Harlow	*Cock Inn*	Upshire	*Horseshoes*
	Dusty Miller	Waltham Abbey	*Angel*
	Hare		*Coach and Horses*
	Herald		*Crown*
	Shark		*Old English Gentleman*
High Beech	*Owl*		*Old Spotted Cow*
Loughton	*Holly Bush*		*Queen's Head*
Ongar	*Stag*		*Volunteer*
Sewardstone	*Plough*		*Welsh Harp*
Tawney Common	*Moletrap*		*Wheatsheaf*
Theydon Bois	*Queen Victoria*		*White Lion*

Greater London

Cambridge Circus	*Spice of Life*	Enfield	*Jolly Farmers*
Chingford	*Royal Oak*		*Plough*, Crew Hill
Covent Garden	*Nag's Head*		*Wonder*
Enfield	*Cricketers*	Finchley	*Windsor Castle*
	Greyhound	Holloway	*Admiral Mann*
	Jolly Butchers	Woodford Green	*Cricketers*

site there was also an old malting and kiln, stores, a house and the Brewery Tap. An 1880 photograph by Arthur Elsden shows it as a complex clutter of timber-clad buildings. There was also a small quay by the river just below a weir making it accessible by barge. The tied estate was never more than seven tied and leasehold properties (Table 13.6).

At an early stage of the ownership two tied properties had been sold to McMullen's and a third had been leased from them. In 1866, Edward's other son William was the owner of the Star Brewery in Ware. He agreed not to poach trade in the territory of the Mill Bridge Brewery. This agreement ceased in 1899 when he stopped brewing.

After the 1938 sale to Wells & Winch the brewery was let as a store. During the Second World War the buildings were requisitioned for use as the Hertford Borough Air Raid Precautions Department. Unfortunately the brewery and Brewery Tap were hit by a flying bomb and demolished in July 1944. The malting survived and has now been converted to private housing

Hertford Brewery – McMullen & Sons Ltd

Peter McMullen began brewing in 1827 in a small brewery in Back Street (now Railway Street). In 1832 he was also brewing on a site at Mill Bridge which was later occupied by the *Woolpack*. He opened his first tied house, the *Robin Hood* at

Figure 13.7 McMullen's Brewery in Hartham Lane

Bengeo in 1836 and his second the *Cricketers* (now the *Lordship Arms*) at Benington in 1841. By 1853 he had a malting at Port Vale, Hertford. He retired in 1860 and was succeeded by his sons Alexander Peter and Osmund Henry. The tied estate increased in size and created a need for greater brewing capacity. Initially the Cannon Brewery in Ware was bought in 1864 to solve the problem. The Star Brewery in Ware was also leased from 1874 to 1878. However brewing on three or four sites was not an ideal solution.

The McMullen family decided to build a new brewery in Hertford in 1891 on a triangular site at the junction of Hartham Lane on the road which led to Cowbridge Station on the Great Northern Railway Line.

The north-eastern side of the triangle was already occupied by a large granary and a bonded store and these were modified to form part of the new brewery. Behind these buildings were the railway goods yards which would form a good bulk transport link. Much of the site was excavated and extensive cellars were constructed for beer conditioning and storage before major building work was started.

The ground floor of the new tower brewhouse housed a horizontal steam engine, liquor and wort pumps, malt crushing rollers and a comprehensive series of screens and sieves. On the first floor was the brewer's room and a purpose built laboratory, which may have been only the second to be

Table 13.8 McMullen's disposals and closures from their tied estate

Herts

Ardeley	Goose 1878	Hertford	Three Tuns
Aston	Beehive BH		Two Brewers to 1966
Barnet	Three Horseshoes after 1880		Unicorn FL to 1983
Bengeo	Robin Hood		Waggon and Horses L.1860
Benington	Cricketers to c.1992		Woolpack to 1929
Bish. Stortford	Cat and Fiddle	High Wych	Queen's Head BH, L.1902
Brickendon	Farmer's Boy to c.1990	Hitchin	Dog closed c.1970
Burnham Green	Duck c.1857		Red Lion closed c.1975
Cheshunt	Bull's Head FL after 1904		OL Ashbrook c.1874
	Horse and Groom 1873	Little Amwell	Horse and Dray BH c.1904
	Two Brewers BH to c.1963	Little Hadham	Cock to c.1963
	Victoria	Little Munden	Rest and Welcome to 1990s
	Vine BH	London Colney	Golden Lion c.1889
Datchworth	Duck BH	Much Hadham	Hoops
Great Munden	Horse and Groom		Rose and Crown BH
Harpenden	Oddfellows' Arms after 1886	Nup End	Three Horseshoes to 1926
Hatfield	Beehive FL, L.1903	Puckeridge	BH Brewery in 1920s
H. Hempstead	King's Arms after 1954	St Albans	Blacksmiths' Arms c.1898
Hertford	Angel to 1917		Golden Harp c.1900
	Bear's Ear closed 1957		Potter's Arms c.1900
	Bell to c.1946	Sandridge	Prince of Wales BH c.1900
	Bell and Crow FL after 1966	Sawbridgeworth	Fox
	Blackbirds' Inn after 1966	Shenley	Lord Nelson 1889
	Black Horse closed 1919*	Standon	Duke of Wellington
	Butcher's Arms closed 1917		Exhibition BH 1904
	Cold Bath closed 1962		Fox and Hounds FL 1904
	Cross Keys closed 1861		Nag's Head 1886
	Dimsdale Arms to c.1966	Stanstead Abbots	Prince of Wales
	Dolphin c.2000	Stapleford	Woodhall Arms L.1904
	Duncombe Arms FL to c.1966		
	Eagle to 1919	Stevenage	Twin Foxes to 1953
	Flower Pot to c.1966		White Swan to 1919
	Gladstone Arms closed 1965	Wadesmill	Windmill
	Gt. Northern Railway to 1920	Waltham Cross	Queen Eleanor to 1960s
	Green Dragon to 1952	Ware	Bird in Hand to 1932
	Highland Chief to 1917		Cabin to 1960s
	King's Head closed 1955		Chequers to 1960s
	Lion's Head closed 1961		Forester's Arms FL 1904
	Little Bell closed 1959		Fox BH, L. 1904
	Maidenhead 1920 to c.1946		Jolly Gardeners BH
	Nelson to 1919		Malakoff BH to c.1918
	New Bridge Inn		New Rose and Crown
	Oak		Red House to 1960s
	Old Ship closed 1970		Red Lion to 1960s
	Punchbowl (Diamond) to 1966		White Swan to c.1900s
	Queen's Head after 1966	Welwyn	Baron of Beef
	Railway Tavern		Boot L. to 1919
	Red Lion to 1961		Moorhen L. & F.
	Reindeer closed 1966		White Hart L.
	Rising Sun closed 1957	Welwyn G.C.	Beehive
	Sawyers' Arms L. 1904		

	Ship to *c.*1966		Whitwell	*Lamb*	
	Talbot Arms to 1966			*White Hart*	
	Three Tuns		Whiteway Bottom	*Green Man*	

Essex

Nazeing	*Lion and Lamb* closed 1906		Waltham Abbey	*Greyhound* to *c.*1920s	
Sheering	*Baker's Arms* 1906				

Beds

Luton	*Inkerman Arms* BH 1874–6		Luton		BH John St

Key: * Station Road
        Bish. Stortford   Bishop's Stortford
        H. Hempstead   Hemel Hempstead
        Welwyn G.C.   Welwyn Garden City

established in Hertfordshire after Benskin's of Watford. The remainder of this floor gave access to piping attached to vessels on the next floor. On the second floor were a re-positioned brewery oak-sided copper-lined mash tun and a new cast-iron mash tun lagged with pitch pine. Spent grain from the mash tuns could be discharged down a shoot to an outside tank. Mr Osmund H. McMullen designed an external mashing machine, built by Pontifex of London, in which the grist (ground malt) was mixed with hot liquor and discharged down a shoot into either mash tun. A cast-iron hot liquor tank was constructed on the third floor together with a grist case capable of independently feeding defined quantities to each mash tun and also three refrigerators. The top floor contained a larger copper cooler. A wing on one side of the tower contained a cast-iron wort back with a steam coil, an open-fire wort copper and a cast-iron circular hop back. The three-storey wing on the other side of the tower was the fermenting hall. On the ground floor was the racking room for barrel-filling containing large slate settling backs to hold the bulk beer. This was connected to the conditioning cellars by a barrel lift. The first floor contained oak fermenting tuns fitted with copper attemperators and parachute yeast skimmers. The second floor contained the malt and hop store and a short direct shoot to the malt screen in the main tower block. On a higher floor was the main cold liquor tank for the whole complex. The beer store with hoists from the cellars and loading bays for brewery drays were built in the apex of the triangle. Most of these buildings have remained for 110 years though obviously there have been internal changes. The majority of the original equipment has been changed but there is still a 1896 mash tun that may be in use.

During 1984 a new brewhouse was built at Hartham Lane using ninety-barrel stainless steel conical fermenters. It was decided in 2004 that a smaller and more flexible facility was needed. The new plant would have a brew length of thirty barrels' capacity.

In 1897 McMullen & Sons registered as a limited company with a tied estate of over ninety public houses. During the same year they acquired the Welwyn Brewery and the *Fox* at Woolmer Green. In the following year they bought the Waltham Abbey Brewery and its tied estate which included the *Maltsters' Arms* and the *Wheelwrights' Arms* at Cheshunt, the *Plough* at Cuffley, the *Queen Eleanor* at Waltham Cross and a number of properties in Waltham Abbey. They bought the Epping Brewery in 1907 to increase their Essex estate. The last major purchase was the Hope Brewery in Old Cross, Hertford with a tied estate of twenty properties belonging to the Baker family. The Hope Brewery House is now part of McMullen's office complex. McMullen's are now Hertfordshire's oldest independent brewery and still managed by the McMullen family. Their tied estate is approximately 140 properties in Essex, Hertfordshire and Greater London (Table 13.7). In 170 years there have been a number of disposals and closures with the greatest number in Hertford (Table 13.8).

In the past McMullen's were also maltsters in Hertford. However the Old Cross Malthouse on the River Lea Navigation is their only malting to survive. This is a two-storey building, about 180 feet in length, which was built partially on sixteenth century brick foundations. The premises have been let to an agricultural merchant.

Hope Brewery

The Hope Brewery was probably established behind Old Cross House at Old Cross near Mill Bridge *c.*1830. Earlier the site had a malting, workshops and outhouses. There may also have been a small brewery. In 1800 a maltster, William Gripper, leased the site for twenty-one years. John Barnard at the *Falcon* in Fore Street purchased the property in 1825 and soon sold it to William Endersby Squire who died shortly afterwards in 1830. This property was put up for auction and bought for £1,500 by William Baker who was a retail brewer. He belonged to a family of bargemasters and maltsters who had been established in Hertford and Ware since 1740.

In 1832 William Baker decided to re-equip the brewery and paid William Pontifex of London £5 5s 0d to act as a consultant and supervise the installation.

Table 13.9 Hope Brewery tied estate

a) Tied estate taken over by McMullen's in 1920

Herts

Benington	*Red Lion* BH	Hertford	*White Lion* FL
Cheshunt	*Plough* BH, Flamstead End		*Maidenhead* FL
Essendon	*Chequers* BH, L. in 1904		*Old Mill Stream* FL
Great Munden	*Horse and Groom* FL 1873		*Red Lion* FL
Hatfield	*Green Man* BH Leased 1904	Standon	*College Arms* FL
	Woodman FL Leased 1904	Walkern	*Yew Tree* FL 1861
Hertford	*Bell* BH	Ware	*Prince of Wales* BH
	Great Northern Railway FL		*Rifle Volunteer* FL
	King's Head BH	Weston	*Rising Sun* FL

Greater London

Waltham Abbey	*Angel*		

b) Tied estate disposed before 1920 sale

Herts

Hertford	OL at brewery	Sandon	*Two Brewers* BH
	Old Waggon and Horses FL	Ware	*Crown and Anchor* FL
	Waggon and Horses BH	Willian	*Fox (Orange Tree)* FL, F.

The final bill from William Pontifex and Sons was as follows: brewing copper and cask £69 9s 6d, set of pumps for liquor and wort £32 0s 0d, mashing machine for a seven feet diameter tun with a ten feet horizontal shaft £32 0s 0d, visit to Hertford £5 5s 0d. Initially he leased the modernised brewery to Thomas Gripper. John Adams Carter then leased the brewery from 1839 to 1847 but unfortunately he died bankrupt in the same year. William Baker then began to brew and remained there until 1886. The business became known as William Baker and Sons. A tied estate gradually was built up in East Hertfordshire and Waltham Abbey (Table 13.9). In 1920 McMullen's bought the brewery and twenty tied houses including five in Hertford. At least five disposals had been made before the sale. During 1927 McMullen's offices, mineral water factory and wine and spirits stores were moved to this site. Most of the old Hope Brewery has now been pulled down and part recently was being used as a staff car park.

Manser's Brewery

It has been claimed that William and J.P. Manser could have been brewing in Back Street as early as 1822. In 1826 only William was still active as a brewer and remained there until 1836. There does not seem to have been any tied estate with this brewery.

Figure 13.8 The Saracen's Head *with part of the Crown Brewery and its malting in the background*

Crown Brewery

Thomas Driver Medcalf had originally leased Manser's brewery in Back Street in 1839 and brewed there until 1854. However, he was established at the Crown Brewery by 1859. This was a small brewery built behind the *Saracen's Head* on the western side of Railway Place. There was also a yard on the opposite side of the street containing a shop, a stable, a harness room, a coach house, a carpenter's shop, a cooper's shed and an open and a closed shed.

Thomas Medcalf began building up a tied estate while he was still leasing Manser's brewery. He bought the *Leather Bottle* in Beacherly Street, Hertford in 1842, the *Sawyers' Arms* at Brickendon in 1843 and the *Saracen's Head* in Ware Road, Hertford in 1854. When the brewery was sold to Percy Hargreaves of the Abridge Brewery, Essex in 1884 there were seven freehold and five leasehold properties (Table 13.10). Medcalf had also previously owned or leased the *Black Horse* and the *White Lion* in Hertford, the *Brewer's Arms* at Hertford Heath and the *Green Man* at Widford. In 1895 Hargreaves sold the brewery and the *Saracen's Head* to Benskin's. Benskin's logos still remain in the glass of the saloon bar of the public house. The remainder of the tied estate was sold to other breweries including McMullen's. The brewery buildings on the other side of the street became a depot for Abridge Brewery. At some later date the brewery

Figure 13.9 Nicholls' Brewery house and the entrance to the brewery in West Street

building would appear to have been converted into a two-storey malting with a furnace chimney at the northern end. This building now has been converted into offices and shops. No traces remain of the other brewery buildings on the opposite side of the street.

Nicholls' Brewery

In 1846 Samuel Ongar Nicholls was the licensee of the *Oddfellows' Arms* in West Street and had become a brewer at the small West Street Brewery by 1853 where a brewhouse had originally been built on the site in 1770. This was a small tower brewery behind the Brewery House, built at right angles to the road and almost reaching the River Lea. His son William Henry succeeded him in 1863. Unfortunately William died in 1879 and his wife Ellen managed the business until she retired in 1896. Their sons William Henry II and George continued as brewers. In 1953 they were trading as W.H. and G. Nicholls with W.H. Nicholls as head brewer. During 1885 this brewery was rebuilt and partially re-equipped by George Adlam of Bristol. The equipment included a six quarter mash tun, a copper of thirty-five barrels' capacity and a large wooden hop back. Hot wort was cooled in a shallow ten feet by five feet cooling trough with extra cooling provided by a dairy-type surface cooler. There were four thirty-barrel capacity

Table 13.10 Crown Brewery tied estate in 1884

Herts				
Brickendon	*Farmer's Boy* F.	Hertford	*Leather Bottle* F.	
	Sawyers' Arms BH, L.		*Saracen's Head* F.	
Hatfield	*Drayhorse* BH, L.		*Turk's Head* BH, L.	
Hertford	*Angel* BH, L.		*Wellington* BH, L.	
	City Arms F.	Much Hadham	*Hoops* BH, L.	
	Flower Pot BH, F.	Wareside	*White Horse* F.	

Table 13.11 Nicholls' Brewery tied estate

Herts	
Bengeo	*Warren House* FL 1853 to 1965, sold to Mr Thomas Matthews
Hertford	*Jolly Farmers* BH, Bengeo St. to 1919
	Oddfellows' Arms, West St 1846
	Two Brewers, Port Vale
	White Horse, Castle St, BH in 1904
	OL at Brewery to 1966
Ware	*Old Victory* FL, sold to Mrs Vospell in 1886

fermenting vats of white cedar wood. This layout suggested a capacity of about ten barrels per day when mashing twice a week. Water was obtained from their artesian well. Beer was sold in pins to hogsheads and included XK, Brown Ale, IPA, Pale Ale, Mild, Family Bitter Ale and Old Nick Strong Ale.

Even when the brewery was operating at maximum capacity it had only five tied houses plus an off-licence at the brewery and would appear to have given up the *Oddfellows' Arms* before 1896 (Table 13.11). Initially much of the other beer sales were to the big mansion houses in the district. As these were pulled down or used for other purposes more limited sales were made to clubs. Since there also was a bottling plant on the site there was also some contract bottling of national beers.

However, by 1965 demand had fallen so much that the brewery was reputed to be mashing only once a month. At this time Hertfordshire County Council decided to build a by-pass round the centre of Hertford. Unfortunately the brewery boiler house was directly on the planned route of the new road. A compulsory purchase order was made and the brewery was pulled down. The Brewery House dating from 1719 is still on the site and there is a converted malting next door.

References

Bedfordshire County Records Office. GK277/1 (1938 deed of Wickham's Brewery).

Connell, E. J. Hertford Breweries, *Industrial Archaeology*, Vol. 4, pp.29–49, 1967.

Hertfordshire Archives and Local Studies. a. D/EL T51 (Baker), b. D/EL B52 (Carter), D/EX 307T1 (Gillman), c. D/EL B69, Acc. 3741, (Crown Brewery), d. D/EL 4286, D/EL 2909–12 (Nicoll), e. 74046 (1696), 73993–4 (1702), 73995 (1703), 74048 (1718), 74003 (1736), 74010 (1770), 74015 (1777), 74073 (1793), 74024 (1803), 74100, 74102 (1847), 74105 and D/EL 2941 (1857), 87411 (1870). All these references in section e. deal with the history of the Young's site.

Messrs. McMullen & Son's New Brewery, Hertford, *Brewers' Journal*, 15 October 1891, p.531.

Petty Sessions Licensing Records for Hertfordshire, Bedfordshire and west Essex.

Poole, H. *Here for the Beer*, Watford Museum, 1984, pp. 22-6.

Richmond, L. and Turton, A. (eds.). *The Brewing Industry: A Guide to Historical Records*, Manchester University Press, 1990, pp.223, 250, 379.

CHAPTER FOURTEEN

Hitchin

Hitchin is an old market town and was on a number of important horse and coach routes during the eighteenth and nineteenth centuries which led to the establishment of approximately one hundred inns and beer houses.

A number of breweries and maltings were built in the town to deal with the demand for beer (Figure 14.1). The brewers included the Draper and Conquest families at the *Red Lion* and in Sun Street (*c.*1600 to 1730s), the Lucas family at the *Red Lion* and in Sun Street (1695 to 1922), Crabb, Marshall & Pierson (*c.*1750 to 1841) and Pierson at the Bucklesbury Brewery (1842–52). There was also the small *Sun* Brewery (1700s to 1902) plus a few brewhouses.

Draper and Conquest families

Although brewing probably began on a small scale in Hitchin in medieval times, the first quoted brewer was Thomas Draper. He was fined in 1602 for operating an unlicensed brewhouse. In 1632 a descendant, Benjamin Draper, was an active brewer, and in 1695 Edward Draper was leasing property and a malting in Sun Street and had leased the *Angel Vaults* and the *Chequers*.

About 1700 William Conquest began brewing in a small brewery on the south side of the yard behind the *Red Lion*, which was demolished in the 1840s when the Corn Exchange was built in the old Market Square. He became the landlord of the *Sun* in 1707, which later had its own brewery, and also owned the *Six Bells* in Baldock, which he later sold in 1729. His son John also became a brewer and took over the business. He married Elizabeth Draper the daughter of another brewer.

John Draper, his wife Anne, together with their daughter Elizabeth and son-in-law John Conquest, collectively took out a loan for £1,100 from William Lucas in 1734. As security they promised their brewery in Sun St, a malting, barns, outhouses and forty-eight acres of land in the manor of Hitchin. Unfortunately they were unable to repay the loan and the Lucas family acquired various properties previously owned by the Draper and Conquest families.

W. & S. Lucas & Co.

The Lucas family, who became Quakers in the late 1600s, were described as farmers and maltsters and were living in 1695 at 10 High Street with a malting behind the house. In 1709 William Lucas formed a partnership with his brother-in-law Isaac Gray I and began brewing at an unknown location. This may have been at a brewhouse with a granary, on the north side of Tilehouse Street that the Lucas family still owned in 1834, or the brewhouse in the yard of the *Red Lion*, after William Conquest had moved to the *Sun* which also had a brewhouse. Lucas and Gray did not take over Conquest's brewery until after 1727 and possibly later than 1734. Samuel Lucas had policy 39820 in 1726 with Sun Insurance for a dwelling house, a malting, wash-houses and lofts, a great barn, stables and hay barns, wood houses and other outhouses for a premium of 2s 6d (12.5p) every quarter day (HALS 51100). Although not stated this insurance presumably was for 10 High Street.

There was also another Isaac Gray, possibly the son or grandson of Isaac Gray I, who was also a Quaker brewer in Hitchin in 1774. However it is not known if he worked at the Lucas Brewery or independently.

In 1748, the Lucas family still owned the malting, barns and a shop in the High Street and had acquired a brewhouse, a malting and five cottages in Sun Street from the Draper family. They also had a tied estate of freehold, leasehold and copyhold property in Hitchin, St Ippollytts, Datchworth, Offley, Willian (all in Hertfordshire) and in Clifton and Shefford in Bedfordshire. The brewery in Sun Street was rebuilt in 1771 and developed at a later stage to include buildings for brewing, storage of beer, a cooperage, cask and bottle washing and mineral water production. In 1780 a large house was built on the site of the five cottages. The early tied estate in Hertfordshire included the *Stag* (Baldock), *Angel Vaults*, *Half Moon*, *Red Lion*, *Swan with Two Necks* and *Wheatsheaf* (all in Hitchin), the *Three Horseshoes* (Nup End, Knebworth), and in Bedfordshire there were also the *White Hart* (Campton), the *Boot* (Langford), the *Five Bells* (Meppershall) and the *Dirt House*, later the *New Inn* (Shillington).

William Lucas's settlement deed of 1834 gives details of thirty tied properties belonging to the brewery. Originally the *Red Lion* was probably one of the

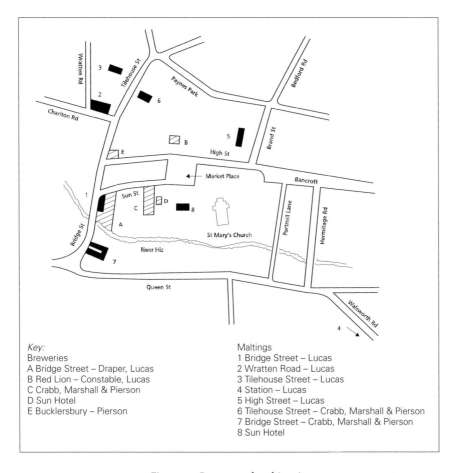

Figure 14.1 Brewery and malting sites

biggest inns in Hitchin with a large yard containing a brewhouse, a washhouse, pumps, shops, a barn, stables, outhouses and other buildings. The *Crown* at Ley Green also had a grocer's shop and a butcher's slaughter house, and there was another grocer's shop next to the *Pig and Whistle* at St Paul's Walden. This deed omits another eleven properties that were owned separately by William Lucas Senior, William Lucas Junior and Samuel Lucas. Very briefly, in 1837 the business was known as Lucas & Jeeves. Members of the Jeeves family were well known as master builders in Queen Street, Hitchin. By the early 1840s the total holding was up to fifty properties and this approximate number was maintained until the brewery sale in 1922 (Tables 14.1 and 14.2). Most of the tied estate outside Hitchin was in villages in North Hertfordshire or South Bedfordshire. It is not known why the brewery never acquired any public houses or beer houses

Table 14.1 Lucas's licensed properties sold to Green's in 1923

Herts

Bendish	Red Lion	1841	Hitchin	Post Boy	1898
Braughing	Axe and Compasses	1898		Railway Inn	1898
Bulls Green	Horns w.j.	1839		Railway Junction	1898
Charlton	Windmill	1898		Rose and Crown L.	1898
Codicote	Goat L.	1920		Wheatsheaf (Pelican)	1834
Datchworth	Three Horseshoes	1834	Ickleford	Cricketers	1898
	Tilbury	1840		Plume of Feathers s.l.	1920
Gosmore	Bull L.	1920	Langley	Royal Oak	1834
Graveley	Fox and Hounds w.j	1920	Ley Green	Crown w.j.	1840
	Waggon and Horses	1898	Lilley	King William IV OL	1920
	Windmill	1841	Little Wymondley	Buck's Head	1841
Hitchin	Adam and Eve	1841	Offley	Red Lion	1840
	Crown	1839	Pirton	Fox	1898
	Half Moon w.s.	1840		Old Hall	1898
	Highlander	1898		Red Lion	1920
	King's Arms	1834	Preston	Chequers L.	1920
	King's Head w.s.	1840	Whitwell	Bull	1845
	Plough and Dial	1898		Eagle and Child w.j.	1834

Beds

Barton	Coach and Horses	1898	Meppershall	Red Lion	
	BH Manor Rd	1898	Shillington	Crown	1898
Campton	White Hart	1776		Five Bells	1834
Leagrave	Sugar Loaf	1834		Red Sign Post	1834
Limbury	Black Swan	1834	Stopsley	First and Last	1876
Luton	Eight Bells	1903		Sun	1920
	Horse and Jockey	1834	Stotfold	Black Lion	1876
	Red Lion	1842			

Key: The dates 1776, 1834, 1839, 1898 and 1920 are taken from Lucas documents
1840 data is taken from tithe maps. Other dates are from Jolliffe and Jones (1995)
In 1839 certain properties were held by William Lucas Senior (w.s.), William Lucas Junior
(w.j.) and Samuel Lucas (s.l.)

in Ashwell, Royston or Stevenage. The brewery had bought the *Clarendon* in Ware by 1830, and the *Vine* shortly afterwards, when the roads were poor and there were no other tied properties within ten miles of this town. Unfortunately there are no records to indicate the source of beer sold by the landlords of these properties.

The Lucas family also owned a number of maltings. The earliest was behind 10 High Street (tithe plot 257) which they were using by 1695, but had been sold to H.J.G. Smith by 1818. Old photographs of the brewery in Sun Street show windows typical of a malting which had been acquired from the Draper family. Two other old maltings from pre-1840 (twelve quarters and sixteen to eighteen quarters) bought from Mr J. Wilshire, were in Wratten Road and owned until at least 1898. They were later sold to a builder to use as a store and pulled down in

Table 14.2 Lucas brewery disposals, closures or finishing of leases before 1923

Herts			Notes
Aston	*Rose and Crown*	1809	Sold to McMullen 1840
Baldock	*Stag*	1732	Sold to John Steed 1776
Charlton	*Seven Stars*		Closed *c.*1890
Codicote	*George and Dragon*	1898	Sold to Trust Houses Ltd 1920
Hitchin	*Angel Vaults*	1785	Sold in 1859
	Bricklayer's Arms*	1918	Short lease *c.*1918
	Bull's Head	1840	Closed 1916
	Dial (*New Robin Hood*)	1834	Amalgamation to *Plough* before 1898
	Peahen	1918	Short lease *c.*1918
	Plough w.s.	1840	Amalgamation to *Dial* before 1898
	Queen's Head	1834	Closed 1862
	Red Lion	1740	Sold to McMullen's after 1850
	Ship	1834	Sold in 1869
	Shoulder of Mutton	1840	Early disposal
	Swan with Two Necks w.s.	1840	Closed in 1915
	Two Brewers	1834	Disposal in 1921
Hook's Cross	*Three Horseshoes*	1839	Sold in 1876
Ickleford	*Green Man*	1834	Sold in 1869
Lilley	*Red Lion*	1842	
	Silver Lion	1918	Short lease *c.*1918
Nup End	*Three Horseshoes*	1790s	
Rabley Heath	*Robin Hood and Little John*	1870	Lease until 1900
St Paul's Walden	*Pig and Whistle*	1842	
Walkern	*Red Lion*	1834	Sold to Wrights in 1869
Ware	*Clarendon* (*Vine*)	1834	Sold in 1840s
	King's Head	1834	Sold after 1876
Welwyn	*Chequers*	1777	Sold in 1883
	Tavern	1904	Lease until 1921
Woolmer Green	*Chequers*	1898	
Beds			
Arlesley	*Three Tuns*	1841	
Dunstable	*Crow* (*Black Raven*)	1834	Disposed in 1866
Langford	*Boot*	1796	Disposed in 1903
Meppershall	*Five Bells*	1796	Disposed in 1903
Polluxhill	*Hoops* w.j.	1839	
Sharpenhoe	*Horseshoes*	1920	Short lease
Shefford	*Crown*	1834	Disposed *c.*1920
	George	1834	Disposed *c.*1920
	White Swan	1834	Lease to *c.*1920
Shillington	*New Inn* (*Dirt House*)	1783	
Streatley	*Red Lion*		

Key: Owned by William Lucas Senior (w.s.) and William Lucas Junior (w.j.) in 1839

the 1960s. In 1898 there were other maltings behind 25 Tilehouse Street and at the junction of Walsworth Road and Nightingale Road. Neither of these maltings was used much later. Much earlier the brewery had also owned the *Red Lion* with its own fifteen quarter malting in Walkern but this property was sold to Wright's Brewery of Walkern in 1869. There was also a malting at the *George* in Shefford but it does not appear to have been used after it was bought by the brewery. As much larger and more economically efficient maltings were built elsewhere in the county between 1850 and 1900 the Lucas family would appear to have gradually given up using or sold most of their maltings early in the 1900s (Figure 14.1).

All of the properties associated with the brewery were put up for sale in 1921. J.W. Green Ltd of Luton bought the business including fifty-one tied houses in 1922 and closed the brewery in 1923 (Table 14.1). Previously the Lucas family had disposed of another twenty-nine properties in Hertfordshire and eleven in Bedfordshire (Table 14.2). The brewery buildings on the corner of Sun Street and Bridge Street were finally demolished in 1963 and replaced by shops and Crown House. Today all that remains is the Brewery House in Sun Street (now Philpott's shop), and the Tilehouse at 25 Tilehouse Street, with inscribed stones in the archways defining Lucas property boundaries.

Crabb, Marshall and Pierson

John Crabb was brewing at 5 Sun Street in a yard behind a Georgian house until he died in 1782. He was succeeded by his son, John Crabb II, who died in 1811.

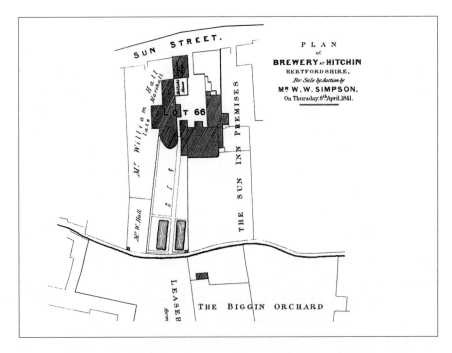

Figure 14.2 Plan of Marshall and Pierson's Brewery in 1841 (Hitchin Museum)

Table 14.3 Crabb's tied estate established between 1786 and 1831

Herts						
Braughing	Brown Bear	1786	Little Munden	Boot	1805
Codicote	Red Lion L.	1785	Little Wymondley	Buck's Head	1806
Gosmore	Bull	1793	St Ippollytts	Greyhound	1785
Hitchin	Adam and Eve	1818	Stevenage	Coach and Horses	1813
	Curriers' Arms	1783	Walkern	White Lion	1796
	Highlander	1827	Welwyn	Rose and Crown	1799
	Red Hart	1805	Weston	Red Lion	1812
	Rose and Crown L.	1818	Whitwell	Red Lion	1831
Holwell	White Hart		Woolmer Green	Red Lion	1818
Knebworth	Roebuck L.	1827			
Beds						
Dunstable	White Swan					

His successor, John Crabb III, died suddenly aged 25 in 1813, and John II's widow Mary, who also owned a malting behind 92 Bancroft, remained in charge of the brewery until she died in 1826. In 1823 she had formed a business partnership with John Marshall who was the brewery manager. At this stage there were about twenty public houses in the tied estate which included the *Adam and Eve, Curriers' Arms, Highlander, Red Hart* and *Rose and Crown* (leasehold) in Hitchin, plus two maltings in Bridge Street and another in Tilehouse Street (tithe plot 291) opposite No. 25.

In 1832 John Marshall formed a new partnership with Joseph Margretts Pierson. Shortly afterwards he was succeeded by his son John Marshall II. The brewery proved to be a success and was brewing 5,500 barrels annually. It had tun rooms, cooler rooms, a cooperage, an engine room, a vat room, a counting house, a cask shed, stores and a hop loft plus a commodious family residence with extensive cellarage. The tied estate had increased to at least forty-six properties extending over a wide area (Table 14.4) making it one of the largest breweries in Hertfordshire. In Hitchin the brewery owned the *Adam and Eve, Boot, Cock, Cross Keys, Curriers' Arms, Red Cow, Red Hart, Robin Hood, Sailor, Six Bells, Three Horseshoes, Three Tuns, Wellington* and *White Lion*.

Unfortunately Marshall and Pierson joined a speculative alkali works venture in Brussels that failed in 1841, and they were forced to sell the brewery and tied estate. Many of the local brewers bought the inns and beer houses. On the second day of the sale on the 8 April 1841, William Lucas (Bryant and Parker, 1934) made the following entry in his diary:

> The sale of Marshall and Pierson's property came on yesterday and concluded today. The attendance of Brewers was very large and the Public houses made

Table 14.4 Marshall and Pierson's tied estate in 1841

Herts			
Bendish	Red Lion	Kimpton	Boot
Braughing	Brown Bear	Lemsford	Sun
Burnham Green	White Hart*	Lilley	Red Lion
Codicote	Bull	Little Munden	Boot
Hexton	Plough	Little Wymondley	Buck's Head
Hitchin	Adam and Eve	Markyate	Sun
	Boot	Pirton	Shoulder of Mutton
	Cock		White Horse
	Cross Keys	Preston	Horse and Groom
	Curriers' Arms	Redbourn	Lion and Lamb
	Red Cow	St Albans	King's Arms
	Red Hart		Post Boy
	Robin Hood	St Ippollytts	Greyhound
	Sailor	Stapleford	White Hart
	Six Bells	Stevenage	Coach and Horses
	Three Horseshoes	Walkern	White Lion
	Three Tuns	Ware	Harrow
	Wellington	Welwyn	Rose and Crown
	White Lion	Weston	Red Lion
Holwell	White Hart		
Beds			
Arlesey	BH	Dunstable	White Swan
Barton	Black Bull	Leagrave Marsh	Three Horseshoes
Caddington	Harrow	Maulden	George
Clifton	Chequers		

Key: * Later Chequers and White Horse

enormous prices, notwithstanding the spread of teetotalism and the very bad state and low trade in consequence of their Beer. We bought the *Adam and Eve* in Hitchin, a Beer shop at Arlesey (*Three Tuns*), the *Buck's Head*, Wymondley, and the moiety of a Public House (*Red Lion*) at Bendish. Dividing the property in this way has been answered completely and it is said to have made £7,000 more than the sum they would have taken for it some time since in one lot.

Today only the old brewery house remains which is owned by the Hitchin Conservative Association, and there is the original brewery coach house in the yard at the back.

Bucklersbury Brewery

After the Marshall and Pierson partnership finished, Joseph Pierson built the small Bucklersbury Brewery in 1842 on the western corner of Bucklersbury and Tilehouse Street. The brewery tap was known as the *Woodman* (20 Bucklersbury) with a five quarter brewery at the rear in the yard. He also worked

Figure 14.3 The entrance to Bucklersbury Brewery in Tilehouse Street and the former
Woodman *at the corner of Bucklersbury*

as a coal merchant in the yard. He acquired several public houses and beer
houses including the *Dog* in Brand Street, a beer house in Walsworth, Hitchin
(Poor Law plot 1128) and the *Two Horseshoes* at Langley (Poor Law plot 1260).
The *Two Horseshoes* was later known as the *Bell,* owned by Phillips of Royston,
and later, as the *Farmer's Boy* it was owned by Simpson's. Joseph Pierson sold the
brewery and tied estate when he decided to leave the country in 1852. The
Woodman building still remains with an altered ground floor that is now shops
and offices, but there is no trace of the brewery in the yard.

Figure 14.4 Converted Brewhouse at the Sun Inn

Sun Brewery

A small brewhouse and a malting in the yard of the *Sun* formed part of a small brewery until 1902. These buildings at one stage were part of a farmyard complex that also contained a cow house, a pig-sty, stables and a cart shed. The close proximity of the farmyard must have made brewing difficult. The brewhouse has now been converted to hotel bedrooms and all the farm building and the malting have been pulled down (Figure 14.5).

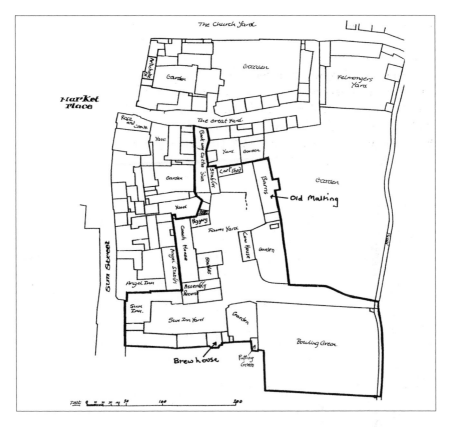

Figure 14.5 Plan of the Sun Inn *and associated buildings (Hitchin Museum)*

Brewhouses

Other small breweries were in operation for a short time in Portmill Lane in 1836 (now a public car park), in Tilehouse Street opposite the Tilehouse in 1860, at the *Peacock* in Queen Street from 1850 to 1900 and at the *Bedford Arms* in Bedford Road from 1866 to 1886.

References

Bryant, G.E. and Parker, G.P. *A Quaker Journal*, London, Hutchinson & Co. Ltd., 1934, pp.237–8.

Hertfordshire Archives and Local Studies. a. 51100 (Sun Insurance), b. 79770–1 (Lucas), c. 10898 (1880 Lucas estate), d. D/P 53/11/8–16 (Hitchin Poor Rate 1847), e. D/Z 99/1 (Marshall & Pierson's sale), f. Acc. 3682. Box 12. Mention of Lucas & Jeeves in 1837, g. Acc. 3682. Box 13. Details of deeds of Lucas properties.

Hitchin Museum. a. Details of sale of Pierson's brewery in 1852, b. Details of sale of *Sun Hotel* in 1952.

Jolliffe, G. and Jones, A. *Hertfordshire Inns & Public Houses: An historical gazetteer*, Hatfield, Hertfordshire Publications, 1995.

Page, K. Personal communication. W. & S. Lucas tied estate in 1920.

Petty Sessions Licensing Records for Hertfordshire and Bedfordshire.

Poole, H. *Here for the Beer*, Watford Museum, 1984, pp.27–31.

Whitbread Archives. a. Extract of W. & S. Lucas Ltd 1898 Trust Deed 82B/2, b. Lucas settlement deed 1834.

CHAPTER FIFTEEN

Hoddesdon

Historically Hoddesdon developed as a small market town on the main road from London to Cambridge. In 1653 Isaak Walton's 'compleate angler' and his companion are reputed to have stopped there for a meal at the *Thatched House*. William Plomer bought the *Thatched House* in the High Street in 1700. William and his son Robert may have used a brewhouse behind the inn which was already well established and possibly supplying the passing coach trade and some other local inns with beer. After Robert Plomer's death, René Briand bought the *Thatched House* and began to increase his brewing capacity and build up a small tied estate. By 1768 he owned the *Thatched House*, the *Bell* and possibly the *Feathers*, which were all in Hoddesdon High Street. Later he bought the *Old George* at Cheshunt (1779), the *Crown and Falcon* at Puckeridge (1779) and the *Sow and Pigs* at Wadesmill (1777). In 1770 a member of his staff was going to London to sell brewery by-products such as excess yeast. This small brewery on the east side of the High Street that later became known as the Hoddesdon Brewery gradually expanded until it became one of the larger breweries in the county when it was finally sold in 1928 to the Cannon Brewery of London (Figures 15.1 and 15.2).

Hoddesdon Brewery

After the historical ownership of the brewery by William Plomer 1700-28, Robert Plomer 1728–42 and René Briand 1742–81 for the first eighty years, the next owner was William Whittingstall 1781–1803. He was to be followed by Christie & Cathrow 1803–42, their executors 1842–3, Christie & Hunt 1843–60, Christie & Co. 1860–1903 and finally Christie & Co. Ltd 1903–28.

William Whittingstall, who lived at Burford House at the north end of the town, bought the brewery in 1781 after René Briand's death. He was already established as a maltster and owned maltings in Hoddesdon and Stanstead

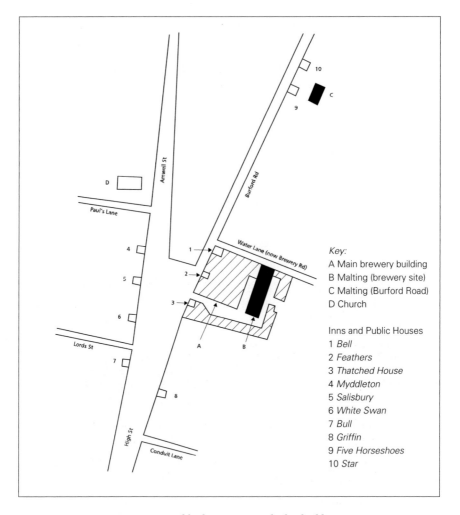

Figure 15.1 Hoddesdon Brewery and other buildings

Abbots. While he owned the brewery he increased the size of the tied estate with at least another twelve properties. He died in 1803, and his brothers sold the brewery to Christie & Cathrow for £59,401. This was a high price at this time but other breweries elsewhere in Hertfordshire were considered to be very valuable sources of investment (Table 15.1).

William Christie and George Cathrow were evidently very capable businessmen who also started a bank in Hertford in 1807. William Christie died in 1811 and his son John became a partner with a 75 per cent share of the brewery until he died in 1831. During the Christie & Cathrow ownership the brewing capacity was increased considerably and the malting operation also may have

Table 15.1 Hoddesdon Brewery early tied estate from 1700 to 1800

Herts			
a) Tied estate in 1800			
Broxbourne	White Bear 1781*	Essendon	Rose and Crown 1790
Cheshunt	Goff's Oak 1778	Hoddesdon	Boar's Head 1792
	Haunch of Venison 1791	Much Hadham	Red Lion 1782
	Old George 1777	Puckeridge	Crown and Falcon 1777
	Ship 1791	Wadesmill	Sow and Pigs 1777
	White Horse 1784	Waltham Cross	Castle 1792
Codicote	Red Lion 1785		
b) Disposals before 1800			
Hoddesdon	Plume of Feathers to 1800		
	Thatched House Inn 1700 to 1800		
Much Hadham	Three Butchers to 1800		

Key: * Now Anne of Cleves

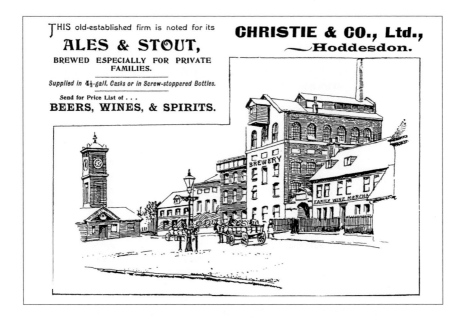

Figure 15.2 A Victorian advertisement showing a front view of the brewery (Anon)

been increased in size both on the High Street site and also in Burford Street near the *Five Horseshoes*. In 1842 the tied estate had already increased to 104 licensed properties which was the largest in Hertfordshire. At a later stage the *Feathers* became the brewery engine room and the *Thatched House Inn* was converted to brewery offices.

George Cathrow died in 1842 and stipulated in his will that a free barrel of beer should be kept filled outside the brewery for passers-by to drink. The

Table 15.2 Tied estate sold to the Cannon Brewery in 1928

Herts			
Anstey	Bell	Hoddesdon	Fox
	Chequers		George
Aston	Crown		Golden Lion
Barnet	Old Rising Sun		Green Man
Bengeo	Globe		Griffin
	Three Harts		King William IV
Bishop's Stortford	Cock*, Hockerill		Old Highway Tavern
	Grapes		Queen's Head
Bragbury End	Chequers		Salisbury Arms
Braughing	Old Black Bull		White Swan
Broxbourne	Railway Station (New Inn)	Hunsdon	Crown*
	White Bear	Little Berkhamsted	Bee Hive
Buntingford	Crown	London Colney	Bull
Cheshunt	Coach and Horses*	Much Hadham	Old Crown
	Goff's Oak		Red Lion
	Green Dragon	Northaw	Two Brewers
	Haunch of Venison	Potters Bar	Robin Hood
	Horse and Groom		
	Jolly Barge Man	Puckeridge	Buffalo's Head
	Jolly Bricklayers		Crown and Falcon
	Moulder's Arms	Roydon	Green Man*
	Old George		New Inn*
	Red Lion		White Hart*
	Rising Sun	St Margaret's	Crown
	Roman Urn	Sawbridgeworth	Queen's Head*
	Rose and Crown	Standon	Bell
	Ship		Falcon
	White Hart		Plough, Colliers End
	White Horse		White Horse
	Windmill	Stanstead Abbots	Five Horseshoes
Codicote	Red Lion		Oak
Cottered	Bell		Retainers Hall
Dane End	Boot		Rye House
Essendon	Rose and Crown	Stevenage	White Hart
Great Amwell	Galley Hall	Tewin	Plume of Feathers
	George IV (King's Head)	Wadesmill	Sow and Pigs
	Woodman		Ye Old White Hind
Great Hornmead	Three Jolly Butchers	Waltham Cross	Black Prince*
Great Munden	Plough		Castle
Hadley	William IV		Fox
			Melbourne
Hatfield	Bull, Stanborough	Ware	Angel
	Crown, Newgate St		Bay Horse
	Rose and Crown**		Bull's Head
Hertford	Albion		Dolphin
	Coffee House Inn		Harrow
	Dimsdale Arms		New Bull
	Globe		Rising Sun
	Plough		Star
	Queen's Head		Three Harts #
	Reindeer	Wareside	Fox
	Three Blackbirds	Watton at Stone	Gate
	Three Tuns		Waggon and Horses

Hertford Heath	*East India College Arms*	Westmill	*Sword in Hand*
	Goat	Widford	*Bell*
	Townshend Arms		*Victoria*
Hoddesdon	*Bell* (Brewery Tap)	Wormley	*Globe*
	Boar's Head		*Old Star*
	Bull		*Queen's Head*
	Duke William		

Essex

Broadley Common	*Black Swan**	Nazeing	*Sun**
Chingford	*Fish and Eels*, Dobbs Weir	Nettleswell Cross	*Greyhound**
Coppersdale Comm.	*Garnon Bushes*	Parndon	*Three Horseshoes**
Epping	*Duke of Wellington**	Potters Street	*Bull and Horseshoe**
	Forest Gate		*White Horse**
	Globe*	Theydon Bois	*Bull**
Epping Green	*Beehive*	Waltham Abbey	*Bull*
	Traveller's Friend*		*Compasses*
Harlow	*Crown**		*Crooked Billet**
Hazelwood	*Rainbow and Dove**		*Good Intent**
Common			*Green Man**
High Beech	*Duke of Wellington*		*Sun**
Nazeing	*Coach and Horses**		*Woodbine**
	Crooked Billet		

Greater London

Edmonton	*Bee Hive*	Enfield	*King and Tinker*
	Cock		*Ridgeway Tavern*
	Jolly Farmers		*Sun and Woolpack*
	Stag and Hounds	Whetstone	*Black Bull*

Key: * Bought by Benskin's from Cannon on 30 March 1928
          ** Tylers Causeway
          # Stoneyhills

landlords of Hoddesdon inns complained that they were losing valuable custom and there were many disturbances. This benevolent practice was soon stopped.

Between 1842 and 1843 executors took over the ownership of the brewery. John Back and Robert Hunt offered £59,500 for the brewery plant and leasehold properties and £27,500 for the copyhold properties (Poole, 1984). In 1842 they had already bought the St Andrew's Brewery in Hertford with 42 tied houses from John Moses Carter. They closed the brewery in Hertford after the Hoddesdon purchase. The freehold properties of the Hoddesdon Brewery may have remained part of the Christie family estate throughout this phase. Families of other deceased brewers often leased the freehold properties to new brewery owners for a few years before finally selling to obtain an investment income.

Initially the company became known as Hunt & Co. However, Peter Christie soon joined the partnership and the company changed the ownership name to Christie & Hunt with a capital of £130,000 (Hunt 50 per cent, Back 25 per cent, Christie 25 per cent). The tied estate increased by another 40 per cent with the

Figure 15.3 Part of Christie's malting on the brewery site from Brewery Lane

104 properties plus at least another 42 properties from the St Andrew's Brewery in Hertford (see Table 13.5). Peter Christie retired in 1858 and his son Charles Peter Christie became a partner. He became the senior partner when Robert Hunt retired in 1860 and the company became known as C.P. Christie & Co. John Back retired in 1865 and Charles Christie bought his share of the business for £100,000 when the brewery had 163 tied properties.

Since the early 1840s, the brewery had increased in size and capacity to cope with the demand for beer from the tied estate and had become the largest brewery in Hertfordshire. The major pieces of equipment in the brewery were recorded in an 1880s inventory and included two malt crushing mills driven by belts connected to a steam engine. There were two cast-iron liquor backs with one thirty-one feet long and thirty feet wide and the other thirty-seven feet long and thirty feet wide. There were also two cast-iron coolers twenty-seven feet long and twenty-four feet wide plus two wooden coolers seventy-four feet long and twenty-four feet wide, sixty-four round wood fermentation vessels, four large iron bound tuns and a refrigerator unit. Power was provided by two steam engines. This equipment was all housed in a four-storey building facing the High Street. It has been claimed that heated water from cooling processes in the

Table 15.3 Hoddesdon Brewery disposals before the takeover in 1928

Herts			
Bengeo	*Reindeer*	Hertford	*White Swan* closed 1909
Benington	*George and Dragon* to 1924		*Woolpack* before 1928
Bishop's Stortford	*Cherry Tree* pre-1810	Hoddesdon	*Harrow* closed 1908
	Cross Keys closed 1920		*Myddleton Arms*
	Crown to 1870		*Old Highway Tavern*
	White Swan L.1806–11		*Old Queen's Head*
Braughing	*Bell* closed 1923		*Plume of Feathers* c.1800
Broxbourne	*Bull*		*Thatched House* c.1800
Buntingford	*Hoops* closed pre-1920	Hunsdon	*Fox and Hounds*
	Sword in Hand pre-1920	Little Munden	*Boot*
	Windmill pre-1920		*Red Lion*
Cheshunt	*Compasses*	Much Hadham	*Three Butchers* c.1800
	Cricketers	Northaw	*Red Lion*
	Magpie C.	Puckeridge	*Anchor*
	Rifle Man	Roydon	*Plough* closed 1906
Colney Heath	*Gardener's Arms* closed 1926	St Albans	*Peacock* c.1857
Great Amwell	*Crane*	Sawbridgeworth	*George IV*
	Fox and Goose	Standon	*Lamb and Flag* L. 1903
	Old Cock c.1903	Ware	*Bricklayer's Arms*
	Red House		*Oriental Tavern* 1903–8
Great Hornmead	*Three Horseshoes* to 1824		*Red Cow*
Hertford	*Crown and Thistle* to 1917		*Standard*
	Falcon L. 1836		*White Hart*
	Red Cow closed 1910	Waterford	*Windmill*
	Ship L. 1855–74	Widford	*White Horse*
	Vine closed 1903	Wormley	*New Star*
	White Hart c.1802		*White Horse*
Essex		*Greater London*	
Epping	*Sun* closed 1907	Edmonton	*Cock*

brewery was circulated through a swimming pool which had been built at the back of the site in Bell Lane.

A brewery tied estate book from the 1890s records that in Hertfordshire there were 125 freehold properties, eight leasehold properties and one copyhold property. In Essex there were 31 freehold properties and two that were leasehold. At the same time in North and North East London there were 25 freehold properties, 12 leasehold properties and four copyhold properties. This gave a total of 208 properties in the tied estate. The licensing survey of 1902 still showed that there were 125 properties in Hertfordshire (see Table 1.2).

Charles Christie died in 1898 and his four sons decided to form a partnership. In 1903 the business became a private company with Charles A. Christie as chairman. Tragically his son John Fairfax Christie, who was expected to become the chairman, committed suicide in 1927. Soon afterwards the Cannon Brewery of Clerkenwell bought the brewery and 159 licensed properties

Table 15.4 Hoddesdon Brewery disposals of uncertain history in Essex and Greater London needing further research

Essex

Benfield End	*Willow*	Northwell	*Horseshoes*
Buckhurst Hill	*British Queen*	Ponders End	*White Hart*
	Duke of Edinburgh		*White Horse*
Epping	*Duke of York*	Waltham Abbey	*Cock*
	Green Man		*Ordinance Arms*
	White Hart		*Red Lion*
	White Swan		*White Horse*

Greater London

Chingford	*Fountain*	Enfield	*Rising Sun*
	King's Head		*Spotted Bull*
Edmonton	*Jolly Farmers*	Finchley	*Fighting Cocks*
	Orange Tree		*New Swan*
Enfield	*British Volunteer*		*Swan & Pyramids*
	Duke of Abercorn	Southgate	*Crown*
	King's Arms	Tottenham	*Nag's Head*
	Prince of Wales	Walthamstow	*Duke's Head*

and brewing stopped at this site in 1928. The tied estate included 119 properties in Hertfordshire, 26 in Essex and 8 in Greater London. The six unidentified properties were probably in North East London. The major concentrations of tied properties were: 17 in Cheshunt, 9 in Hertford, and 14 in Hoddesdon. Evidently the directors of the Cannon Brewery studied this tied estate in some detail because on 28 March 1928 they sold at least eight tied houses in Hertfordshire and eighteen in Essex to Benskin's of Watford (marked * in Table 15.2). The reasons for justifying this sale to Benskin's are not known but transport logistics may have been an important factor. Benskin's already had distribution depots in Bishop's Stortford and Essex. The Petty Sessions records for Cheshunt and Ware show that there were further sales of the Cannon Brewery estate in 1945 to Benskin's.

During the last eighty years of the Hoddesdon Brewery's operation there had been a significant number of disposals by sale, closure or completion of lease (Table 15.3). Further research is needed to identify the other licensed properties in Essex and Greater London, whose history cannot be verified, which may have been initially bought by the Cannon Brewery in 1928 before disposal (Table 15.4).

The brewery frontage has been demolished and been redeveloped. However other original buildings that were in the brewery yard are still there. The large malting is being used as a night club. The old brewery tap, the *Bell* (*Blue Bell*) is still a public house (Figure 15.4).

Figure 15.4 The Bluebell *at the corner of the High Street and Brewery Lane*

References

Hertfordshire Archives and Local Studies. a, D/ECb T1–42 (Inventory in 1866) alsoD/Ebu E2, b. Tithe Map of Hoddesdon 1841, c. Acc. 3883. Box 24, Property register for Essex – details of a few Christie & Cathrow properties sold to Cannon and resold to Benskin's, D/Z 110 Z1 (Details of estate 1889–1903).

Petty Sessions Licensing Records for Hertfordshire and west Essex.

Poole, H. *Here for the Beer*, Watford Museum, 1984, pp.31–3.

Richmond, L. and Turton, A. (eds). *The Brewing Industry: A Guide to Historical Records*, Manchester University Press, 1990, p.103.

Tregelles, A. *A History of Hoddesdon*, 1908.

CHAPTER SIXTEEN

Kimpton

Lion Brewery

Joseph Kingsley established the Lion Brewery on the north side of the High Street in 1835. This small brewery had a series of owners and leaseholders in a relatively short time. Chronologically the known occupants were Joseph Kingsley 1835 to 1839, William Coleman 1839 to 1850, William Coleman and John Sibley in 1855, Henry Kingsley 1859, Henry Kingsley and William Coleman in 1862, Henry Kingsley 1870 to 1892, Hornsey & Co. 1899 to 1900, Herts Brewing Company 1900 to 1902, Brass & Abbott 1903 to 1905 and finally George Chalkley 1906 to 1910.

Joseph Kingsley started building up a tied estate in 1836 when he purchased the *Nelson* (*Melbourne Arms*) on Marford Road, Wheathampstead. Four more properties were acquired at the sale of Marshall and Pierson's brewery in

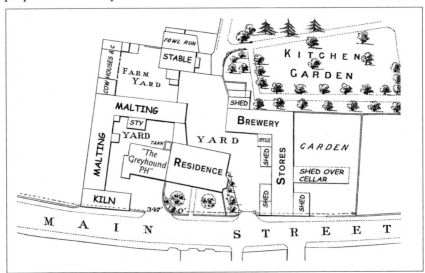

Figure 16.1 Plan of Lion Brewery (HALS)

158

Table 16.1 Lion Brewery tied estate

a) Retained in 1892			
Herts			
Bendish	*Harrow* BH 1868 #	Kimpton	*White Horse* BH
Kimpton	*Black Horse* L.	Kinsman Green	BH
	Boot FL 1841*#	Marford	*Nelson* FL 1836 #
	Goat BH, L.	Whitwell	*Fox* BH #
	Greyhound BH		
Beds			
Eggington	*Plough* L	Slip End	*Shepherd's Crook* BH, L
b) Disposed before 1892			
Herts			
Amwell	*Red Cow* 1841*	Pirton	*White Horse* 1841–80*
Hitchin	OL Queen St 1874		
Beds			
Barton	*Sow and Pigs* 1872	Luton	*Volunteer* BH 1872
Kemsworth	*Packhorse* 1843–76	Toddington	*Fancot Arms* L.

Key: * Bought in 1841 at Marshall and Pierson's Brewery sale
Bought by Pryor, Reid & Co. in 1892

Hitchin in 1841 followed by a few other purchases and leases. The tied estate would appear to have reached its maximum size about 1880. After this time single properties would seem to have been sold or leases not renewed. In some cases this may have been due to the Kingsley family having re-occurring financial problems which were solved by selling a tied property to another brewery.

By 1892 the brewery consisted of a three-storey brick and tile six quarter brewhouse with a nearly new copper, a mash tun, an underback, square brewing vessels, a twelve quarter malting, other buildings, stabling for six horses, a brewer's house and the *Greyhound* brewery tap. Claims were made at this time that the brewery was producing up to 1,200 barrels of beer per year. There was also a farmyard and this must have made good brewing practice extremely difficult because of potential contamination.

This brewery and tied estate was finally put up for sale in 1892 as Henry Kingsley had large debts. Pryor, Reid & Co. of Hatfield bought one public house with a full licence and three beer houses. At this time no one bought the brewery. Later when William Hornsey bought the brewery he named it the Lion Brewery. Herts Brewing Co. were the next owners who had financial problems in 1902 and again put the brewery up for sale. This company was dissolved in 1903 and the brewery finally closed in 1911 after two more owners had not been very successful.

Figure 16.2 Part of the kiln and malting from Main Street

Figure 16.3 The Brewery house and the Greyhound *(white building) from Main Street*

Afterwards, the brewery building was used by a laundry then an Art Centre, and finally was pulled down and replaced by a small housing development in the 1990s called Lion Yard. The *Greyhound* and the brewery house are now private residences. The malting has been converted for commercial use and is currently used by a hairdresser, an estate agent and a motor car repair business.

References

Hertfordshire Archives and Local Studies. a. D/EL B236 (sales details for 1858), b. D/Ery B287 (sales details for 1893), c. D/EL 5006 (sale of *Harrow*, Bendish in 1868).

Petty Sessions Licensing Records for Hertfordshire and Bedfordshire.

Poole, H. *Here for the Beer*, Watford Museum, 1984, pp.33–4.

CHAPTER SEVENTEEN

King's Langley

There were two long-established breweries in King's Langley High Street started by the Godwin and Cromack families.

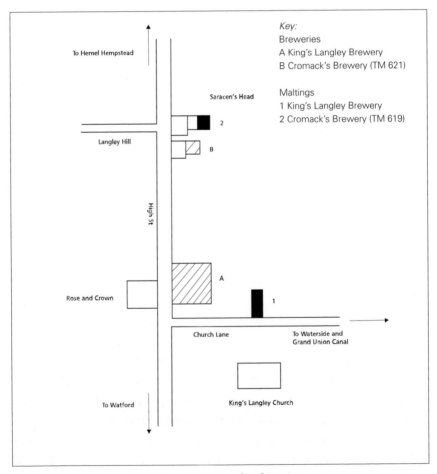

Key:
Breweries
A King's Langley Brewery
B Cromack's Brewery (TM 621)

Maltings
1 King's Langley Brewery
2 Cromack's Brewery (TM 619)

To Hemel Hempstead

Saracen's Head

Langley Hill

High St

Rose and Crown

Church Lane

To Waterside and Grand Union Canal

To Watford

King's Langley Church

Figure 17.1 Brewery and malting sites

Table 17.1 King's Langley Brewery tied estate

a) Bought by Benskin's in 1897

Herts

Abbot's Langley	*Compasses* F.	King's Langley	*Rose and Crown* F. 1838
Apsley End	*Fountain* FL, F.	Leverstock Green	*Crabtree* BH, F.
Bovingdon	*Royal Oak* BH, L.	London Colney	*White Lion* L., C. 1844
Boxmoor	*Fishery Inn* L.	Markyate	*Green Man* F.
Bricket Wood	*Fox* BH, L.	Nash Mills, H.H.	*Three Crowns* BH, F.
Bucks Hill	*Rose and Crown* F. 1765	Piccotts End, H.H.	*Crown* BH, F.
Bushey	*White Horse* F. 1756	St Albans	*Pineapple* BH, L. 1836
Chipperfield	*Royal Oak* BH, C.		*Post Boy* F. 1841
Flamstead	*Bell* F. 1853	Saratt	*Plough* F.
	Wheatsheaf C.		*Red Lion* F. 1840
King's Langley	*Boatman* BH, F.	Two Waters, Apsley	*Albion* BH, F.
	Eagle FL, F. 1779		*Boot* F. 1765
	Old Palace BH, F. 1843	Watford	*King's Arms* BH, F.

Beds

Dunstable	*Shoulder of Mutton* F.	Kemsworth	*Half Moon* F.
Edlesborough	*Bell* F. 1853	Tottenhoe	*Duke's Head* L.

Bucks

Chesham	*New Inn* BH, F.	Ivinghoe	*Raven* C.

b) Disposed before 1897

Herts

Bovingdon	*Friend at Hand* BH 1876	Piccotts End, H.H.	*Cock* 1810
Bury Mill End, H.H.	*Three Horseshoes* 1783	Radlett	*Red Lion* L. 1756*
Chipperfield	*Eagle* 1779	Rickmansworth	*Vine*, Mill End 1836**
Hemel Hempstead	*Albion* BH	Trowley Bottom, Flam.	*Blue Boar* 1847
King's Langley	*Royal Oak* BH 1876		

Key: * Sold separately to main sale in 1897
** Sold to Wild's of Rickmansworth
H.H. Hemel Hempstead
Flam. Flamstead

King's Langley Brewery

The Godwin family are reputed to have started brewing in 1720. Mordecai and Henry Godwin were buying and leasing inns between 1740 and the 1760s. They leased the *Red Lion* at Radlett in 1756 and bought the *White Horse* at Bushey in 1756, the *Rose and Crown* at Bucks Hill in 1765 and the *Boot* at Two Waters in 1767. Unfortunately Mordecai Godwin was the last male member of the family. When he died *c*.1766, the brewery was bequeathed to his daughter Sarah, who had married Thomas Groome before 1765. Thomas took over the management of the brewery. He was succeeded in turn by his son Thomas Godwin Groome, grandson John Andrew Groome (1837 to 1864), great-grandson Henry Abbott Groome during 1865 and finally John Edward Groome. By 1803 the Groomes owned eight public houses and a brewhouse.

Table 17.2 Cromack's Brewery tied estate

Herts		Year acquired
Bovingdon	Bell	1838
King's Langley	Red Lion, Waterside	Possibly 1820
	Saracen's Head	1790
Leverstock Green	Plough	Possibly 1843, definitely by 1851
	Red Lion	Possibly 1820
Nash Mills, Hemel Hempstead	George and Dragon	

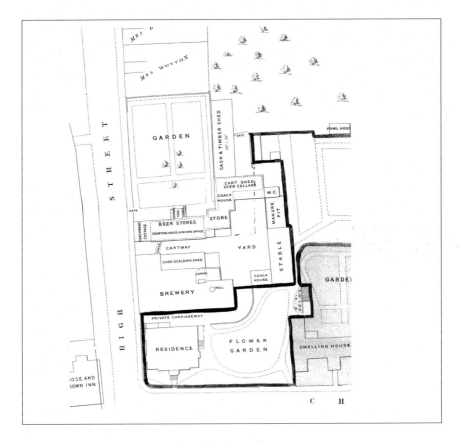

Figure 17.2 Plan of King's Langley Brewery in 1897

The original site of the King's Langley Brewery was behind the *Boot* at Two
Waters, Apsley, near the Grand Union Canal (Richmond and Turton, 1990). In
1826 a purpose-built brewery was constructed on tithe plot 631 on the corner of
the High Street and Church Lane in King's Langley. A fifteen quarter malting
was built at the same time in Church Lane on tithe plot 630 opposite the village
church and next to the Rev. John Butt's vicarage.

At the same time the Groomes increased their tied estate, which was a

Figure 17.3 King's Langley Brewery malting in Church Lane

mixture of freehold, leasehold and copyhold properties. Most were in Hertfordshire together with a few in Bedfordshire and Buckinghamshire. Identified disposals are given in Table 17.1. When John Edward Groome decided to retire in 1897, he had no sons to take over the brewery and put it up for sale by auction on 18 October 1897.

By this time the brewery contained a copper of forty barrels' capacity, a liquor back of thirty barrels' capacity, a ten quarter mash tun, five fermenting vessels with a total capacity of 200 barrels plus a cooler, a refrigerator and a deep well. Sales were 4,500 barrels of beer per year. The other buildings included a cooper's workshop, a cask scalding shed, beer stores and cellars, offices, cask and timber stores, stabling, a cart shed, a coach house and a manure pit.

Benskin's bought the brewery and tied estate of thirty-two licensed properties for £64,000 at the auction in 1897 (Table 17.1). John Groome's wife and daughter survived him and gave the malting to the vicar and churchwardens of King's Langley to use as a church hall in 1904. More recently it has been converted and occupied by a printing company. No trace is left of the brewery complex in the High Street.

Cromack's Brewery

The 1835 tithe map of King's Langley shows one brewery in the High Street on plot 621 beside the *Saracen's Head* (plot 620) where there was a brewhouse and a

Figure 17.4 The Saracen's Head *in the High Street*

malting on tithe plot 619 behind the brewery house. Francis Cromack originally owned the brewery in 1790. Much later he left the brewery to his son Thomas. By 1820 this brewery is thought to have owned three more licensed properties plus slightly later additions in Leverstock Green and Nash Mills (Table 17.2).

The family had stopped using their brewery by 1849 and they were leasing all the tied houses except the *Plough* at Leverstock Green to the Watford Brewery (Whittingstall, Sedgwick) and later to John Lloyd of the Kingsbury Brewery in St Albans. These five properties were bought by Weller's of Amersham in 1876 and afterwards became part of Benskin's of Watford tied estate when they bought Weller's in 1929. The *Plough* at Leverstock Green which may have been owned separately by other members of the Cromack family, was sold to Bennett's of Dunstable in 1901. Now all that is left of Cromack's small brewery is the brewery house besides the *Saracen's Head* in King's Langley. Both the brewhouse and the malting have long since been pulled down.

References

Hertfordshire Archives and Local Studies. a. D/Els/B436 (Groome), b. D/E/Be T1 (Cromack), c. Acc 3883, Box 12. Volumes of *Pennant*.
Petty Sessions Licensing Records for Hertfordshire, Bedfordshire and Buckinghamshire.
Poole, H. *Here for the Beer*, Watford Museum, 1984, pp.34–5.
Richmond, L. and Turton, A. (eds.). *The Brewing Industry: A Guide to Historical Records*, Manchester University Press, 1990, p.161.

CHAPTER EIGHTEEN

Little Hadham

The *Nag's Head* at Hadham Ford was licensed as a beer house from 1735 to 1781 and re-licensed in 1862.

In the early 1860s a small four-storey brewery was built beside the beer house. It had a malt crusher, three iron liquor tanks, a four and a half quarter mash tun, a ten barrel copper, an underback, two wooden coolers and four fermentation vessels plus piping for cooling. The ancillary buildings included hop and malt stores, beer and small beer stores, a cask store, a three-stall stable and hay and corn lofts.

Shortly after the brewery was built George Felstead leased it to George Stracey who later bought it. George Stracey brewed there until 1892 when he sold the part freehold and part copyhold property to Andrew Lawson and Mr Drake. They sold the *Nag's Head* and the brewery to Rayment's in 1912.

References

Hertfordshire Archives and Local Studies. E1187 (details of 1892 sale).

Jolliffe, G. and Jones, A. *Hertfordshire Inns & Public Houses: An historical gazetteer,* Hertfordshire Publications, Hatfield, 1995, pp.55, 57.

Poole, H. *Here for the Beer*, Watford Museum, 1985, p.37.

CHAPTER NINETEEN

Markyate

At least three small breweries were active in the village in the 1800s. Pickford Hill Brewery at 25-27 Pickford Hill was reputed to have started in the 1700s. During the 1830s, this business belonged to Mary Griffith and James Pearman was the brewer. He was replaced later by Albert Rowley and Thomas Parslow. At no. 27 there is still a very long cellar and a deep well.

Later Albert Rowley and his son A.W. Rowley owned the Lion Brewery at 8 Albert Square from the 1850s to 1890. This was a small brewery with a boiler house, a malting, an office and stables. They brewed up to nine beers for sale to the public. In 1859 their beers included XXXX Old, XXX Old, XX Old, X Old, Pale Ale and Porter Table Ale. By 1877 their beers were XXX, XX Mild, XXB bottled B (dinner wine), BK, Pale Ale, Double Stout, XX, Single Stout and Porter. Their only tied property was the *Three Horseshoes* in Markyate in the 1870s.

During the 1850s Robert Shemelds was a brewer and maltster at 11 High Street. He owned a small brewery, a malting, a barn and stables. All the buildings were thatched.

References

Markyate Local History Society. *The Book of Markyate*, Halsgrove, 2002.
Poole, H. *Here for the Beer*, Watford Museum, 1984.

CHAPTER TWENTY

Puckeridge

A small brewery was built in Puckeridge High Street in the 1880s and closed in 1907. It was owned by Matthew Fleming before 1886 and by Chapman & Co. afterwards. In 1898 there was a timber and tile brewhouse with a tiled fermenting room, plus a steam plant, a copper, a beer store, a sugar store, a cellar, a mineral water plant and stabling for five horses. There was also a dwelling house and an off-licence. The off-licence was later converted to a beer house and sold to McMullen's in the 1920s.

Reference

Hertfordshire Archives and Local Studies. a. D/Elc B19 (sale in 1898).

CHAPTER TWENTY-ONE

Redbourn

There were evidently a number of active maltsters in Redbourn in the 1600s. However it was the passing coach trade on the High Street (Watling Street) which probably stimulated some of the innkeepers in the early 1800s to brew their own beer. Robert House brewed at the *Bull* in 1854 and James Hawkes and J. Puddephat were active elsewhere in the village (Featherstone, 2001). However the Redbourn Brewery was the one with a tied estate.

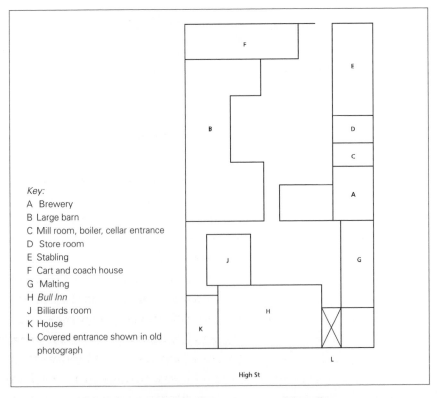

Figure 21.1 Plan of Redbourn Brewery and the Bull Inn

Table 21.1 Redbourn Brewery tied and leased estate

Herts		Original and later ownership if known
Bendish	*Woodman* BH	Leased from the Earl of Strathmore
		Later sold to Bennett
Flamstead	*Horse and Groom* BH	Later sold to Bennett
Harpenden	*Leather Bottle* BH*	Leased from Bowes Lyon family
		Later sold to Bennett
Markyate	*Bull and Butcher* BH*	Leased from Hon. Bowes Lyon
		Later sold to Green of Luton
	Horse and Groom BH	Edwards, later sold to Bennett and
	(*Sportsman*)	to Adey & White
Offley	*Bull* BH*	Leased from the Earl of Strathmore
		Later sold to Bennett
Redbourn	*Bull* FL*	Leased from the Lady Bowes Lyon
		Later sold to McMullen
	Lark BH*	Later sold to Green of Luton
	Punch Bowl FL*	Later sold to the Kingsbury Brewery
St Albans	*Crystal Palace* FL*	Later sold to Benskin's
	Hope BH*	Later sold to Benskin's
	Spotted Bull BH	Edwards, later sold to Bennett
		and to Adey & White
St Paul's Walden	*Strathmore Arms* BH	Leased from the Earl of Strathmore
		Later sold to Bennett
Beds		
Eaton Bray	*Victoria* BH	Owned by Bennett family
		Later leased by Adey & White
Luton	*Blue Lion* FL*	Leased from Lady Glamis
		Later sold to Bennett
	Duke of Cambridge BH*	Leased from Bowes Lyon family
	Later became OL	to Bennett
Studham	OL no name	Leased from Lady Glamis

Key: * These were all advertised for sale in the *Herts Advertiser* on 1 May 1897 on instruction from the Hon. F. Bowes Lyon

Redbourn Brewery

Thomas and John Edwards established a small five quarter brewery behind the *Bull* in the High Street in 1866 employing three other men. Some of the buildings may already have been there and adapted for brewing. A major part of the brewery tied estate in Hertfordshire and Bedfordshire was created by leasing public houses and beer houses from members of the Bowes Lyon family, whose main residence still is at St Paul's Walden, south of Hitchin. Some other members of the Bowes Lyon family lived in Redbourn in the 1800s. The Edwards brothers independently bought the *Horse and Groom* at Markyate and the *Spotted Bull* at St Albans. The brewery also increased its beer sales by supplying local family customers with ale and porter at 1 shilling per gallon and XXX strong ale at 1s 6d per gallon. The Edwards operated the brewery for twelve years until 1878.

In 1879 the brewery and the tied estate were leased for £360 a year on a long lease until 1900 by the brewer Benjamin Bennett of Dunstable (see also the Dunstable chapter). He also bought the *Horse and Groom* at Flamstead and the *Victoria* at Eaton Bray in Bedfordshire. He appears to have used the brewery for part of the time as a depot.

However, in 1897 the brewery and tied estate were auctioned on the instructions of the Bowes Lyon family. The 1897 sales document stated that there was a brewhouse, a boiler house, a mill room and a storeroom, a malting and kiln, a cooperage, a coach house and stabling for ten horses.

The public houses and beer houses were sold to Bennett, Pryor, Reid & Co. of Hatfield, Green's of Luton, the Kingsbury Brewery of St Albans and Healey's of Watford. The *Bull* at Redbourn was sold slightly later to McMullen's of Hertford. Unfortunately no buyer could be found for the brewery. There are now no traces of the brewery or associated buildings behind the *Bull*.

In the 1897 sale the *Bull* at Offley which had not formed part of the leasing package with the Redbourn Brewery was sold to Bennett's and the *Holly Bush* at Potters Crouch was sold to T. & J. Nash of Chesham.

References

Featherstone, A. *Redbourn's History*, Redbourn Books, 2001, p.163.
Herts Advertiser, 1 May 1897, sale advertisement for Redbourn Brewery.
Petty Sessions Licensing Records for Hertfordshire and Bedfordshire.
Poole, H. *Here for the Beer*, Watford Museum, 1984, p.40.

CHAPTER TWENTY-TWO

Rickmansworth

There have been two breweries in Rickmansworth started and owned by the Salter and Wild families plus a number of brewhouses attached to some of the old inns and one of the farms.

Salter & Co.

The Salter family established a brewery in Rickmansworth and this remained an active family business until being taken over in 1924. Members of the family are thought to have been brewers in the 1600s. Samuel Salter I had bought the *Coach and Horses* in Rickmansworth High Street by 1741 and possibly the *Angel* at Watford in 1750. He died in 1750 and was succeeded by his son Stephen Salter who began to build up a tied estate within a fifteen-mile radius of the brewery. His early purchases included the *Green Man* and the *White Hart* at Bushey, the *Black Horse* at Chorley Wood, the *Red Lion* at Elstree, the *Three Blackbirds* at Hemel Hempstead, the *Cross* at Maple Cross, the *Feathers* and the *Rose and Crown* (Mill End) at Rickmansworth, the *White Horse* at Watford, the *Green Man* at Sparrow's Hearn in Buckinghamshire and the *White Hart* at Edgware. During the time he was the brewery owner he was probably responsible for initiating the building of the brewery and the malting at the east end of the High Street (Figure 22.1.) The brewery also owned a malting on the east side of Watford High Street opposite the *Maidenhead* before 1840.

Stephen Salter died in 1795 and was succeeded by his nephew Samuel Salter II, who paid for the construction of a short branch off the Grand Junction Canal which had been constructed as far as Rickmansworth in 1796. A wharf at the end of the branch canal was only 400 yards from the brewery. The canal may have been used to transport beer into London or for the transport of barley or malt. In 1803 Samuel II's daughter Sarah married William Capel, the vicar of St Mary's, Watford.

Samuel increased the size of the tied estate particularly in Bushey, Rickmansworth, Watford and the nearby towns and villages. He also entered into a partnership with Job Woodman, a brewer from Watford, in 1820 and later had Thomas Fellowes as a partner. In 1829 when Samuel II died, Thomas Fellowes became a trustee to look after Samuel's share of the brewery on behalf of his wife Jane, his daughter Sarah Capel and her son William Capel. Samuel II also gave instructions in his will that a barrel of free beer should be placed outside the brewery for the benefit of local townspeople and travellers. Unfortunately this philanthropic action regularly led to disturbances and was eventually stopped in 1857.

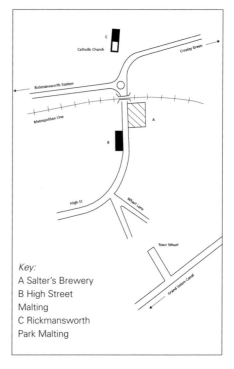

Figure 22.1 Brewery and malting sites

William Capel joined Thomas Fellowes in management of the brewery which continued to be known as Salter & Co. Thomas died in 1858 and his son Harvey Fellowes was eventually appointed manager on behalf of the Salter family trust. The brewery buildings were enlarged in 1887 and a second malting was built before 1896 on the north side of the Metropolitan Railway line.

Salter & Co. became a limited company in the late 1800s and much later in 1924 it was sold with seventy-six public houses to the Cannon Brewery of Clerkenwell. It only has been possible to identify from available records sixty-four of these licensed properties, of this total, forty-five were in Hertfordshire, thirteen in Buckinghamshire and six in Middlesex (now Greater London). More research is needed to identify the remaining twelve properties that were probably in Middlesex or Buckinghamshire. The disposals before 1924 are listed in Table 20.2. Brewing stopped immediately after the sale and the buildings were used later by Adco Ltd who were fertiliser manufacturers. The old brewery buildings were demolished in 1970 and an office block was built on the site. The original malting was used in turn by a photographic film manufacturer, a winery

Table 22.1 Salter's known tied estate sold to Cannon Brewery in 1924

Herts

Abbot's Langley	*King's Head* 1808	Rickmansworth	*Cart and Horses* 1838
Bovingdon	*Bull* 1802		*Coach and Horses* 1741
Bushey	*Queen's Arms* 1798		*Feathers (Cock)* 1780
	Red Lion 1799		*Fisherman*
	White Hart 1782		*Fox and Hounds*
Chorley Wood	*Black Horse* 1772		*George and Dragon*
	Gate		*Golden Cross*
	White Horse 1838		*Green Man* 1838
Croxley Green	*Coach and Horses*		*Halfway House*
	Fox and Hounds		*Rose and Crown** 1767
Elstree	*Green Dragon*		*Rose and Crown***
	Red Lion 1786		*Victoria Hotel* #
Flaunden	*Green Dragon* 1838		*Whip and Collar* 1838
Hemel Hempstead	*Bell* 1843		*White Bear* 1838
	Fountain 1843	St Albans	*King Harry* 1848
	Three Blackbirds 1783		*King William IV* 1900
	White Horse	Sarratt	*Boot* 1840
Hunton Bridge	*King's Head* 1874		*Cock* 1800
Maple Cross	*Cross* 1770	Shenley	*Black Lion* 1840
Northchurch	*Old Grey Mare* 1840	Watford	*Angel* 1750
	White Horse		*Essex Arms*
Radlett	*Railway Inn* ##		*Three Horseshoes*
			Wheatsheaf

Bucks

Beaconsfield	*George*	Chesham	*King's Arms*
Chalfont St Giles	*Crown*		*Swan*, Ley Hill *c.*1820
Chalfont St Peter	*White Hart c.*1820		*Waggon and Horses*
Chesham	*Cock c.*1820	Little Chalfont	*Sugar Loaves*
	*Crown c.*1820	Seer Green	*Three Horseshoes c.*1900
	George and Dragon	Sparrows Green	*Green Man* 1773
	Hen and Chickens		

Greater London

Edgware	*Boot* 1873	Pinner	*George*
Little Stanmore	*White Hart*	Pinner Common	*Bell*
Northwood	*True Lovers' Knot*	Uxbridge	*Three Tuns*

Key: * Mill End
          ** Woodcock Hill
          # Licence transferred from *Sugar Loaves* in 1888
          ## Was previously the *Cross Keys*

and Reckitt & Colman. The newer malting now forms an ancillary part of the local Catholic church.

Wild's Brewery

A smaller brewery was established *c.*1870 in Mill End by Thomas Wild on a site opposite Mill End Farm, between the main road and the River Chess, with a

Table 22.2 Salter's tied estate disposed before 1924

Herts

Berkhamsted	*Red Lion* OL to 1876	Rickmansworth	*Prince of Wales** to 1912
Bushey	*Green Man* 1770 to 1840		*Prince of Wales*** to 1923
	Royal Oak		*Queen's Head* 1838 to 1911
Chorley Wood	*Finchs Arms* 1800		*Red House*
Croxley Green	*Green Man*		*Royal Oak*
Elstree	*Farmer's Boy*		*Sugar Loaf* # to 1888
Hemel Hempstead	*Bull* Two Waters		*White Horse* 1838
	Lamb 1876	Watford	*Angel* to 1903
	Royal Oak BH		*Chequers* 1844 to *c.*1865*
London Colney	*Swan* before 1844		*Chequers* Waterdell to 1900
Oxhey	*Victoria* 1850s to1877		*Essex Arms*
Rickmansworth	*Anchor and Hope* to 1903		*King's Arms* 1852
	Bear 1795		*Maidenhead* 1844
	Chequers to 1911		*True Blue c.*1840 to 1914
	Finches 1838		*Victoria* BH to 1877
	Mines Royal Arms 1838		*White Horse* 1762 to 1838

Bucks

Amersham	*King's Arms*	Chesham	*Royal Oak*
Beaconsfield	*Elm Tree*		*Three Tuns*
	Old Hare	Langley Marsh	*Three Horseshoes* L.
Chalfont St Giles	*Three Sugar Loaves*	Sparrows Hearn	*Green Man* 1773
Chesham	*One Star*	Wooburn	*Royal Oak* closed in 1912
	Punch Bowl		

Greater London

Edgware	*George* L. 1873	Ruislip	*Old Bell*
	White Hart 1762		*Old Swan*

Key: * High Street
      ** Woodcock Hill
      # Licence transferred 1888

tannery to the west and a paper mill to the east. Members of the Wild family were already farming in this locality. The relevant Petty Sessions licensing records indicate that this brewery had a small tied estate of approximately ten to twelve owned or leased properties in Bushey, Chorley Wood, Oxhey, Rickmansworth and Watford, and for a short while it leased the *Fox and Hounds* at Chalfont St Giles (Table 22.3).

The *Vine* at Mill End served as the brewery tap. When the brewery was finally sold to Sedgwick's of Watford in 1900 there were six public houses but Sedgwick's already had obtained three more in earlier sales after 1874. Both Benskin's and Healey's of Watford also previously had purchased other public houses. The brewery site was used later by the Royal Herts Laundry.

Table 22.3 Wild's tied estate

a) Sold to Sedgwick's after 1891	
Herts	Notes
Chorley Wood	Jolly Brickmakers
	Old Shepherd
Rickmansworth	Horseshoes
	Red House, Two Hatches
	Vine, Mill End
	Halfway House, Cassio Bridge *
b) Disposed before 1891	
Herts	
Bushey	Live and Let Live BH – c.1855 to c.1874 when pulled down
	Swan BH – lease transferred to Benskin's in 1887
Oxhey	Royal Oak – from 1860s, sold to Sedgwick's after 1874
Rickmansworth	Western Inn – sold to Healey's after 1874
Watford	Bedford Arms – sold to Mr Kemp of Watford
	Golden Lion – sold to Benskin's after 1874
	Oddfellows' Arms – sold to Sedgwick's after 1874
	Royal Oak – sold to Sedgwick's after 1874
Bucks	
Chalfont St Giles	Fox and Hounds BH – lease in 1867
Key:	* Leased from the Grand Union Canal Company and later bought

Other small breweries and brewhouses

The *Swan Hotel* in the High Street had its own brewhouse until 1820. The 1838 tithe map shows that Richard Biggs had a brewhouse at Horn Hill Farm, north west of Rickmansworth and the *Bell* beer house on the side of the road by his drive entrance. At this time King's College, Cambridge was the landlord of a malting at Troy Farm.

References

Arnold, D.R. The day they burned down the maltings, *Rickmansworth Historian*, Vol. 33, 1977, pp.836–7.

Hertfordshire Archives and Local Studies. a. Tithe Map of Rickmansworth 1838.

Jacques, A. and C. *Rickmansworth, A Pictorial History*, Chichester, Phillimore, 1996.

Petty Sessions Licensing Records for Hertfordshire, Buckinghamshire and North London.

Poole, H. *Here for the Beer*, Watford Museum, 1984, p.41.

CHAPTER TWENTY-THREE

Royston

Royston is an ancient market town that developed around the crossing of the prehistoric Icknield Way and Ermine Street, the Roman road from London to Lincoln. In modern times these roads are better known as the A505 from Hitchin to Newmarket and the A10 from London to Huntingdon. More than fifty licensed properties are known to have existed in Royston but there were only seven left in 2000. During the 1700s at least three small breweries were being operated by Robert Phillips at the Royston Brewery, the Bedlam family and the Sharp family, to deal with the local demand for beer.

Royston Brewery

In 1725 Robert Phillips, a Quaker living in Radwell and already established as a maltster in Royston, bought land on the south side of Baldock Street for £500 from a man named Haggar and established a small brewery there (Figure 23.1). It is evident that members of the Haggar family were also Quakers. This brewery became known as the Royston Brewery and was to remain associated with the Phillips family for over 200 years. A malting was added to the brewery complex in 1759. Robert is not known to have married and when he died he left the brewery to John Phillips I. John's relationship to Robert is not known. Four more John Phillips were to be involved in the management of this brewery during the next 200 years, hence it is important to designate them by numerals to minimise confusion.

In 1720 there was also a Michael Phillips, a Quaker maltster of Royston, and another John Phillips, a Quaker yeoman living in Radwell, who were trustees for an Ashwell Quaker annuity. Unfortunately their relationship to Robert or to John Phillips is not known either.

John I died in 1786 and bequeathed the brewery to his nephew John Phillips II, the son of Thomas Phillips. He was described as a Royston brewer when he

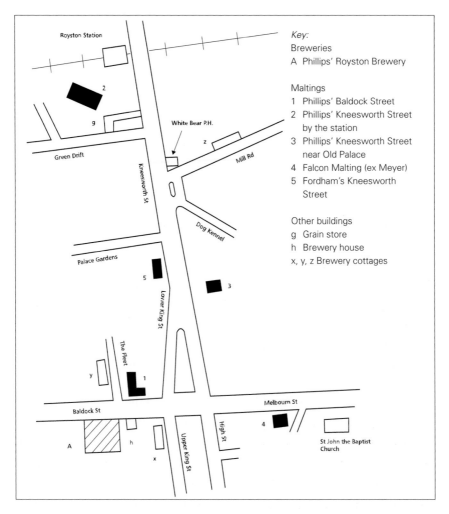

Key:
Breweries
A Phillips' Royston Brewery

Maltings
1 Phillips' Baldock Street
2 Phillips' Kneesworth Street
  by the station
3 Phillips' Kneesworth Street
  near Old Palace
4 Falcon Malting (ex Meyer)
5 Fordham's Kneesworth
  Street

Other buildings
g Grain store
h Brewery house
x, y, z Brewery cottages

Figure 23.1 Brewery and malting sites and also other brewery buildings

was appointed as a trustee for the Ashwell Quaker annuity when it was updated in 1788. John II was responsible for starting to build up the tied estate in Royston. During 1786 he bought the *Bull*, and *Coach and Horses* and the *Green Man* much later during 1803. In 1805 he bought the other rival Royston brewery and its tied estate from William Bedlam for £8,000 (Table 23.1).

John Phillips II never married and died in 1821. The brewery and tied estate were left as a bequest to two nephews, John Phillips III of Royston and John Phillips IV of Stamford. In a brewery inventory prepared by Crocket and Nash in 1825, there was a fifty quarter mash tun made from oak timbers with an ash rim and curb on joists. Additional equipment included a horse wheel, a wort engine

Table 23.1 Bedlam's tied estate and free trade

a) Tied estate sold to J. Phillips on 14 November 1805 for £8,000

Herts

Barley	Fox and Hounds C.*	Royston	Queen's Head F.
Barkway	White Horse F.		White Bear F.
Reed End	White Horse C.		White Hart F.*
Royston	Jolly Butchers C.		White Horse F.*
	Plough F.		White Lion F.

Cambs

Bassingbourn	Red Lion C.*	Melbourn	Chequers C.
Guilden Morden	Swan F. & C.	Thriplow	Gardener's Spade C.
Litlington	Seven Stars F.*		

b) Bedlam's free house trading agreements presumably transferred to J. Phillips

Herts

Buckland	Red Lion	Puckeridge	Rising Sun

Cambs

Barrington	Catherine Wheel	Shepreth	Plough*
Kingston	Chequers*	Toft	Red Lion*
Orwell	Red Lion		

Key: * Sold to Green's of Luton in 1949

and a malt mill. The other buildings mentioned were a cooper's shop, a carpenter's shop, a counting house, a granary, yeast houses and stables.

Unfortunately John Phillips III died soon afterwards in 1826 and his share of the investment in the brewery was bought by John IV. The next major project in 1829 was to rebuild the large brewery house to the east of the brewery in Baldock Street (Figure 23.2). In 1830 the brewery estate already consisted of thirty-seven tied public houses with eleven tied properties in Royston. John IV married twice and had two sons, John Phillips V (first marriage) and Joseph Edward John Phillips (second marriage) were later to become partners in the business. John IV bought a small malting at 27 Kneesworth Street from Edward Prime. He also commissioned the building of a thirty quarter malting opposite the brewery (Figure 23.3) and a sixty quarter malting with its own railway siding near Royston station *c*.1854. The larger malting had its own drive-through grain store where sacks could be hoisted direct from carts to a first-storey storage facility. In 1865 he bought from a relative, Charles Phillips, a small brewery in Newmarket with six public houses for £8,000, but by 1870 he had resold this brewery and four of the public houses. The two that were retained were possibly the *Horse and Groom* in Newmarket and the *White Horse* at Exning.

John Phillips IV died in 1871. During his ownership and the early shared management by John V and Joseph Edward John, the brewery underwent a

Figure 23.2 Phillips' Brewery house

Figure 23.3 Phillips' Baldock Street malting

Table 23.2 Meyer's tied estate taken over by Phillips in 1897

Cambs			
Barrington	Queen Victoria BH	Histon	Rose and Crown FL*
Bassingbourn	Rose FL	Kneesworth	Rose BH & W*
	Tally Ho FL	Kingston	Rose and Crown FL*
Bourn	Golden Lion FL*	Landbeach	Red Cow FL
Caldecote	Fox FL*	Litlington	Royal Oak BH*
Cambridge	Town Arms FL	Little Gransden	Chequers FL*
Caxton	Bricklayer's Arms FL*	Melbourn	Red Cow BH*
Comberton	Three Horseshoes FL*	Meldreth	British Queen FL*
Coton	Plough FL*	Orwell	Duke of Wellington FL*
Croydon	Queen Adelaide BH*		Fox and Hounds FL*
Dry Drayton	Black Horse FL*		Queen Victoria BH*
Etisley	Leeds Arms FL*		White Hart FL*
Gamlingay	Hardwicke Arms FL*	Over	Red Lion FL*
Great Gransden	Crown and Cushion FL*	Steeple Morden	Diggings BH*
	Diggings BH*		One Bell FL*
Great Wilbraham	White Swan BH*	Swaffham Prior	Black Swan FL
Hardwicke	Chequers FL*	Thriplow	Shoulder of Mutton FL
Harston	Pemberton Arms FL*	Toft	Red Lion FL*
Haslingfield	Marquis of Granby FL	Waterbeach	Jolly Anglers FL
Hauxton	Chequers FL*	Whittlesford	Village Blacksmith BH*

Herts			
Royston	Falcon FL*		

Beds			
Dunton	Three Horseshoes FL*	Potton	Rising Sun BH*

Key: * Sold to Green's of Luton in 1949

major refurbishment to increase the brewing capacity, improve the stores, cellars, other ancillary buildings and stabling. By 1894 the tied estate consisted of 118 freehold properties (fifty-six in Hertfordshire, forty-eight in Cambridgeshire, five in Essex, four in Bedfordshire, three in Huntingdonshire and two in Suffolk) and forty-three copyholds (twenty-five in Cambridgeshire, thirteen in Hertfordshire and five in Essex). In Royston, the *Bell and Anchor*, the *Black Swan*, the *Fox and Duck* and the *White Lion* had been closed in the early 1890s. The brewery also owned a number of houses, cottages, shops and many small plots of land. In Royston there were brewery workers' cottages in Baldock Street, the west side of the Fleet off Baldock Street, Upper King Street and in Mill Road by the *White Bear*.

In 1897, John V and Joseph Edward John bought Orwell Brewery in South Cambridgeshire plus forty-three public houses from Arthur Hugh Meyer and Philip Meyer. Four of these properties were in Orwell, one in Cambridge and the remainder were in other Cambridgeshire villages, except the *Falcon* in Royston and two others in Bedfordshire. This sale also included a brewery, stabling and a

Table 23.3 Tooth's tied estate taken over by Phillips in 1898

Cambs

Cambridge	Boot and Shoe FL	Linton	Crown FL*
	Clairmont FL	Longstanton	Railway Tavern FL*
	Rose and Crown FL*	Newnham	Red Bull FL*
Chatteris	George FL	Oakington	Butcher's Arms BH*
Cherry Hinton	Brookfield House FL*	Over	Admiral Vernon FL*
Cottenham	Cross Keys FL*	Soham	Cherry Tree BH
Great Shelford	De Freville Arms FL*	Trumpington	Green Man FL*
Great Wilbraham	King's Head FL*		

Key: * Sold to Green's of Luton in 1949

Table 23.4 Phillips' tied estate taken over by Green's in 1949

Herts

Anstey	Castle FL	Reed	Cabinet FL, C.
Aston	Pig and Whistle (Boot) FL		Red Lion FL
Barley	Fox and Hounds FL, C.	Royston	Angel FL
	Shah BH		Bull FL
	Three Crowns FL, C.		Chequers FL
	Waggon and Horses FL, C.		Coach and Horses FL
Barkway	Cross Keys FL		Eagle FL **
	Wheatsheaf FL		Falcon FL
Brent Pelham	Black Horse FL		Green Man FL
Buckland	Royal Oak FL		Hoops FL
	White Horse FL, C.		North Star FL
Buntingford	Chequers FL		White Bear FL
	George and Dragon FL		White Horse FL
Cottered	OL		William IV BH
Graveley	Waggon and Horses BH, C.		OL Mill Rd
Hertford	Nag's Head FL	Sandon	Chequers FL
Hitchin	Red Cow FL	Standon	Bay Horse FL
	Three Horseshoes FL	Therfield	Fox and Duck FL, C.
Hoddesdon	Duncombe Arms BH		Red Lion FL, C.
Kelshall	Crown FL, C.	Wadesmill	Anchor FL
Meesden	Fox FL	Ware	Albion BH
Munden, Great	Three Horseshoes FL		

Cambs

Abington	Princess of Wales FL	Histon	Rose and Crown FL
Barrington	Royal Oak FL		William IV BH & W
Bassingbourn	Black Bull FL, C.	Ickleton	Greyhound FL
	Carpenters' Arms BH		Jolly Butchers BH, C.
	Red Lion FL, C.	Kingston	Chequers FL, C.
Bourn	Golden Lion FL		Rose and Crown FL
Burwell	Bushel BH	Kneesworth	Red Lion BH
Caldecote	Fox FL		Rose BH & W
Cambridge	Rose and Crown FL	Linton	Crown FL
Caxton	Bricklayer's Arms FL	Little Eversden	Plough FL
Cherry Hinton	Brookfield House FL	Little Gransden	Chequers FL
Chishill	White Horse FL	Little Shelford	Prince Regent FL
Comberton	Three Horseshoes FL	Litlington	Royal Oak BH
Coton	Plough FL		Seven Stars FL
Cottenham	Cross Keys FL	Longstanton	Railway Tavern FL

Croydon	Axe and Compasses FL	Melbourn	Carriers' Arms BH
	Queen Adelaide BH		Red Cow BH
Dry Drayton	Black Horse FL		Rose FL
Duxford	Plough FL	Meldreth	British Queen FL
Elsworth	Fox and Hounds FL		Railway Tavern FL
Etisley	Leeds Arms FL	Milton	Waggon and Horses FL
Eversden	Hoops FL	Newbridge	Coach and Horses FL
	Plough FL	Newnham	Red Bull FL
Fenstanton	Woolpack FL	Newton	Queen's Head FL, C.
Fowlmere	Black Horse FL	Oakington	Butcher's Arms BH
Foxton	Black Boy FL	Orwell	Chequers FL, C.
	Railway Tavern FL		Duke of Wellington FL
Fulbourn	Assylum (Windmill) BH		Fox and Hounds FL
	Railway Tavern FL		Queen Victoria BH
	Rising Sun BH		White Hart FL
Gamlingay	Hardwicke Arms FL	Over	Admiral Vernon FL
	White Swan FL		Red Lion FL
Grantchester	Red Bull FL	Pampisford	OL
Great Gransden	Crown and Cushion FL		
	New Diggings BH	Reach	Black Swan FL, C.
Great Shelford	Black Swan FL, C.	Sawston	Greyhound FL
	De Freville Arms		Queen's Head FL
	Greyhound FL, C.	Shepreth	Plough FL
Great Wilbraham	King's Head FL		Railway Tavern FL
	White Swan BH	Stapleford	Rose FL, C.
Hardwicke	Chequers FL	Steeple Morden	Diggings BH
Harlton	Hare and Hounds FL		One Bell FL
Harston	Pemberton Arms FL	Swaffham Bulbeck	Black Horse FL
Haslingfield	Jolly Brewers BH	Thriplow	Green Man FL, C.
	Marquis of Granby FL	Toft	Red Lion FL
	Waggon and Horses FL	Trumpington	Green Man FL
Hauxton	Chequers FL		Red Lion FL, C.
	King's Head FL	Whaddon	Queen Adelaide BH, C.
Heydon	King William IV FL	Waddon Gap	Waggon and Horses BH
Hilton	Prince of Wales BH	Whittlesford	Exhibition BH*
Hinxton	Red Lion FL		Railway Tavern BH
	Village Blacksmith BH		

Essex			
Berden	King's Head BH, C.	Duddenhoe End	Woodman FL
Chishill	Red Cow FL	Widdington	William the Conqueror
Clavering	White Swan BH, C.		BH

Beds			
Dunton	Three Horseshoes FL	Potton	Rising Sun BH

Suffolk			
Exning	White Horse FL		

Key: * Bees in the Wall
        ** Originally in the parish of Barkway

malting in Orwell. A limited company, J. & J.E. Phillips Ltd. with a capital of £140,000 was created in 1897 to finance this purchase. The six company directors were John Phillips V, Joseph Edward Phillips, John Robert Phillips

(John V's son), James Jarvis and James Edward Jarvis, also Arthur Hugh Meyer. The *Falcon* in Melbourn Street, Royston had a malting that was later converted into three cottages. This building conversion was reported to the local licensing magistrates because these three private dwellings had their entrances in the public house yard. Two years later in 1899, the company bought Alexander Frederick Tooth's Wootens Brewery in Castle Street, Cambridge and fifteen tied houses for £29,000. In both these purchases the majority of the tied houses had full licences. Later documents belonging to the Whitbread archives show that these two tied estates were always identified separately as Meyer's and Tooth's tied houses in the Phillips' estate until the brewery was sold to Green's of Luton in 1949 (Tables 23.2 and 23.3).

By 1909, the brewery had sixty staff and controlled 153 freehold and fifty-seven copyhold properties. During that year in August, sparks from a stray piece of flint in the malt grist mill started a major fire at the brewery. In spite of prompt action by the works staff and the local fire brigade there was considerable damage to parts of the brewery. Until brewing could be restarted, beer for the tied estate was obtained from an unnamed source, possibly Simpson's brewery in Baldock, and transported to the brewery by a traction engine with three waggons. The Simpsons were related to the Phillips family and the two families had a long-standing agreement never to buy licensed properties in each other's hometown. Joseph Edward John Phillips died in 1910 but John Phillips V lived another fifteen years, dying at the age of ninety.

During the 1930s, the directors of the company began to realise that many of the tied public houses in the rural parts of North East Hertfordshire and South Cambridgeshire had relatively low beer sales giving poor economic returns. Negotiations for an amalgamation or sale were made to other local breweries but without any success. Finally in 1949, J.W. Green Ltd of Luton bought all the Ordinary and Preference shares and therefore obtained control of the Company. The estate included the brewery, 151 public houses and beer houses (Table 23.4).

This sale included thirty-four properties from Meyer's tied estate and eleven from Tooth's tied estate. There were also the thirty and sixty quarter maltings plus a number of shops, houses, land, etc. Lt. Col. H.P.J. Phillips and Maj. E.G.M. Phillips subsequently joined the board of directors of J.W. Green. The brewery in Baldock Street was closed in 1950. A study of the appropriate Petty Sessions licensing records indicates that approximately another fifty of the former Phillips estate with low sales and needing major structural changes such

Table 23.5 Phillips' disposals before takeover by Green's in 1949

Herts

Ashwell	Bull's Head FL	Puckeridge	White Hart
	Cat FL	Royston	Bell and Anchor BH
	New Found Out BH		Black Horse FL
	Slip Inn		Black Swan BH
	Waggon and Horses BH		Catherine Wheel
Aspenden	Red Lion FL		Crown
Barley	BH		Crown and Anchor FL
	Woolpack BH, C.		Crown and Dolphin FL
Barkway	Bell FL		Fox and Duck BH
	Swan FL		Griffin
	White Horse FL		Plough BH
Braughing	Bird in Hand FL		Prince of Wales BH
Buckland	Chequers FL		Robin Hood BH
	Royal Oak		Sun FL
Buntingford	Black Bull FL		Three Horseshoes BH
	George and Dragon FL		Three Jolly Butchers
	Railway (Shah of Persia)		White Hart FL
Clothall	Barley Mow		White Lion
Furneux Pelham	Yew Tree FL		OL Gas House Rd
Great Munden	Three Horseshoes FL		OL Market Hill
Hertford	Victoria BH	Sandon	Carrier BH
Hitchin	Britannia BH	Therfield	Buffalo's Head BH
	Duke of Wellington BH, C.		Cricketer's Arms
Hoddesdon	Sun		White Horse, Reed End
Hornmead, Great	Bell FL		Yorkshire Grey BH
	Swan FL, C.	Ware	Royston Crow FL
Kelshall	Welsh Harp FL	Westmill	BH
Langley	Bell BH	Weston	Swan BH, C.
Nuthampstead	Bell FL		

Beds

Potton	Bell BH	Potton	King's Head BH
	Cock BH	Wrestlingworth	King's Hussar BH
	William IV BH		

Cambs

Barrington	Boot and Shoe FL	Guilden Morden	Black Swan FL, C.
	Catherine Wheel FL	Hardwicke	Rose and Crown
	Queen Victoria	Harston	White Swan FL
Bassingbourn	Axe and Compasses BH, C.	Kneesworth	Red Lion BH
	Boys Bridge BH	Landbeach	Red Cow FL
	Hoops BH	Linton	George and Dragon BH, C.
	John O'Gaunt BH, C.	Little Shelford	Carrier's Cart BH
	Rose BH		Three Horseshoes FL
	Tally Ho BH	Litlington	Chestnut Tree BH
	Yew Tree BH, C.	Longstowe	Fox
Bourn	Cock and Bottle BH	Madingley	Three Horseshoes L.
	Duke of Wellington	Melbourn	Chequers
Cambridge	Bell and Crown FL		Coach and Horses FL
	Boot and Shoe FL		Elm Tree BH
	Brewery Tap Magdalen St		Hoops FL
	Bushel and Strike		Tailor's Arms BH, C.
	Clairmont FL	Meldreth	Bell FL, C.

	King's Head BH		*Green Man* BH, C.
	Little Rose BH		*Queen Adelaide* FL
	Osborne Arms FL	Orwell	*Old English Gentleman* BH
	Tally Ho BH		*Red Lion*
	Town Arms FL	Shepreth	*Green Man*
	Three Tuns FL	Soham	*Cherry Tree* BH
	Waggon and Horses FL	Stapleford	*Hammer and Anvil* BH
	OL Castle St	Steeple Morden	*Hoops* BH
Chatteris	*George* FL		*Little Wonder* BH, C.
Comberton	*Plough* BH, C.	Swaffham Prior	*Black Swan* FL
Croydon	OL	Thriplow	*Fox under the Hill* FL
Duxford	*Butcher's Arms* BH		*Gardener's Spade*
	King's Head FL, C.		*Shoulder of Mutton* FL
Fowlmere	*Shoulder of Mutton*	Trumpington	*Coach and Horses* L.
	Swan House Inn FL		*Green Man*
Fulbourn	*Royal Oak* BH		*Red Lion* FL, C.
Gamlingay	*Dolphin* FL	Waterbeach	*Jolly Anglers* FL
Great Eversden	*Fox and Duck*	Whittlesford	*Waggon and Horses* BH
Great Gransden	*William IV* BH		

Essex

Arkesden	*Ancient Shepherd* BH, C.	Clavering	*Bleak Lodge* BH, C.
	Red Cow FL		*Swan* BH
	Woodman BH	Heydon	*William IV* FL
Chesterford	*Horseshoes* BH, C.	Widdington	*William the Conqueror*

Suffolk

Newmarket	*Horse and Groom* FL

as water-flushed toilets, etc. were later closed and sold to be used as private dwellings by Green's, Flowers and Whitbread. Details of the tied property disposals before the sale in 1949 are summarised in Table 23.5.

The brewery buildings were initially sold to a sweet manufacturer who adapted them without making any major changes. Later the site was cleared and is at present occupied by a supermarket. The brewery house together with the thirty quarter and sixty quarter maltings plus the grain store still remain although all are now used for other purposes and the malting in Kneesworth St has been converted to a house.

Bedlam's Brewery

In 1776 Joseph Bedlam leased a property in Icknield Street, Royston which had a house, outhouses, a malting, barns, stables, etc., but there was no mention of a brewhouse. When William Bedlam sold the tied estate in 1805 to the Phillips family it included seven inns in Royston, three in local Hertfordshire villages and five in South Cambridgeshire villages. There were also another seven free houses (volunteers) with trade agreements to buy Bedlam's beers (Table 23.1).

This sale did not include leases for the *Talbot* in Royston or the *Adam and Eve* at Buntingford or for any brewery horses. Cash book records show that William Bedlam sold beer directly to the local gentry.

Sharp's Brewery

In the 1740s Jane Sharp was the owner of Quern House in Upper King Street, that had a yard containing a barn and a malting next to the Market Place. She also owned a brewhouse, a barn, a stable, a shop and a well that were leased to William Mans. She stipulated in her will in 1750 that her daughter, Susannah Sharp should have joint use of the brewhouse and the well. This is possibly one known example of a number of other small-scale breweries in the town that did not get much larger or remain in business for very long.

References

Cornell, M. Phillips' Royston Brewery. *The Brewery History Society Journal*, No. 49, pp.6–12.

Crocket and Nash's 1825 Inventory. A brief summary in *Brewery History Society Newsletter*, No. 20, 2000, p.26.

Flood, B. Personal communication about Meyer's and Tooth's tied estates in Cambridgeshire.

Hertfordshire Archives and Local Studies. a. D/EB 650 T12 (Bedlam's Brewery tied estate sale), b. Herts and Cambridge Reporter 14 August 1909 (Brewery fire), c. Acc. 3682. Box 5 (Details of Phillips', Meyer's and Tooth's tied estates that were sold or closed) and J. & J.E. Phillips' trade for year ending December 1948 for tied estate, e. 81801 (Sharp's brewery).

Jones, A. (ed.) *Royston Inns and Public Houses*, Royston and District Local History Society, 1990.

Kingston, A. *A History of Royston*, Royston, Warren Bros., 1906.

Petty Sessions Licensing Records for Hertfordshire, Bedfordshire, Cambridgeshire and west Essex.

Poole, H. *Here for the Beer*, Watford Museum, 1984, p.42.

Richmond, L. and Turton, A. (eds.) *The Brewing Industry: A Guide to Historical Records*, Manchester University Press, 1990, pp.262–3.

Whitbread Archives. Deed of 1897 of Phillips' brewery, tied estate and other properties.

CHAPTER TWENTY-FOUR

St Albans

In St Albans in the 1800s the main choice of beers came from the Kingsbury, St Albans, St Peter's and Holywell breweries. The locations of these breweries and their own maltings are shown on Figure 24.1. They supplied most of the old inns and public houses either side of the London to Holyhead horse and coach route which went along the Old London Road, Sopwell Lane, Holywell Hill, the High Street, George Street, Fishpool Street and through St Michael's. Thomas Telford was responsible for the construction of the new London Road in 1825 which came above the *Peahen* at the top of Holywell Hill on the site of the *Woolpack* and left the High Street as Verulam Road between the *Great Red Lion* and the *George*. Because of this major route change, many of the old inns on Holywell Hill and in

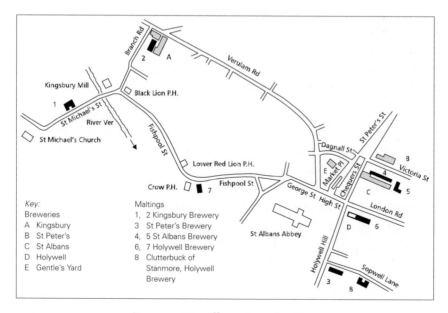

Figure 24.1 Sites of breweries and maltings

George Street and Fishpool Street lost the passing coach trade and eventually were closed. There were also other old inns in Chequer Street, the Market Place and St Peter's Street.

Kingsbury Brewery

The Kingsbury Brewery was probably started in the late 1600s by the Carter family who were succeeded by the Niccoll family. One of their descendants, Francis Carter Niccoll, who twice became mayor of St Albans, married Anne Searancke whose family owned the Hatfield Brewery. Their son, another Francis Carter Niccoll, changed his surname to Searancke in 1781 so that he could inherit the Hatfield Brewery. He owned this brewery in Hatfield in a partnership with his brother Joseph until 1815 when they sold it with a tied estate to Joseph Bigg. At this stage Francis took over the ownership of the Kingsbury Brewery and remained in charge until he died in 1835. In 1825 he was in a partnership with a Mr Seward for a lease of the *Chequers* in Stevenage owned by the Lytton family.

Before the construction of Verulam Road, it is not known where the original Kingsbury Brewery was situated in or behind Fishpool Street or any details of its brewing capacity or the full extent of the tied estate. None of the trade directories of 1820s give precise details of position or street number. It has not been possible to find any relevant information in the Benskin's archives. The Verulam Road brewery dating from *c.*1827 may have been built on the site of an earlier smaller brewery. The 1843 tithe map of Fishpool Street and St Michael's shows the replacement brewery in Verulam Road near to the corner of Branch Road. It would appear that this brewery had the capacity to brew between 250 and 300 barrels per week and a malting on the site producing thirty to fifty quarters each batch-cycle depending on its efficiency. A good description of the brewery and the brewery manager's house with five bedrooms and a plan of the whole complex at a later time including Kingsbury Lodge survives as a sale document (Figure 24.2). The Brewery Tap, the *Angel* was originally in Branch Road. However it was demolished later when the stable block for Kingsbury Lodge was built. In 1843 the brewery was still leasing another malting owned by Samuel Smith in St Michael's next to the *Rose and Crown*. This malting was later pulled down and the St Michael's parish school was built on the site.

A detailed study of various tithe maps of St Albans and local towns and villages (1840 to 1843) and other sources indicates that the early brewery tied estate in Hertfordshire included those properties given in Table 24.1.

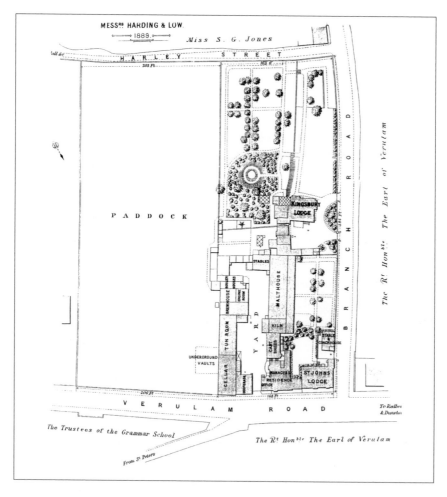

Figure 24.2 Plan of Kingsbury Brewery in 1898 (HALS)

Unfortunately no records exist for 1700 to 1798. Branch Johnson (1962) thought that all the Redbourn inns except the *Chequers,* could have been acquired by the Searancke family in the early 1800s while they were still living in Hatfield. These did not form part of the Hatfield Brewery tied estate included in the sale in 1815 to Joseph Bigg. In 1816 or slightly later the *Angel* and the *Rose and Crown* in St Michael's were probably bought from the Wykes family of St Michael's.

From 1837 to 1838 the sons Francis and Joseph Searancke, who were managing the brewery, were registered as electors in St Albans, because they owned property in Abbey Mill Lane and the High Street, but there is no evidence that either of them were actually living in the city. Francis Searancke retired in 1868 and the brewery and about thirty public houses were leased to John Lloyd,

Table 24.1 Kingsbury Brewery tied estate in the 1840s

Herts			
Hemel Hempstead	Six Bells* 1840	St Albans	Green Man
Redbourn	Chequers L. c.1843		Great Red Lion
	Cricketers 1820		Jolly Sailor
	George 1820		Reform Beer Shop
	Hollybush 1798		Royal Oak
St Albans	Angel c.1843	Stevenage	Chequers L.**
	Cock and Flowerpot c.1843		

Key: * Tithe plot 692, Bury Mill End, Hemel Hempstead
     ** Lease from the Lytton family

Table 24.2 Kingsbury Brewery tied estate sold to Bingham Cox in 1889

Herts			
Barnet	Old Windmill FL	St Albans	Fighting Cocks FL
Berkhamsted	Bull BH		Great Red Lion FL
Colney Street	Jolly Farmer BH		Green Man FL
Flamstead	Rose and Crown FL		Harrow FL
Hemel Hempstead	Six Bells FL		Jolly Sailor FL
London Colney	Bell FL		Midland Railway
Redbourn	Crown FL		Prince of Wales BH
	George FL		Rose and Crown
	Holly Bush FL		Royal Oak FL
	Running Horse FL*		Unicorn FL
	Waggon and Horses BH		White Lion FL
Ridge	Old Guinea FL		White Swan FL
St Albans	Cock and Flowerpot FL	Smallford	Four Horseshoes BH*
	Crow FL	South Mimms	Red Lion FL *
Beds			
Dunstable	Horse and Groom FL	Kemsworth	Red Lion BH
Kemsworth	Chequers FL*	Studham	Bell FL

Key: * These were not bought by Bingham Cox in 1889
Note: The Five Horseshoes and the White Hart in Markyate were bought by the Kingsbury Brewery
         between 1890 and 1897

a Welshman, for £1,500 a year. He also bought and leased more licensed properties independently. When Francis Searancke died in 1889 and John Lloyd retired, the brewery and the tied estate were sold to William Bingham Cox for £25,000. Six other brewers bought a few of the public houses from John Lloyd's own separate estate of licensed properties when it was sold a week later for £24,000.

The sale on 15 July 1889 of the brewery and its tied estate from Searancke to Bingham Cox included thirty-two tied properties given in Table 24.2. Bingham Cox bought thirteen of Lloyd's estate at this sale giving him a final total of forty-five tied houses. Weller's of Amersham took over the leases of Cromack of King's

Figure 24.3 Kingsbury Brewery yard (Michael Whitaker)

Langley's tied estate and bought two other properties. Five other breweries bought the remainder of the properties (Table 24.3).

During the next five years Bingham Cox increased beer production by a third and tried to sell the brewery in July 1894. As the offer price was not considered sufficient he decided to form a limited company registered as the Kingsbury (St Albans) Brewery Co. Ltd in December 1894. Shortly afterwards in 1898, the Kingsbury Brewery was bought by Benskin's and all brewing was transferred to their brewery in Watford.

Almost all of the original Kingsbury Brewery buildings remain, except for some of the cellars and the high level footbridge which have been adapted for other purposes by a number of small businesses. The ex-brewery manager's house, Kingsbury Lodge and stables and some very distinctive boundary walls of brick and knapped flint in Branch Road survive to this day.

St Albans Brewery

Thomas Kinder, who was a brewer in St Albans, bought the *Three Horseshoes* in Smallford in 1737. It may have been his son, another Thomas, who was responsible for building the original St Albans Brewery, or a replacement, in

Table 24.3 Kingsbury Brewery sale 22 July 1889 – Lloyd's disposal of his own tied estate or transfer of lease

		b.b.			b.b.
Herts					
Abbot's Langley	*George*, Nash Mills L.*	W	Leverstock Green	*Red Lion* FL,L.*	BC
Berkhamsted	*Castle Hotel* C.	BC	London Colney	*Golden Lion* FL	Mc
Bovingdon	*Bell* FL, L.*	W	Redbourn	*Queen Victoria* BH	Gn
Boxmoor	*Three Crowns* BH	BC	St Albans	*Acorn*	BC
Hemel Hempstead	*Coach and Horses* BH	BC		*Blockers' Arms* BH	BC
King's Langley	*Red Lion* L.*	W		*Garibaldi* BH	BC
	Saracen's Head L.*	BC		*Great Northern* BH	BC
	William IV BH	W		(*Alma*)	
Beds					
Luton	*Bute Arms* FL	Gn	Luton	*Moulder's Arms* FL	Be
	Hearts of Oak FL	Gn		*White Hart*	BC
	Lea Bridge Inn	AW			
Bucks					
Chesham	*Bell* BH	W	Chesham	*Sun Inn* BH	BC
	Eagle BH	BC		*White Lion* BH	BC
	New Inn BH	Ge			

Key: * These leases were all from the Cromack family of King's Langley
b.b. Brewery buyer
AW Adey & White
BC Bingham Cox
Be Bennett
Ge Groome
Gn J.W. Green
Mc McMullen
W Weller's

Chequer Street. This brewery was reputed to date from 1776. In 1822 a descendant, another Thomas Kinder had a house, a brewhouse, a malting and a storehouse in the yard and stables and granaries. In the same year he leased a cottage and a malting behind the *Rose and Crown* in Sandridge for 14 years from William and Solomon Burr of Luton. Subsequent generations of the family continued to brew in Chequer Street. Kinder's tied estate included the properties listed in Table 24.4, of which at least thirteen had been acquired by 1822 and about forty by 1868 when the brewery was bought by Adey & White.

After the sale of the brewery many of the tied houses were retained by the Kinder family and leased to Adey & White until 1910, when these licensed properties were finally sold and became part of the tied estate of the brewery. Adey & White gradually increased their own tied estate independently by buying or leasing other properties quoted in Table 24.5.

Later Adey & White bought the St Peter's Brewery and Kent's Holywell Brewery. In 1936, as Harold Adey had no son, he and Reginald Kent agreed to

Table 24.4 Kinder's tied estate in the 1860s

Herts

Abbot's Langley	*Asylum Tavern* BH	St Albans	*King's Head* FL 1745*
	Rose and Crown 1841		*Little Red Lion* FL*
Colney Heath	*Queen's Head* 1797		*Lower Red Lion* FL
Harpenden	*Cross Keys* c.1760		*Mermaid* BW 1835*
	Gibraltar Castle F		*Midland Arms* 1864
London Colney	*King's Head* BH 1742		*Mile House* FL 1826
Markyate	*Swan* FL 1822		*Plough* 1845
Park Street	*White Horse* FL 1805		*Portland Arms* FL 1845
Redbourn	*Bell and Shears* FL 1795		*Queen's Hotel* FL 1771*
St Albans	*Antelope* FL 1846		*Two Brewers* FL 1799*
	Bell FL 1765*		*White Horse* FL*
	Black Lion FL 1842*		*Windmill* FL*
	Boar's Head 1746		*Woolpack* FL*
	Cock FL pre 1834*	Sandridge	*Queen's Head* FL
	Cricketers L. 1846	Shenley	*Green Willows* BH
	Cross Keys FL		*King William IV* BH, L.
	Fleur de Lys FL 1760		*Lord Nelson* L.
	Goat FL 1854	Smallford	*Three Horseshoes* FL 1737
	Hare & Hounds FL 1748*		

Key: * These were transferred from leasing to ownership in 1910 by Adey & White

Table 24.5 Adey & White's own additions to their tied estate after 1868

Herts

Abbot's Langley	OL Nash Mills L.	St Albans	*Inkerman Stores* OL
East Barnet	*Harts Horn* BH		*Lamb* FL
Flamstead	*Britannia* BH		*Noah's Ark* OL
	Spotted Dog BH		*Peacock* FL
Harpenden	*George IV* BH, L.		*Robin Hood* BW, L.
	Railway Inn BH		*Spotted Bull* BH
	Woodman's Arms BH		*Stag* FL
Hemel Hempstead	*Henry VIII* BH		*Steeple Chase* BH
	Spotted Bull BH		*Sugar Loaf* BH
	True Blue BH		*Ten Bells* OL
King's Langley	*Rose and Crown* BH		*Wheatsheaf* FL
Leverstock Green	*Rose and Crown* BH		*Woolpack* FL
	White Horse BH	St Peters rural	*King's Arms* FL*
Markyate	*Horse and Groom* BH	Shenley	*Green Willows* BH
	Plough BH		*Lord Nelson* BH
	Star and Garter BH		*William IV* BH
	White Horse BH	South Mimms	*Plough*
New Barnet	*Cambridge Arms* FL, L.	Tyttenhanger	*Plough* BH
Redbourn	*Prince's Head* FL	Welwyn	*Queen's Head* BH
	Red Lion FL		*Vine* FL
St Albans	*George* FL	Wheathampstead	*Gibraltar Castle* FL**

Beds

Dunstable	*Goat* FL	Luton	*Parrot* FL, L.
	Swan with Two Necks		*Ship*
Eaton Bray	*Victoria* BH, L.		OL North St
Luton	*Goat*		OL Vicars Rd
	Lea Bridge Inn FL		

Key: * Now London Colney
     ** Now in Batford, Harpenden

Table 24.6 Parsons' tied estate leased to Adey & White in 1878

Herts			
Bovingdon	*Wheatsheaf* BH 1864	London Colney	*King's Arms*
Colney Heath	*Crooked Billet* 1854	Markyate	*White Horse*
Flamstead	*Spotted Dog*	Sandridge	*Rose and Crown* 1870s
Great Gaddesden	*Chequers* 1862	Watford	*Leviathan* 1838
Harpenden	*Railway Inn** 1863		*Retreat*
Hemel Hempstead	*Mason's Arms*		
Beds			
Luton	*Highlander*** 1876	Luton	*Midland Railway Tavern*
	Mason's Arms		

Key: * Great Northern
        ** Farley Arms

accept an offer for the St Albans Brewery and fifty-two tied public houses plus four off-licences from J.W. Green of Luton. Table 24.9 shows the composition of the 1936 tied estate indicating which had originally belonged to Kinder, bought directly by Adey & White plus those retained after buying Parsons' and Kent's breweries.

Later in 1936, St Albans City Corporation bought the brewery site. Most of the buildings were pulled down. Part of the land was used to build the Chequers cinema and the remainder was used as a car park. The brewery cellars were used as air raid shelters during World War II. All that now remains of the brewery is the Brewery House in Chequer Street which has an Adey & White monogram and the date 1887. This building has been modified and now forms part of the large Maltings shopping complex that covers the rest of the original brewery site.

St Peter's Brewery

Members of the Parsons family were brewers in Sandridge as early as 1765 where they owned the *Maltster* (location in village not known), the *Queen's Head* and the *Rose and Crown* and used the malting behind the latter. In 1813 Ann Parsons, the widow of Jonathan Parsons, was living at the *Rose and Crown*. During 1832 members of the family built the St Peter's Brewery behind 8 St Peter's Street, St Albans and a brewery house (now a solicitor's office) next to it at 6 St Peter's Street. They bought licensed properties in central Hertfordshire (Tables 24.6 and 24.7). The brewery also owned another malting on Holywell Hill, St Albans, just south of the entrance to Sopwell Lane. This is shown behind a house on the 1840s tithe map and the 1897 OS 25 inch to the mile map. This brewery was bought later by Adey & White in 1878 and it remained in use until burnt down by a fire in 1902.

Table 24.7 Parsons' tied estate sold or closed before the sale of St Peter's Brewery to Adey & White in 1878

Herts			
Abbot's Langley	OL Nash Mills	Hemel Hempstead	OL Water End
Bedmond	*Swan* BH *	Leverstock Green	BH No name
Croxley Green	*Traveller's Arms* BH	Redbourn	*White Hart* BH
Flamstead	*Britannia* BH	St Albans	*White Hart Tap* BH
Hemel Hempstead	*Henry VIII* BH		*White Swan* FL**
	Queen's Head BH	Sandridge	*Queen's Head* FL #
	Spotted Bull BH		

Beds			
Caddington	*Plough* BH	Kemsworth	*California* BH
	Sheepshearers BH	Luton	*Compasses* BH
Humbershoe	*White Horse* BH		*Plait Hall* FL

Key: * Sold to Kent's
         ** Sold to Benskin's
         # Sold to Kinder's in 1820

Table 24.8 Kent's Holywell Brewery tied estate

Herts			
Ayot St Peter	*Waggoners* BH, L	St Albans	*Blue Anchor* BH 1872
Bedmond	*Swan* BH		*Blue Lion* BH 1872
Redbourn	*Chequers* FL*		*Thomas Oakley* OL
St Albans	*Bat and Ball* BH 1808	Shenley	*Queen Adelaide* BH
	Beehive (Brewery Tap) BH		

Key: * Ownership transferred to Earl of Verulam after 1910

Parsons had previously disposed of some of the properties which they had owned or leased, mostly in 1876, before leasing the remaining fourteen properties to Adey & White when they sold the St Peter's Brewery. Before 1903 Parsons' leased properties were finally sold to Adey & White. Much later this brewery site became the site of Thomas Oakley's shop which had originally belonged to Kent's when it was at 1 High Street.

In the late 1800s there was possible confusion of breweries and tied estate ownership in Bedfordshire because there was also Thomas Parsons' brewery in Princes Risborough. This brewery owned the *White Hart* in Dunstable, the *Bird in Hand* in Houghton Regis, the *Dolphin* in Leighton Buzzard and leased the *Swan* in Leighton Buzzard to Adey & White.

Holywell Brewery

Kent's leased and later owned the small Holywell Brewery at 1 Holywell Hill (first archway) which is claimed to have been founded in 1826 by a Thomas Kent who owned the *Bat and Ball* in Chequer Street. However the brewery may not

Figure 24.4 Kent's Brewery house on Holywell Hill next to the Peahen

originally have been at this address. His nephew, Thomas Weedon Kent (1806–1900), is thought to have been the first of the Kent family to actually manage the brewery.

In 1878 the Kent's brewery house was described as a brick-built residence with a spacious entrance hall, drawing and dining rooms, office, the usual domestic offices, five bedrooms fitted with cupboards and closets, store rooms, a bathroom and three attics. At the rear were an extensive range of buildings, including the brewery with cellarage and store rooms, a twelve quarter malting with barley and malt storage lofts and a four-stall stable with lofts over it. All buildings had a good water supply. Behind the brewery was a large and productive garden planted with espalier fruit trees and a paddock. At the east end of the paddock was the timber-built licensed beer house known as the *Beehive* which is still a public house. In 1878 T.W. and T. Kent were 6 years into a 21-year lease for the entire brewery property which they purchased as a freehold

Table 24.9 Tied estate when Adey & White sold the St Albans Brewery to J.W. Green and Sons of Luton in 1936

Herts

Bedmond	Swan BH	Ke	St Albans	Fleur de Lys FL	Ki
Bovingdon	Wheatsheaf BH	P		Goat FL	Ki
Colney Heath	Crooked Billet BH	P		Hare and Hounds FL	Ki
	Queen's Head FL	Ki		Inkerman Stores OL	AW
Flamstead	Spotted Dog BW	P		King's Head FL	Ki
Great Gaddesden	Crooked Billet BH	P		Lower Red Lion FL	Ki
Harpenden	George IV BH	AW		Mermaid BW	Ki
	Gibraltar Castle FL	Ki		Mile House FL	Ki
	Railway Inn BH	P		Noah's Ark OL	AW
Hatfield	Boar and Castle BH	AW		Peacock FL	AW
Hemel Hempstead	Henry VIII BH	AW		Portland Arms FL	AW
	Spotted Bull BH	AW		Queen's Hotel FL	Ki
Leverstock Green	White Horse BH	AW		Robin Hood BW	AW
London Colney	King's Head BH	Ki		Spotted Bull BW	AW
Markyate	Swan F	Ki		Ten Bells OL	AW
Park Street	White Horse F	Ki		White Horse FL	AW
Redbourn	Chequers FL	P	Sandridge	Queen's Head FL	Ki
	Red Lion FL	AW		Rose and Crown FL	P
St Albans	Bat and Ball BW	Ke	Shenley	King William IV BH	Ki
	Beehive BH	Ke		Queen Adelaide BH	Ki
	Bell Hotel FL	Ki	Smallford	Three Horseshoes FL	Ki
	Black Lion FL	Ki	Tyttenhanger	Plough BH	AW
	Blue Lion BW	Ke	Watford	Leviathan FL	P
	Cock Inn FL	Ki	Welwyn	Vine FL	AW
	Cross Keys FL	Ki			

Beds

Dunstable	Queen's Head FL	Ki	Luton	Midland Railway FL	AW
Luton	Goat FL	AW		Parrot FL	AW
	Highlander FL	P		Vicars Road OL	AW
	Lea Bridge Inn FL	P			

Key: AW Adey & White
       Ke Kent
       Ki Kinder
       P Parsons

estate from Mr Hollingworth. The other public houses that made up the tied estate of the Holywell Brewery are given in Table 24.8.

In 1840 Kent's were leasing a malting near the *Crow* in Fishpool Street (plot 340 on the tithe map). Later they took over the ex-Clutterbuck malting in Sopwell Lane. The brewery malting is not recorded on the 1897 large-scale map.

Thomas Weedon Kent bequeathed the brewery to his eldest son Thomas who died relatively young in 1917. His other son Reginald took over, but in 1918 he decided to merge his brewery with Adey & White and became a partner at the St Albans Brewery. At this time the Holywell Brewery ceased brewing. The brewery house is still standing and was a restaurant in the 1950s and 1960s. It is now used as an antique furniture/soft furnishings business while the small brewery at the rear has been converted to a house/office.

Gentle's Yard brewery

Samuel Wildbore was a brewer and maltster living in Dagnall Street in 1839. It is possible that he was using the small brewery in Gentle's Yard which had direct access to Dagnall Street. He leased the *Vine* in Spicer Street during the 1820s and 1830s.

Micro-breweries

After the closure of the St Albans Brewery in Chequer Street, there was no active brewery in St Albans for over fifty years. Two micro-breweries, the *Philanthropist and Firkin* in the old Carnegie public library in Victoria Street and the *Farmer's Boy* in London Road began brewing in the 1990s. Only the *Farmer's Boy* Verulam Brewery is still brewing.

References

Dunk, G. *Around St Albans with Geoff Dunk*, St Albans and Hertfordshire Architectural and Archaeological Society, 1985, pp.26-7 (Gentle's Brewery), pp.30–1 (Kinder and Adey & White's Brewery).

Hertfordshire Archives and Local Studies. a. D/Eby B83 (Kingsbury Brewery sale), b. D/EL B220 Bundle 8 (Kent's Brewery and *Bee Hive* BH).

Kilvington, F. The Kent family, *Herts Past & Present*, Spring 2004, 3rd Series No. 3, pp.17–21.

Petty Sessions Licensing Records for Hertfordshire and Bedfordshire.

Poole, H. *Here for the Beer*, Watford Museum, 1984, pp.42–5.

Richmond, L. and Turton, A. (eds.) *The Brewing Industry: A Guide to Historical Records*, Manchester University Press, 1990, p.37.

Whitbread Archive. List of Adey & White's tied estate properties sold to Green's of Luton.

CHAPTER TWENTY-FIVE

Stevenage

In spite of its size and position on the Great North Road, Stevenage has never had a major brewery. Historically there are known to have been brewhouses in the old town at the *Marquis of Lorne, Swan, White Lion* and *Yorkshire Grey* and later at the *Buckingham Palace* and *Prince of Wales*. At least three small common breweries have existed who sold to beer houses and the public. In 1834 William Moulden began brewing at 115–17 High Street. He later owned a beer house and the *Royal Oak*. Hicks & Richards used a small brewery near the *Swan* in 1839. They were succeeded by John Deacon in 1841 and Griffin Cant in 1844. Robert Hart was active in Albert Street in 1870. Brewing ceased for over one hundred years until micro-breweries were established for short periods at the Hollywood Bowl (bowling alley) in 1996 and at the *Buckingham Palace* in 2000.

There is an old malting at the north end of the High Street in the old town. Records indicate that it never belonged to a large brewery. After malting ceased the building was used by Vincent Motor Cycles and later became part of Thomas Alleynes School.

References

Madgin, H. Brewing in Stevenage in Ackroyd, S. (ed.) *Aspects of Stevenage 1700–1945*, Stevenage Museum, 2001, pp.42–4.
Poole, H. *Here for the Beer*, Watford Museum, 1984, p.48.

CHAPTER TWENTY-SIX

Tring

Brewing and malting became established industries in Tring during the 1800s when three small breweries were built in the town. Demand for beer dramatically increased during the 1830s when hundreds of navvies became involved in the construction of the three-mile cutting for the railway line between London and Birmingham. There were at least seventeen inns and beer

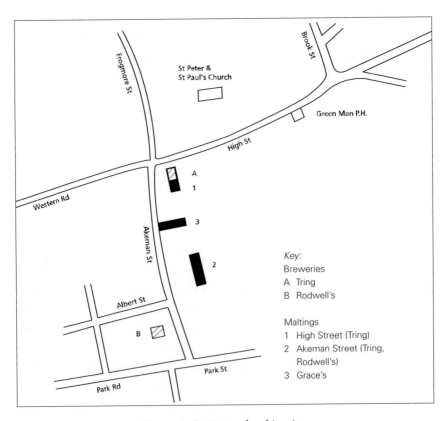

Figure 26.1 Brewery and malting sites

Table 26.1 Tring Brewery tied estate

a) Sold to Locke & Smith in 1898			
Herts			
Long Marston	*Boot* BH	Tring	*Pheasant* BH
Tring	*Britannia* BH		*Queen's Arms* FL
	Castle FL		*Royal Oak* FL
	King's Arms FL	Wiggington	*Greyhound* FL
Bucks			
Aston Clinton	*White Lion* FL		
b) Disposals before 1898 by the Brown family			
Beds			
Eaton Bray	*Bedford Arms c.*1876		
Bucks			
Aylesbury	*Angel* BH *c.*1872	Waddesdon	*Red Lion* FL *c.*1872
Quainton with Shipton Ley	*George* FL *c.*1872		

houses for a population of 4,500. Some of them had their own brewhouses. The last of the three breweries closed in the 1930s. However in 1992 the Tring Brewing Company was established to brew the first beer in the town for over fifty years.

Tring Brewery

The Tring Brewery at 24 High Street, where there is still a sign over the archway, is claimed to have been founded *c.*1800. The earliest known owner was Thomas Amsden who has been described as a common brewer who also owned the *White Lion* at Aston Clinton. James Field was the next owner of this brewery *c.*1828. It is thought that James Brown bought the brewery two years later and remained there for the next fifty years. He came from Okeford Fitzpaine in Dorset where he was born in 1795. During the 1830s he built the *Britannia* and the *King's Arms* in Tring and the *Harcourt Arms* (*Royal Hotel, Railway Hotel*) at Albury (Tring Station). By 1851 he was described as a farmer as well as a brewer, a maltster and a wine and spirit merchant. His eldest son John Herbert Brown was managing the brewery and a malting in 1881 when he employed nine men. John Brown finally died in 1890 aged 95 years and left the brewery to John Herbert Brown and a younger son Frederick William Brown. John Herbert died in 1896. Frederick William sold the brewery, a malting and nine freehold public houses to Locke & Smith of Berkhamsted in 1898 (Table 26.1). The brewery was initially

Figure 26.2 Tring Brewery entrance and Brewery House in the High Street

converted to a slaughterhouse but is now used by a small printing and stationer business and a resin casting and moulding company.

On the site at 24 High Street there was also the brewer's house, possibly with a shop for wines and spirits plus an off-licence and the brewery, stores and stabling in the yard at the rear. The shape of some of the windows would indicate that one of the old buildings in the yard has been a small malting. In 1890 the Brown's bought the large malting in Akeman Street behind the *Royal Oak,* which had previously belonged to Liddington's Manor Brewery and is now part of Rodwell's site. This is a large two-storey malting (approximately 150 feet long and 30 feet wide) which had a kiln at the north end. This has been modified and is now used for storage purposes. Besides the nine public houses that were sold with the brewery in 1898, the Brown family had previously owned four other properties and remained owners of the *Royal Hotel* until it was sold to Benskin's in 1923.

Table 26.2 Manor Brewery tied estate in 1876			
Herts			
Albury	OL No name	Tring	*Pheasant* BH
Bulbourne	*Grand Junction Arms*		*Uncle Tom's Cabin*
Long Marston	BH No name		*Victoria*

Rodwell's Brewery

William Olney established a small brewery in Akeman Street in 1839. He was later succeeded by his daughter Sarah Olney in 1854. John Batchelor bought the brewery and a beer house in 1886 and formed a partnership with William Jesse Rodwell in 1895. Rodwell's of 28 Akeman Street were established in 1843 as a soft drinks manufacturer. William Rodwell married John Batchelor's daughter Emily. He managed the brewery on his own from 1902 to 1923. This small brewery, which is now a private house, was on the opposite side of the street to Rodwell's present business and south of Albert Street.

The identified tied estate consisted of the *Anchor Inn* at Tring (sold to Benskin's in 1926), the *Fish* at Berkhamsted, the *Pheasant* at Wiggington, the *Black Horse* BH at Wilstone and an off-licence at the brewery. It is claimed that the brewery and five public houses, not including the off-licence, were sold to Meux & Co. of London between 1923 and 1935. The remaining properties have not been identified. Rodwell's have continued to operate as a soft drinks manufacturer and distributor.

Manor Brewery

Seabrook Liddington was brewing at the Manor Brewery at 172 High Street from 1839 to 1874. He was succeeded by James Liddington, a relative who had been at the *Victoria* in Frogmore Street. In 1886 Mrs Rebecca Liddington took charge of the brewery and its small tied estate (Table 26.2). The Rothschild family owned the land where the brewery had been built and had it pulled down in 1895. Memorial gardens were subsequently established on this site.

Tring Brewing Company

The Tring Brewery Company Ltd of 81-82 Akeman Street was established in 1992. There is a micro-brewery of thirty-two barrels' capacity on Tring Industrial Estate. The brewery supplies about 100 free-trade outlets. At the present time there is a lease of the *Two Brewers* in Luton that is run as a free house with two or three Tring beers normally available.

Other brewers

The 1877 plan of the town centre shows a small brewery on a plot behind the Baptist Chapel in Frogmore Street. Trade directories of this date do not indicate the ownership or use of the building.

A few of the inns had their own brewhouses. The *Green Man* in the lower High Street also had its own brewhouse where John Philby was brewing in the 1840s and John Woodman from *c*.1878 to 1895. This brewery was also demolished by the Rothschilds to form part of the memorial gardens. The *Rose and Crown* brewed its own beer from the 1600s to 1865. Timothy Northwood was the brewer between 1829 and 1839 and James Sharman in 1854.

There was also another large malting in Akeman Street that has never belonged to any of the town brewers; Amsden and Brown used it as a source of malt. This malting was owned by the Grace family, who used some of the malt to brew beer for personal drinking until *c*.1900. They were also large-scale flour millers. This complex was converted into private housing during the 1980s.

References

Grace's malting. *Brewery History Society Newsletter*, No. 30, 2005, p.20.

Hertfordshire Archives and Local Studies. a. D/EVy B43 (Sales details of Tring Brewery 1898).

Petty Sessions Licensing Records for Hertfordshire, Bedfordshire and Buckinghamshire.

Poole, H. *Here for the Beer*, Watford Museum, 1984, pp.48–50.

Woodhouse, B. *Tring, A Pictorial History*, Chichester, Phillimore, 1996.

CHAPTER TWENTY-SEVEN

Walkern

Samuel Wright I began working as a maltster in the village of Walkern in the 1790s. His son, Samuel Wright II, continued to run the family business and began commercial brewing in the 1860s in old farm buildings in the village on an unidentified site. In 1869 he bought the *Red Lion* in Walkern High Street and a malting on the property for £845 from the Lucas Brewery of Hitchin. The malting was part boarded and part brick with a part-tiled and part-reed thatched roof. The lead cistern could take sixteen quarters of barley to be later spread on two floors. This malting was pulled down when surplus to requirements and the *Red Lion* is now a private house.

Unfortunately this first brewery was destroyed by fire a few years later. The diarist George Beaver of Hitchin recorded that, "the bursting vats sent volumes of beer down the road. Down went the good people of Walkern on hands and knees and, well, all that beer was not wasted".

Victoria Brewery

Because of the fire a new tower brewery, named the Victoria Brewery, was built at the south side of the village on the High Street opposite the village school. Good quality water was obtained from a 300-foot well sunk into the chalk beds underneath the brewery. Samuel II continued to manage the brewery until he died in 1875. Initially the brewery was then managed by J. Bullen, an executor, and J. Holland the brewery manager until Samuel II's two sons Samuel III and Herbert were old enough to take control.

As the business developed, the brewery was gradually enlarged to brew ale, stout and porter and included a cask-washing department, a bottle-washing department, an engine house, stores, a hop room, a malt store and stables. There were about thirty horses and eight to ten draymen to deliver beer. At a later stage the horses were replaced with a fleet of lorries. A new malting was

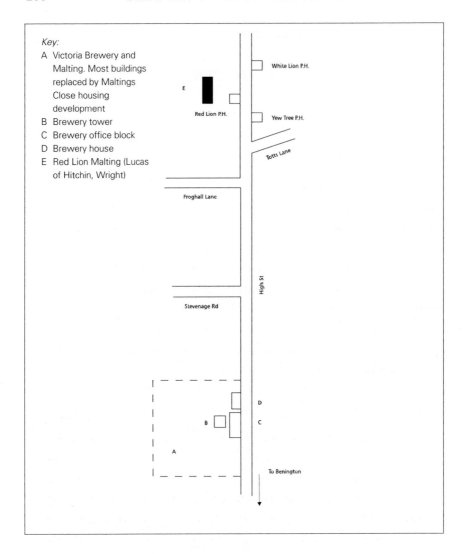

Figure 27.1 Brewery and malting sites

built on this site with two germination floors of 150 feet long by 40 feet wide which was about fifty quarters capacity.

On 13 August 1909 the Victoria Brewery placed an advertisement in the *Royston Crow*:

Important statement by S. Wright & Co. An unqualified denial of libellous reports. Perhaps you have heard among other things that our water supply is contaminated, and that we are prohibited by the Excise

Table 27.1 Wright's tied estate

a) Sold to Simpson & Co. in 1924

Herts

Ashwell	*Stag's Head*	Stevenage	*Crooked Billet*
Ayot St Lawrence	*Brocket Arms** L.		*Marquis of Lorne* L.
Benington	*White Horse*	Titmore Green	*Hermit of Redcoats*
Breachwood Green	*Red Lion*	Walkern	*Red Lion*
	Sugar Loaf	Ware	*King's Head*
Datchworth	*Plough* L.		

Beds

Luton	*Jolly Butchers*	Stotfold	*Pig and Whistle*
	Yorkshire Grey		

Cambs

Steeple Morden	*Fox*		

b) Disposals before 1924

Herts

Albury	*Fox* L.	Layston	*Globe*
Aston	*Fox* L.	Stevenage	OL High St
Hitchin	OL Walsworth Rd	Ware	*White Swan*

Beds

Luton	BH Newtown St	Stotfold	*White Swan*

Key: * Was *Three Horseshoes* until 1935

from Brewing. Our present purpose is to give an unqualified denial to all these reports, and to thank the kind friends who have been responsible for them. The facts of the case are as follows: About three weeks ago we had two brewings develop an abnormal flavour, a very common experience among brewers at this time of the year. Our stock being very low we had to buy beer for a short time, two neighbouring Brewers of good standing very kindly coming to our aid. The crisis is over. We are going on as usual. Our Malt, Hops and Water have been examined by an expert and pronounced above suspicion. Our water Supply and Finished Drinks, have been analysed by Dr Bullock, of the London Hospital, and passed as pure. Our Factory is Certified by the Medical Officer of the City of London. May we have the pleasure of convincing you that our Beers are First Class? Let us send you a Free Sample. Send us a Post Card with your Name and Address; we will do the rest.

This was a very positive way of dealing with a problem that sometimes occurred and demonstrated the degree of co-operation that existed among the local brewers.

Figure 27.2 Victoria Brewery (Michael Whitaker)

The tied estate, which included off-licences, was gradually expanded in Hertfordshire, Bedfordshire and Cambridgeshire reaching its greatest size in the early 1900s. Brewing ceased in 1917 because of reduced demand due to competition and twelve freehold properties and three leasehold properties were sold to Simpson's of Baldock. Other properties previously disposed of are also given in Table 27.1. There was also an off-licence at the brewery until at least 1924.

Cider making was started in 1924 to complement mineral water and lemonade manufacture. The Wright brothers' factory became the only cider producer within the county using locally grown apples. However, after a few

years the cider was obtained in bulk from other sources. Cider bottling ceased in
1955 and mineral water production, which reached a production volume of
400,000 gallons per year by the late 1970s, stopped because of competition from
supermarkets. The empty malting was then used for a short time as Mickles
micro-brewery and other buildings by a plastics company. The whole site was
finally sold for development. When Walkern Parish Council learned that it was
proposed to clear the site and build luxury houses they called a public meeting
and protested to the planning authorities. A small housing estate was eventually
built on the land, but the brewery tower and a building nearer the road were
saved and adapted for housing. The old brewer's house is still there, next door
(Figure 27.2).

References

Hertfordshire Archives and Local Studies. a. D/Ery B50 (Details of tied estate in 1906),
    b. *Herts & Cambridge Reporter*, 15 August 1909, Wright's denial of libellous reports.
North Herts Gazetteer, 20 February 1987, Ale and Farewell.
Page, K. Personal communication. Details of tied estate sold to Simpsons & Co.,
    Baldock, in 1924.
Petty Sessions Licensing Records for Hertfordshire, Bedfordshire and Cambridgeshire.
Poole, H. *Here for the Beer*, Watford Museum, 1984.
Tyler, D. Hertfordshire's only cider makers, in *Hertfordshire Countryside*, Vol. 31, No. 201,
    1976, pp.22, 24.

CHAPTER TWENTY-EIGHT

Ware

Historically Ware was a major malting town providing large quantities of malt to the London breweries because it could be easily transported by barge along the River Lea. Many of the maltsters lived on the south side of the High Street and had private wharves at the ends of their plots. In the middle of the nineteenth century there were approximately seventy operational maltings, many of which covered large tracts of land north of the High Street. When the Victoria Maltings was built in 1907 it was the largest malting complex in England. Malting finally ceased in 1994 when Pauls of Ipswich closed their last maltings in the town.

Ware was also on an important north–south coach route. There were at least forty inns established by 1700, the most important being in the High Street. Originally many would have brewed their own beer on the premises. Much later Carter, McMullen's and Young's of Hertford, and Christie & Cathrow of Hoddesdon became the major owners of licensed properties in the town. However, the High Street, Cannon and Star Breweries were established as small local breweries. There were also brew-pubs such as the *Barge,* the *Two Brewers* and the *Saracen's Head.* Part of the Victorian maltings in Broadmeads was adapted for use as the Victoria Brewery in 1981.

Cannon Brewery

The Cannon Brewery was built on a site between Princess Street and Whitehorse Road. In 1853, when Blake & Co. sold the brewery, there was a six quarter mash tun and a tied estate of twelve licensed properties, but only three of them were in Ware (Table 28.1). Thomas Cox operated the brewery between 1852 and 1864. It was then acquired by McMullen & Sons who used this brewery until 1891. However McMullen's do not appear to have ever bought or leased a major part of this tied estate.

Table 28.1 Cannon Brewery tied estate in 1864

Herts			
Bengeo	*New* BH	Stevenage	*Cross Keys*
Bishop's Stortford	*Coach and Horses* BH	Wadesmill	*Wheatsheaf* BH
Colliers End	*New* BH	Ware	*Bugle Horn*
Fanhams Hall Green	*Wellington* FL		*Union Jack*
Hertford	BH Back St		FL West Mill Rd
	BH Honey Lane	Widford	*Fox and Duck* BH

Star Brewery

The Star Brewery on Watton Road, was initially owned by members of the Hitch family, who were already well established in Ware as maltsters. It was a three-storey tower brewery with fermenting and tun rooms, malt and cask stores. Caleb Hitch was there from 1862 to 1866 and leased the brewery to Isaac Everitt from 1866 to 1874 and later to McMullen's of Hertford from 1874 to 1878. It was then owned by William Wickham from 1879 to 1899 and leased to Holt & Co. Marine Brewery, East Ham, London E7 (1900–12) and leased once more to McMullen's during 1914. Subsequently they bought it by 1931 but had sold it again by 1938 to Herbert Lynn who in turn sold it to Ware Brewing Company from 1938 to 1951 and finally sold to Wells & Winch of Biggleswade during 1952. Brewing had ceased by 1952. The buildings have now been sensitively restored.

Caleb Hitch does not appear to have had a known tied estate when he owned the Star Brewery between 1862 and 1866. However, this was at a time when no Petty Sessions licensing records exist. When he was no longer an active brewer he bought the *Rose and Crown* and the *Victoria* in Ware from William Wickham *c*.1889 and leased them both later to Holt's Marine Brewery. These new owners bought and leased a number of other local properties (Table 28.2).

High Street Brewery

In 1829, Edward Wickham had bought the Mill Bridge Brewery in Hertford from John Ireland. His son Edward took over this brewery and his other son William moved to Ware in 1866 to establish the High Street Brewery behind the *Brewery Tap* at 83 High Street. He was here until 1878 until he bought the Star Brewery. He remained at this second brewery until 1899 when he sold his business to Holt's Marine Brewery. Between 1868 and 1899 William Wickham acquired a small tied estate in Ware and near by villages (Table 28.3).

He had an agreement with his brother not to buy or lease properties in his

Table 28.2 Holt's tied estate until 1910–12

Herts		Notes
Great Amwell	*Cherry Tree* BH	Bought from W. Wickham
Hunsdon	*Turkey Cock* FL	Later sold to Rayment's
Ware	*Bird in Hand* BH	Bought from W. Wickham
	Cherry Tree BH	Bought from W. Wickham
	Green Dragon BH	
	John Barleycorn BH	Bought from W. Wickham
	Rose and Crown FL	Later leased to McMullen
	Saracen's Head FL, L.	
	White Swan FL	Later leased to McMullen
	Windsor Castle BH	Bought from W. Wickham
Wareside	*Railway Tavern* BH, L.	Bought from W. Wickham and later sold to E.J. Wickham of Hertford

Table 28.3 Star Brewery tied estate of W. Wickham

Herts		Notes
Amwell End	*Spread Eagle* FL	Sold later to McMullen
Ware	*Bird in Hand* BH	Sold later to McMullen
	Black Swan BH	Sold later to Capt Parker
	Cherry Tree BH	Sold later to Holt's Marine Brewery
	High Street Brewery Tap BH	Sold later to J. Kempston
	John Barleycorn BH	Sold later to Holt's Marine Brewery
	Rose and Crown FL	Sold later to Caleb Hitch
	Star Brewery Tap BH	Sold later to Caleb Hitch
	Victoria FL	Sold later to Caleb Hitch
	Windsor Castle BH	Sold later to Holt's Marine Brewery
Wareside	*Railway Tap* BH	Sold later to Holt's Marine Brewery

brother's Hertford territory and vice versa. When William owned the Star Brewery, the *Brewery Tap* in the High Street was renamed the *Star Brewery Tap*. This can cause confusion unless the High Street or Watton Road is included with the name.

References

Hertfordshire Archives and Local Studies. a. D/Ex 613 T2 (Sale of Cannon Brewery and tied estate 1853), b. D/Ele B19/3 (Sale of Star Brewery 1912).

Petty Sessions Licensing Records for Hertfordshire.

Poole, H. *Here for the Beer*, Watford Museum, 1984, pp.51–3.

Richmond, L. and Turton, A. (eds.) *The Brewing Industry: A Guide to Historical Records*, Manchester University Press, 1990, pp.119–20 (Cannon Brewery), p.223 (Cannon and Star Breweries), p.309 (Star Brewery).

The Brewer's Journal, 15 July 1907 (Details of Page & Co.'s Victoria Malting).

CHAPTER TWENTY-NINE

Watford

Historically Watford was one of the smaller Hertfordshire towns that began as a ribbon development along the High Street. A number of inns were established to cater for the local and passing coach trade. In 1835 there were already three small breweries and eight maltings. The town rapidly expanded in size after the building of the London to Birmingham railway line in 1838. In 1843 there were 589 houses and a reported population of 2,960. By 1880 the population was 15,500 and is now probably in excess of 100,000. Unfortunately later redevelopment of the town centre has led to the destruction of the breweries, maltings and many of the old inns.

The brewing history of Watford from 1700 to the 1950s involved four major breweries and a number of owners. These were the Cannon Brewery, 296 High Street (Pope, Dyson, Benskin), Watford Brewery, 323 High Street (Smith, Whittingstall, Sedgwick), King Street Brewery (Healey) and St Albans Road or Lion Brewery, 141 St Albans Road (Thorpe, Wells) (Figure 29.1). Benskin's Cannon Brewery became the most successful brewing business and later bought the other three town breweries between 1898 and 1952 as well as many more breweries in other towns and villages and individual and small group purchases of licensed properties.

Cannon Brewery

John Pope was born in Hemel Hempstead *c.*1662 and later became a miller and baker in Watford. He is thought to have been baking at Pope's Head in the High Street in 1693. This building was later converted in to a public house known initially as the *Barley Mow* and later as the *Eight Bells* until it was demolished in 1959. In 1708 he leased a malting, barns and stables in the Lower High Street. Some time between 1714 and 1722 he became a brewer and established a brewhouse in Pope's Yard behind the *King's Head* and to the north of St Mary's

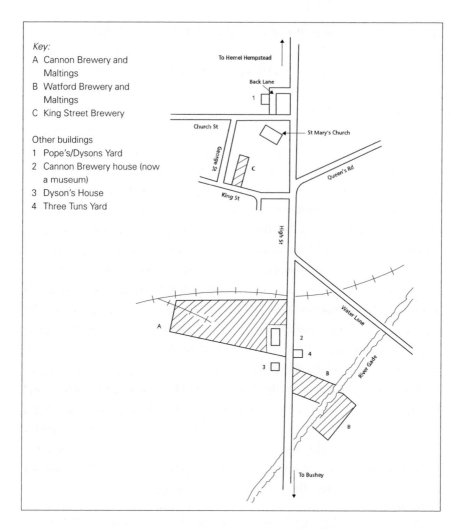

Figure 29.1 Breweries and associated buildings

Church. In his 1722 will he left his brewery, brewing equipment, drays and two
horses to his second son Daniel when he became of age. Daniel was only 14 when
his father died and he himself died relatively young and unmarried in 1741.

One of Daniel's sisters, Sarah, had married William Dyson, a Watford
maltster, and they had a son John Dyson I and two daughters. Both the parents
died while John I was relatively young and he was therefore brought up by his
grandmother, Sarah Pope, evidently a very independent lady, who eventually
bought the business properties that her husband had originally leased.

John Dyson I was brewing in Pope's Yard in 1751. He was fortunate to have inherited from his grandmother and parents a cottage in Abbots Langley (later the *Bell*), Pope's Yard Brewery, the Lower High Street malting, the *King's Head* and the *Three Crowns* in Watford and the *King's Head* in Aldenham. In the same year he bought the *Red Lion* at Coney Butts (later Vicarage Road) and soon afterwards he opened the *Three Tuns* in the Lower High Street. He married in 1761 and his eldest son, John Dyson II, was born in 1763. When John Dyson I died in 1790 he bequeathed the *Three Tuns* and a third share of the brewery to John II. The remainder of the business was left to his widow Mary. After her death in 1800, John II gradually bought her share of the business which she had bequeathed to his other brothers and sisters.

John Dyson II had bought Leaden Porch, a property next to the *Three Tuns* yard in 1794, presumably to allow for further expansion. However when the substantial property on a large site on the opposite side of the Lower High Street came up for auction in 1810, he decided to buy it also for potential expansion. He began to build the Cannon Brewery on this large site before 1829 and closed the Pope's Yard site behind the *Eight Bells* in 1830. By 1836 he had rebuilt the malting on the *Three Tuns* site.

In 1806 John II had married Maria Erhet and they later had three sons and three daughters. After John II's death in 1845, two of his sons, John Dyson III and his brother Ralph, inherited the brewery estate and the third son inherited a family farm. John III purchased Ralph's half share of the brewery and estate for £7,700 in 1858 and continued to expand the business. He died in 1867 and the family decided to auction the business. A sale notice in the *Watford Observer* on 2 November 1867 described the Cannon Brewery as follows:

> as being a most complete establishment with two private residences suitable for principals surrounded by luxuriantly planted gardens and orchards, in the rear of which is a meadow known as Watford Field, the whole being freehold and occupying a site of nearly eight acres, in the heart of the town, close to the High Street railway station. The home property further embraces two capital malthouses together wetting 22 quarters with capacious stowage, a timber yard, and kitchen garden extending to the River Colne, two cottages and two small houses, one occupied by the brewer. Also 31 freehold and 11 leasehold public houses and beerhouses situated in Watford and the surrounding neighbourhood. The whole of the forgoing, together with the fixed plant of the brewery and the goodwill of the trade (of 9000 barrels per annum)

Table 29.1 Dyson's known tied estate

Herts			
Abbot's Langley	*Bell* 1758	Watford	*One Crown* 1750
Aldenham	*King's Head* 1750		*Queen's Arms* 1839
Bushey	*King William IV*		*Railway Arms** c.1839
	Robin Hood		*Railway Arms*** 1858
Cheshunt	*Britannia* 1846		*Railway Tavern* L. 1854
Hemel Hempstead	*Royal Oak* by 1843		*Red Lion #*, Coney Butts 1751
Oxhey	*Railway Arms* 1861		*Rising Sun* 1830
Watford	*Crystal Palace* 1854		*Stag* 1852
	King's Head		*Three Crowns* c.1750
	King William 1840		*Three Tuns* 1756
	Leathersellers' Arms		*Verulam Arms*
	Nascot Arms 1866		

Greater London	
Edgware	*Crystal Palace*

Key: * St Albans Road
          ** Aldenham Road
          # Later Vicarage Road

will be sold in one lot, offering one of the most solid investments ever offered in the brewing business ever submitted to public competition.

Joseph Benskin, a retired London hotel owner, and his partner William George Bradley, a Watford draper, bought the business for £34,000.

It has only been possible to identify twenty-four of the public houses previously owned or leased by the Dyson family because of the absence of Petty Sessions licensing records or any other relevant documents in County Archives. However, if the licensed properties owned by Joseph Benskin before 1875 are considered, it is highly likely that many of those in Harrow and other locations might have originally belonged to John Dyson III. There might also be some among a number of other single and small group purchases by Joseph Benskin.

The early history of the Benskin's brewery ownership involved numerous changes in a relatively short time. William Bradley resigned from the partnership in 1870 and Joseph Benskin became the sole partner until he died in 1877 at the age of 63. His widow Maria Benskin then took over the management of the brewery with her second son John Pusey Benskin and her son-in-law Walter Green, the Head Brewer. Maria retired in 1884 and her third son Thomas became a partner. In 1885 John Benskin retired because of ill health and Walter Green left the company. Thomas Benskin appointed James Albert Panton from Dorset as a partner. He claimed to be the first qualified brewer to have studied with Professor Graham at University College, London. Henry Mildmay Husey became a third partner in the business. The brewery was registered as a

Table 29.2 Benskin's early tied estate c.1867–73 (some possibly from John Dyson III)

Herts

Barnet	Old Windmill	Letchmore Heath	Bricklayer's Arms
Bedmond	Green Man	Markyate	Green Man
Berkhamsted	Gardener's Arms		Sebright Arms
Bovingdon	Swan		White Hart
Boxmoor	Plough	Rickmansworth	Bell
Chipperfield	Traveller's Friend		Halfway House*
Chorley Wood	Jolly Brickmakers	Ridge	Guinea
Croxley Green	Gladstone Arms	South Mimms	Greyhound
Hadley	Old Windmill		Red Lion
Hemel Hempstead	Boar's Head	Watford	Anglers' Arms
Leavesden	Hammer in Hand		Oddfellows' Arms

Greater London

Harrow	Bell**	Harrow	Royal Oak**
	Case is Altered L.**	Little Stanmore	Crystal Palace**
	Duck in the Pond**	Pinner	White Hart**
	North Star**	Temple Fortune	Royal Oak**
	Red Lion**		

Key: * Cassio Bridge
      ** Owned or leased before 1873

Table 29.3 Benskin's later independent and small brewery purchases by 1903

Herts

Abbot's Langley	Bricklayer's Arms	Hertford	Leather Bottle
	Brickmakers' Arms		Lion's Head
Aldenham	Fishery Inn		Saracen's Head
Berkhamsted	Carpenters' Arms*		Turk's Head
	Rising Sun		Wellington
	Royal Oak	King's Langley	Griffin
	Traveller's Friend		King William IV
Bishop's Stortford	Bricklayer's Arms	Letchmore Heath	Bricklayer's Arms
	Maltsters' Arms	Northchurch	Anchor BH
	Red Bull	Redbourn	Punch Bowl
	Robin Hood	St Albans	Crown and Anchor
	BH Barrell Down Rd		Crystal Palace
	BH Slant Hill		Hope
Boxmoor	Albion		King's Arms
	Anchor		London and North Western
	Railway Hotel		Midland Station
	Swan		Queen Adelaide
	Three Crowns		Rats' Castle
Bricket Wood	Fox		Verulam Arms
Bushey	Railway Arms		White Hart
	Swan		White Hat Tap
Cassio Bridge	Halfway House		OL Bernard St
Chorley Wood	Stag L.		OL Lattimore Rd
Croxley Green	Sportsman	St Stephen's	Three Hammers
Flamstead	Bell	Smug Oak	Fox and Hounds
	Rose and Crown	Ware	Royal Oak
	Wheatsheaf	Watford	Bedford Arms

Hemel Hempstead	Boot		Bell
	Compasses		Escourt Arms
	Crab Tree		Fox
	Halfway House		Golden Lion
	Sebright Arms		Greyhound
	Windmill*, Piccotts End		Old Berkley Hunt
Hertford	Barge		Prince of Wales
	Britannia		Wellington
	City Arms	Wheathampstead	Bell and Crown
	Flower Pot		Walnut Tree

Beds

Dunstable	Plume of Feathers*	Leighton Buzzard	Black Lion
	Red Lion		Cross Keys**
	Waggon and Horses*		Peacock*
Edlesborough	Traveller's Rest*		Roebuck**
Hawridge	Rose and Crown*		Sun**
Heath and Reach	Axe and Compasses*	Linslade	Buckingham Arms
	Cock BH**	Luton	Painter's Arms
	Duke's Head FL**		Royal Hotel
Hockcliff	Red Lion*		White Hart
Houghton Regis	Chequers FL**	Potton	George and Dragon
Kempston	OL College St	Wavendon	Plough*
Leighton Buzzard	Brewery Tap BH**		

Greater London

Harrow Weald	Red Lion	Mount Pleasant	Old Cheshire Cheese
Islington	Druids' Arms	Pimlico	Stanhope Arms
	Golden Cross	Pinner	Railway Inn
	Falkland Arms	Tower Hill	Grapes L.
Marble Arch	Whitaker Arms	Wealdstone	Royal Oak

Essex

Epping	Royal Oak	Stisted	Red Lion
Harlow	George Hotel	Thaxted	King's Head
	Marquis of Granby		

Sussex

Brighton	Good Intent L.		

Key: * Bought from Fuller's of Chiswick in 1903
         ** Estate of George & Dragon Brewery, Leighton Buzzard, 1897

company in 1894 and again in 1898. Thomas Benskin died in 1903 and his son Eric Segrave Benskin became a director. Colonel William Briggs married Doris Benskin in 1903 and became a company director in 1908. He later became the managing director from 1914 until 1946 and company chairman until he died in 1951 aged 75. His son J. Aidan Briggs was the assistant managing director in 1954 and later became the managing director after the merger with Ind Coope in 1957.

During the 1880s Thomas Benskin and James Panton initiated a major increase in beer production. They succeeded in tripling output in a relatively short time. Much of this beer was being sold directly through their Camden

Town depot to hotels and theatres in London, as the tied estate was thought to initially only have been fifty-four public houses. It is fortunate that Barnard visited the Cannon Brewery and described it in his *Noted Breweries in Great Britain and Ireland* based on his visit in 1890 or 1891 providing a fairly detailed description of the brewery and its operation.

Malted barley grain was lifted from wagons in a railway siding using a steam driven hoist to malt stores capable of holding 2,000 quarters of malt. The malt was then fed through screens to two malt crushers with sets of steel rollers encased in pitch pine. Each unit was capable of crushing fifteen quarters per hour. The grist (crushed malt grains) fell into a shoot and was mechanically fed into a thirty quarter grist hopper placed over the mash tuns. Meanwhile water obtained from a well was pumped into a cast iron cold water tank with a capacity of 400 barrels (14,400 gallons). This water was used to fill two copper plated hot liquor tanks of 100 barrels' capacity and heated by steam coils to 145° to 150° F.

The grist and heated water were mixed and held in two twenty-five quarter mash tuns for two hours at 145° to 150° F to ensure an efficient extraction of the soluble fractions in the grain. The waste grain (spent grain) from the mash tuns was removed and collected by local farmers for animal feed. The liquid component (wort) was fed into one of two coppers heated directly by a coal/coke furnace. At this stage Kent hops were added and the wort was boiled for two hours. The wort was then passed through a hop back, a square copper vessel with perforated draining plates to remove the hop debris. Filtered wort was pumped into a large shallow cooling vessel in the roof of one of the fermenting rooms to reduce the temperature and finally through two refrigeration units to cool it to 60° F.

Cooled wort was piped to fermenting rounds or squares of pitch pine, up to 100 barrels' capacity, fitted with attemperators (coolers) for temperature control and parachutes for excess yeast collection. Appropriate quantities of yeast suspended in wort were used to inoculate these vessels. This part of the process was undertaken in three large rooms that were 123 feet long. All the excess yeast was pressed to remove any wort and packed in 28 lb blocks in buckets to sell to bakers in London.

Beer from the fermenting vessels was transferred to the basement of the fermenting room block where there was a slate settling back (twenty feet by twenty feet) being used as a temporary holding tank to fill the clean barrels. There was also a series of cellars (110 feet x 60 feet) for maturation and the

Table 29.4 Benskin's acquisitions between 1897 and 1951

Year	Acquisitions by Benskin's	Subsidiary acquisitions
1896	1. Ashdowns, George & Dragon Brewery, Leighton Buzzard (7 p)	
1897	1. Groome of King's Langley (32 p)	
	2. Kingsbury Brewery, St Albans (45 p)	
1898	1. Healey's King St Brewery, Watford (18 p)	1. Victoria Brewery, Watford 1898 (1 OL)
	2. Hawkes', Bishop's Stortford (156 p)	1. Black Lion Brewery, Braintree 1890 (8 p)
		2. Smiths of Gr. Bardfield 1898 (4 p)
	3. Downs Beer Agency, Woburn Sands	
1903	1. Fullers & Co., Chiswick (10 p)	1. Part of Three Counties Brewery, Dagnall
1913	1. Locke & Smith, King's Langley (32 p)	1. Tring Brewery 1898 (9 p)
1915	1. New Bell Brewery, Aston Clinton (5 p)	
	2. Fox Brewery, Bishop's Stortford (1 OL)	
1919	1. Watney East Anglian estate (79 p)	1. Saffron Walden Brewery 1899 estate
1920	1. Pryor, Reid & Co., Hatfield (107 p)	1. Park St Brewery, Hatfield 1878 (3 p)
		2. Newtown Brewery, Hatfield 1888 (7 p)
		3. Youngs Brewery, Hertford 1893 (56 p)
		4. Lattimore, Wheathampstead 1897 (9 p)
	2. Peacock Brewery, Harpenden (3 p)	
1923	1. Sedgwick, Watford (97 p)	1. Colne Brewery, Uxbridge 1896 (16 p)
		2. Speedy's Brewery, Clapham 1923 (6 p)
		3. Wilds, Rickmansworth 1900 (6 p)
1927	1. Roberts & Wilson, Ivinghoe (48 p)	
1928	1. Cannon East Anglian estate (20 p)*	1. Christie & Co., Hoddesdon 1928
1930	1. Weller, Amersham (132 p)	1. Cromack, King's Langley 1889 (5 p)
1951	1. Wells, Watford (25 p)	

Key: The term 'p' includes full licences, beer houses and some off-licences, both freehold and leasehold
        * Benskin's may have bought more than 20 p from Cannon Brewery on 28 March 1923 but this is not shown in records in Herts Archives

storage of thousands of barrels. The Camden Town depot had storage for another 3,400 barrels.

On the brewery site in Watford, Benskin's also had facilities for making malted barley. Firstly there were two old traditional maltings 100 feet and 200 feet long and probably 20 feet wide with stores for 2,000 quarters of barley and 1,200 quarters of malt. A new malting of five storeys (155 feet by 55 feet) of eighty quarters capacity with a double kiln had also recently been constructed. The steeping cisterns had mechanical discharge to the three germination floors and germinated grain was mechanically transferred to the drying floors. In 1910 Benskin's still owned another malting at The Dell in Bishop's Stortford that they had bought as part of the Hawkes brewery estate.

Transport logistics have always been important in any big business. In 1898 the brewery had forty horses in Watford and thirty-eight in London. This increased to 138 in 1899 after taking over other breweries and two depots were established at Bishop's Stortford and Braintree. There were normally three

Figure 29.2 Cannon Brewery house

horses per dray which might leave the yard by 2.30 a.m. for long distance deliveries and not return until 10.00 p.m. The lead horse in a team of three might travel 140 to 150 miles in a week. Horses had a ration of 21 lbs of crushed oats per day. The drivers were paid twenty shillings per week plus one shilling for a third horse. With overtime bonuses they might be paid as much as thirty shillings per week. By 1919 only twenty horses remained at the old Hawkes' Brewery in Bishop's Stortford. The first two steam lorries were bought between 1904 and 1906 and a Commer truck in 1913. The fleet of motor vehicles had increased to fifty-nine by 1931 (*The Pennant* 1930–1).

Between 1897 and 1951 Benskin's pursued a very ambitious expansion plan both in terms of capacity in the brewery and in increasing the size of their tied estate by take-overs of many breweries in Hertfordshire and elsewhere (Table 29.4).

Watford Brewery

It is claimed that William Smith had a deed of conveyance in 1655 for the Mansion House, a brewhouse, a malting and a public house known by the name of the *Swan* in Watford High Street (*Watford Observer* Jubilee Supplement 1913). Unfortunately there are known to have been three *Swan* public houses in Watford which gives rise to much confusion. Members of the Smith family continued to become brewers. During 1758 they acquired a malting and two

Table 29.5 Smith's tied estate in 1790

Herts			
Bedmond	*White Hart* C.	Watford	*Crown*, Garston C.
Berkhamsted	*Five Bells* F.		*Dog* (*Holly Bush*) C.
Bushey	*Robin Hood* C.		*Eight Bells* F.
Leavesden Green	*Hare* C.		*George* F.
Letchmore Heath	*Three Horseshoes* C.		*One Bell* F.
London Colney	*Green Dragon* F.		*Swan* F. 233 High St
Park Street	*Falcon* C.		*Three Compasses* F.
Shenley	*Bricklayer's Arms* C.		
Bucks			
Chesham	*Crown*, Ley Hill F.		

adjoining cottages in the High Street. They converted one of these cottages into a public house named the *Swan*, probably at 216 High Street, which had a eighteenth-century brewhouse at the rear and was finally demolished in 1959. Eventually he was succeeded by his son, another William Smith, who was also a brewer and maltster. The two of them also acquired the freehold or copyhold of a number of other public houses. In 1790 the brewery and fifteen public houses were sold to George Whittingstall.

George Whittingstall undertook a major expansion of the brewery and tied estate and was probably responsible for initiating building expansion on the other side of a tributary of the River Colne. When he died in 1822 he left £500,000 to a distant cousin Edmund Fearnley provided that he was prepared to change his name to Edmund Fearnley Whittingstall. This was legally recognised by 1825 and Edmund F. Whittingstall became the owner of the brewery. He subsequently increased the capacity of the brewery and the size of the tied estate. This included leasing the tied estate and a malting of Cromack's brewery in King's Langley and a malting by the *Greyhound* in Albury. He also decided to become a partner in a bank in Hemel Hempstead with a William Smith who was a descendant of the original owners of the brewery. Many other brewers in Hertfordshire also became bankers. At the time when Edward F. Whittingstall died the bank had major financial problems and his estate was apparently liable for claims of £30,000. This was obviously one factor that forced his son George Whittingstall into deciding to lease the brewery plus sixteen men and nine horses and its tied estate to William. F. Sedgwick (Tables 29.6, 29.7 and 29.8). This was initially done in three stages. In 1862 he transferred the leases of twenty properties in Hertfordshire and five in Greater London. A year later a further sixteen leases were transferred. Finally in 1875

Table 29.6 Whittingstall's leases transferred to Sedgwick in 1862

Herts

Aldenham	*Volunteer*	Nash Mills, H.H.	*George and Dragon**
Bovingdon	*Bell**		*Railway Arms*
Bushey	*Lord Nelson*	Potters Bar	*Pilot Engine*
Chipperfield	*Anchor*	Rickmansworth	*Wheelwrights' Arms*
Hemel Hempstead	*Compasses*	Ridge	*Sovereign*
	Lamb	St Albans	*Boot*
King's Langley	*Red Lion**		*Railway Tavern*
	Saracen's Head*	Watford	*Anchor*
	BH*		*Coachmakers' Arms*
Leverstock Green	*Red Lion**		*Jolly Gardeners*

Greater London

Edgware	*Load of Hay*	Willesden	*Crown*
Enfield Chase Gate	*Railway Tavern*		*White Horse*
Uxbridge	*Bell Inn*		

Key: * Cromack of King's Langley
            H.H. Hemel Hempstead

Table 29.7 Whittingstall's leases to Sedgwick's in 1863

Herts

Abbot's Langley	*Royal Oak* C. Kitters Gr.	King's Langley	*Swan* C.
Barnet	*Three Elms* L.& C.	St Albans	*Crown (Mermaid)* F.
	Woolpack F.	Sarratt	*Cricketers* L.
Bushey	*Devonshire Arms* F.	Watford	*Brewer's Arms* F.
East Barnet	*Cat* F.	Watford Heath	*Load of Hay* C.
Hemel Hempstead	*Cupid* F. Cupid Gr.	Welwyn	*Red Lion* C.
Hunton Bridge	*Dog and Partridge* C.		

Beds

Edlesborough	*Axe and Compasses* F.

Greater London

Eastcote	*Ship and Sun* F.	Wembley	*Greyhound* F.

Table 29.8 Whittingstall's estate sold to Sedgwick's in 1874 and more leases transferred

Herts

Barnet	*Mitre* F.	London Colney	*Green Dragon* F.
Bedmond	*White Hart* L.	Park Street	*Falcon* F.
Berkhamsted	*Crown* F.	Radlett	*Red Lion* F.
	Five Bells F.	Watford	*Compasses* F.
Bricket Wood	*Black Boy* F.		*Crown* F. High St
Chipping Barnet	*Edinburgh Castle* F.		*Crown* F. Garston
Hemel Hempstead	*Swan* F.		*Dog* C.
Leavesden Green	*Hare* F.		*Eight Bells* F.
Letchmore Heath	*Three Horseshoes* L.		*George* F.
	Two Wrestlers L.		*One Bell* F.
London Colney	*Cross Keys* L.		*Swan* F.

Bucks   *Greater London*

Chesham	*Crown* F., Ley Hill	Whetstone	*Blue Anchor* L.

Table 29.9 Release of leases by Frederick James Sedgwick to his mother
Mrs May Ann Sedgwick in 1885

Herts

Albury	*Greyhound*	Potters Bar	*Red Lion*
Aldenham	*Chequers*	Rickmansworth	*George*
	Volunteer	Shenley	*Red Lion*
Bushey	*Royal Oak*	St Albans	*Boot*
Cassio Bridge	*Halfway House*	Tring	*Cow Roast*
Chipperfield	*Swan*		BH 18 Akeman St
Chorley Wood	*Old Berkeley Arms*	Watford	*Coach and Horses*
Great Gaddesden	*Crown and Sceptre*		*Coachmakers' Arms*
	Horse and Jockey		*Jolly Gardeners*
Hemel Hempstead	*Lamb*		*Queen's Arms**
	Rose and Crown		*Queen's Arms***
Leverstock Green	*Leather Bottle*		

Beds

Leighton Buzzard	*Bridge Hotel*

Bucks

Aylesbury	*County Arms*	Aylesbury	*Cross Keys*

Greater London

Harefield	*Prince of Wales*	Stratford	*Steam Hammer*
Hillingdon	*Militia Canteen*	Uxbridge	*Victoria Chop House*
Pinner	*Victory*		

Key: * Queen's Road
          ** Watford Station

another five leaseholds and one copyhold were transferred and seventeen freehold properties were sold to the Sedgwick family. J. Fellowes of the Rickmansworth Brewery was involved as an executor in these negotiations. Meanwhile William Sedgwick had died in 1869 and been succeeded by his widow Mary Ann Sedgwick and their son Frederick James Sedgwick. The company traded as Mrs Mary Ann Sedgwick & Co. and, after buying the business for £60,000 by 1875, a major rebuilding programme was started.

Unfortunately some years later Frederick Sedgwick became seriously ill and on 29 July 1884 he was certified insane, so his mother legally took over a number of leases in Hertfordshire, Bedfordshire, Buckinghamshire and Greater London (Table 29.9).

This transaction also included the malting near the *Greyhound* in Albury. The company had opened a depot at 3 South Wharf, Paddington by 1886, also stores at 29 High Street, Berkhamsted and 13/15 Station Road, Croydon. Bottling of beer was started in 1892 and later proved to be very successful. In 1896 Sedgwick's bought the Colne Brewery on Uxbridge High Street from Mr J. Mercer and others for £9,200. The sale included seven tied properties and leases

Table 29.10 Sedgwick's Brewery acquisitions

a) Colne Brewery, Uxbridge 1896

Greater London

Cranford	*Jolly Gardeners* BH	Uxbridge	*Aubrey Arms* L.
Headstone	*Goodwill to All* BH		*General Elliott*
Hillingdon	*Cricketers* L.		*The Lynch* L. to 1909
North Hyde	*Canteen* L.		*Prince of Wales* L.
Pinner	*Oddfellows' Arms* L.		*Spotted Dog* L. to 1907
Southall Green	*Bricklayer's Arms*		BH
Uxbridge	*Abrook Arms*		

Herts

Croxley Green	*Rose* L.	Rickmansworth	*Sportman's Arms* BH

Bucks

Chalfont St Giles	*Duke of Wellington* L.		

b) Speedy's Brewery, Clapham 1923

Greater London

Brixton Hill	*Windmill* L.	Clapham	*Seven Stars*
Clapham	Horsham Grocery OL	Peckham	Beer Market OL
	Little Wonder OL	Southville	*Surprise* OL

for nine more (Table 29.10a.). Brewing stopped but the buildings were used as a depot. Because this brewery backed onto the Grand Union Canal access was also gained for barges to the quay on the property. One condition of the sale stipulated that Mr Mercer should not start another brewery within forty miles of Uxbridge.

Mrs Sedgwick continued as sole owner of the business until she died in 1897. Her executors, Gordon and Thomas Arnold Sedgwick ran the business with a manager named V.S. Harvey. In 1900 they bought Wild's Brewery in Rickmansworth with six tied properties (see Table 22.3). In the 1903 survey of licensed properties the brewery owned sixty-five public houses and off licences in Hertfordshire. In 1913 it has been reported that Sedgwick's had a brewery staff of 150 plus sixty-two horses and a barge for transporting beer to their depots in London and Uxbridge. During 1923 the brewery bought Speedy's Brewery in Clapham (Table 29.10b) presumably to have a presence in South London. Later in the same year when the brewery owned ninety-seven public houses it was sold as a thriving business to Benskin's for £597,000 (Table 29.11). During the time Sedgwick's had owned the brewery a number of disposals were made and it may not have been possible to identify all of these in Greater London (Table 29.12). In 1927 Benskin's converted some of the brewery buildings in Watford into maltings. Most of these buildings that had belonged to Sedgwick's finally were demolished between 1965 and 1966.

Table 29.11 Sedgwick's tied estate taken over by Benskin's

Herts

Abbot's Langley	Dog and Partridge	Park Street	Falcon
	Royal Oak	Potters Bar	Lion Hotel L.
Barnet	Albion	Rickmansworth	Sportsman L.*
	Arkley Hotel L.	St Albans	Boot L.
	Edinburgh Castle		Vine L.
	Mitre	Sarratt	Cricketers
	Woolpack	Shenley	Red Lion L.
Bedmond	White Hart	Watford	Anchor
Berkhamsted	Crown		Coachmakers' Arms
	OL Kittsbury Rd		Compasses
Bricket Wood	Black Boy		Crown
Bushey	Devonshire Arms		Dog (Holly Bush)
	Royal Oak		Eight Bells
Cassio Bridge	Halfway House		Escourt Tavern
Chorley Wood	Old Shepherd		George
Croxley Green	Red House L.		Heydon Arms
East Barnet	Cat		Jolly Gardeners
Flamstead	Horse and Groom		Load of Hay
Garston	Crown		Malden Hotel L.
Great Gaddesden	Crown and Sceptre L.		Oddfellows' Arms
Hemel Hempstead	Cupid		One Bell
	Railway Arms		Queen's Arms L.
	Rose and Crown		Swan
	Swan		Victoria Tavern
King's Langley	Swan		OL Langley Rd
Leavesden	Hare		OL Merton Rd
Letchmore Heath	Three Horseshoes	Welwyn	Red Lion
London Colney	Green Dragon	Wheathampstead	Cross Keys L.
Oxhey	Royal Oak	Wiggington	Cow Roast

Beds

Edlesborough	Axe and Compasses

Bucks

Aston Clinton	Bell	Aylesbury	OL Mill St
Aylesbury	County Arms L.	Beaconsfield	OL London End
	Cross Keys	Chalfont St Giles	Fox and Hounds L.

Greater London

Common Wood	Cart and Horses	Pinner	Oddfellows' Arms
Cranford	Jolly Gardeners L.*		Victory L.
Eastcote	Ship and Sun	Southall	Bricklayer's Arms*
Edgware	Royal Oak	Uxbridge	Abrook Arms*
Harefield	Prince of Wales		Crooked Billet L.
Harrow	Flora		General Elliott*
	Iowa Tavern		Hut
Hatch End	Letchford Arms		King's Arms
Hillingdon	Canteen L.*	Wandsworth	Seven Stars
	Hut		Surprise
Mill Hill	Railway Hotel	Wealdstone	Goodwill to All*
	Three Hammers	Wembley	Greyhound L.
Northwood	Clifton Hotel	Whetstone	Anchor
Pinner	Goodwill to All	Willesden	Fisherman's Arms L.

Key: * Part of Colne Valley Brewery estate

Table 29.12 Sedgwick's disposals before sale to Benskin's

Herts

Abbot's Langley	Red Lion	Letchmore Heath	Two Wrestlers L.
Albury	Greyhound L.	Leverstock Green	Leather Bottle L.
Aldenham	Chequers		Red Lion L.
	Volunteer	London Colney	Cross Keys
Amwell, Great	Holly Bush	Much Hadham	White Horse
Barnet	Three Elms	Potters Bar	Pilot Engine
Berkhamsted	Five Bells		Red Lion L.
Bishop's Stortford	Peacock	Radlett	Red Lion F.
	Pewter Pot	Rickmansworth	George L.
	Six Bells		King's Arms **
Bovingdon	Bell L.		Wheelwrights' Arms
Boxmoor	Leather Bottle	Ridge	Sovereign
Bushey	Lord Nelson	St Albans	Crown (Mermaid) F.#
	Robin Hood C.		Railway Tavern L.
Chipperfield	Anchor L.	Sarratt	Coach and Horses
	Swan L.	Shenley	Bricklayer's Arms
Chorley Wood	Jolly Brickmakers	Thorley	Green Man
	Old Berkeley Arms L.	Tring	OL Akeman St
Croxley Green	Rose L.*	Watford	Bedford Arms
Great Gaddesden	Horse and Jockey		Brewer's Arms F.
Hemel Hempstead	Compasses		Cart and Horses
	George and Dragon		Coach and Horses
	Lamb		Leathersellers' Arms
Hunton Bridge	Dog and Partridge		Pointer and Birds
King's Langley	Red Lion L.		Three Compasses F.
	Saracen's Head	Watford Heath	Load of Hay

Beds

Caddington	Horse and Jockey	Leighton Buzzard	Bridge
Dunstable	Horse and Groom L.	Marsworth	Lock House

Bucks

Chalfont St Giles	Duke of Wellington L.*	Denham	Hare and Hounds
Chesham	Crown, Ley Hill	Iver	Crooked Billet

Greater London

East Moseley	OL	Uxbridge	Aubrey Arms L.*
Edgware	Load of Hay		Bell
Enfield Chase	Railway Tavern		Lynch L.*
Friern Barnet	Anchor		Prince of Wales L.*
Hillingdon	Cricketers L.*		Spotted Dog L.*
Pinner	Oddfellows' Arms L.*		Victoria Chop House L.
Stanmore	Load of Hay	Wembley	Greyhound L.
Stepney	New Inn	Whetstone	Swan
Stratford	Steam Hammer L.	Willesden	Crown L.
	Mitre	Willesden Junction	White Horse

Key: * Part of Colne Valley Brewery estate
         ** Supplying although a 'free house'
         # Holywell Hill location

Table 29.13 Healey's tied estate in 1898

a) Sold to Benskin's			
Herts			
Abbot's Langley	Asylum Tavern c.1875	Rickmansworth	Prince of Wales
	Leathersellers' Arms		Western Inn
	Railway Arms, Nash Mills	Watford	Duke of Edinburgh
Bushey	Duke of Edinburgh c.1860		Jolly Anglers 1850
	Horse in Chains c.1877		Lamb 1854
	Villiers Arms 1874		New Inn (Brewery Tap)
Croxley Green	Duke of York		Old Berkeley Hunt
Elstree	Railway Arms		Red Lion
Rickmansworth	Plough, Mill End		Woodman
b) Earlier disposals			
Albury	Valiant Trooper L.	Bushey	Sawyers' Arms F. to 1870
Bushey	Holly Bush F.1860 to1890	Croxley Green	Sportsman F.

King Street Brewery

Healey's King Street Brewery was established in 1851 when Charles Healey I bought the stable block of the Watford Place Estate and two adjoining plots. Both Charles and his elder brother George (he bought Curtis's brewery in Harpenden) and their father previously had worked for the Whittingstall family at their Watford Brewery. Charles built the *New Inn* on the empty site and converted the stable block into a brewhouse. George Wakeford was appointed Head Brewer. In 1861 his son Charles Healey II became owner of the brewery employing nine men and boys. Tragically he died of a brain disease aged forty-one in 1863 but his wife Elizabeth Julie continued to own and manage the brewery until she died in 1891. Their son Charles III, who was only seven when his father died, eventually became a partner in the business and the company became registered as E.J. & C. Healey Ltd. In 1892 the company received a royal warrant for its beers by appointment to HRH Princess Mary of Cambridge, Duchess of Teck.

During 1898 Healey's took over the Victoria Brewery at 147 St Albans Road, Watford and an off-licence on this site. In less than fifty years this small brewery had belonged to Samuel Roate (1854–71), Frederick Cocks (1872–91), William Clarke (1892–6) and the Chesham Brewery (1896–8). However, in the same year Healey's themselves were taken over by Benskin's with eighteen public houses. The estate included seven public houses in Watford and the remainder in local towns and villages. No obvious traces now remain of the brewery a hundred years later.

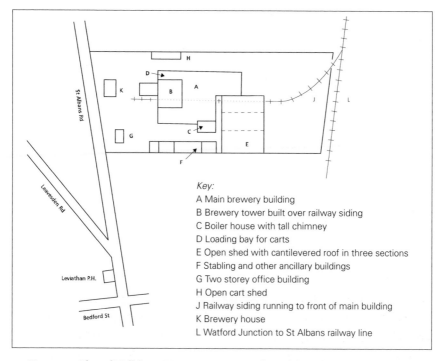

Key:
A Main brewery building
B Brewery tower built over railway siding
C Boiler house with tall chimney
D Loading bay for carts
E Open shed with cantilevered roof in three sections
F Stabling and other ancillary buildings
G Two storey office building
H Open cart shed
J Railway siding running to front of main building
K Brewery house
L Watford Junction to St Albans railway line

Figure 29.3 Plan of Wells' new Lion Brewery in 1902 derived from the architect's sketch in
The Brewer's Journal, *15 April 1902*

Lion Brewery

Ralph Thorpe founded the Lion or St Albans Road Brewery in June 1890. His young nephew J.R. Godson later worked for him. Initially this was a six quarter brewery obtaining its water from the underlying chalk strata. Most of the early business appears to have been contract brewing, in particular orders from the London Cooperative Wholesale Societies. An etching from *The Brewer's Journal*, when a new thirty quarter brewery was being erected, shows a railway siding running the whole length of the premises. A bottling plant was built and much of the output was transported by rail to a depot at Chalk Farm. Wells bought the brewery before 1909 and J.R. Godson became a company director. At this stage there was a tied estate of twenty properties that were all in Greater London. None were in Hertfordshire, Bedfordshire, Buckinghamshire, Cambridgeshire or Essex at that time.

In 1932, Wells opened their first off-licence in Watford. It is interesting to note that three years later the Watford Licensing Court stipulated that there should be no shop at the brewery, no sale to the general public and only sale to

Table 29.14 Wells' tied estate on 25 May 1951

Herts

Bushey	Cold Harbour Hotel F	Watford	Leggatts Rise OL
St Albans	Camp Stores OL		*Tudor Arms* F
Watford	Bushey Mill Lane OL		

Beds

Eaton Bray	White Horse F		

Greater London

Battersea	Meyrick Stores OL	Holborn	*George and Dragon* F
Bethnal Green	*Three Crowns* OL	Islington	*Albion* B & W
Bishopsgate	*Magpie* F	Kilburn	Granville Stores OL
Clerkenwell	*Corner Pin* B & W, L.	Knightsbridge	*Nag's Head* F
	Crown F	Regent's Park	*Crown and Anchor* F
	Norfolk Arms B & W, L.	South Harrow	Roxeth Stores OL
Deptford	*Earl Douglas* OL	Upper Norwood	*Colby Arms* F
Finsbury	*Fountain* F	Walworth	*Providence* OL
Greenwich	*Old Loyal Britons* B & W	Woolwich	*Duchess of Wellington* F
Hammersmith	Cardross Stores OL		

Table 29.15 Wells' disposals from their tied estate and closing of accounts before 1951

Herts

Abbot's Langley	Working M.C. 1946	Hemel Hempstead	Working M.C. 1945
Bricket Wood	Working M.C. 1945	Markyate	Stores OL 1939

Greater London

Albany St NW	*Victory* F. 1945	Northolt	British Legion 1946
Commercial Rd E1	*Boundary Tavern* 1941	Wealdstone	Social Club 1946

Key: M.C. Men's Club

trade customers. Wells opened another off-licence in Watford and later bought the *Tudor Arms* in Watford and the *Cold Harbour Hotel* in Bushey.

When sold to Benskin's in 1951 there were nineteen freehold properties and six leasehold properties in their tied estate (Table 29.14). This consisted of eleven full licences, four beer and wine licences and ten off-licences. The main part of the estate was in Greater London (nineteen properties). In Hertfordshire there were five plus another one in Bedfordshire. Previously there had been a closure or disposal of three properties (Table 29.5). During the Second World War the *Boundary Tavern* in Commercial Road, London, was destroyed by a bomb. Five accounts with social clubs had also been closed.

References

Allied Brewery Archives. *Benskin's Annual General Meeting*, 1929.

Barnard, A. Cannon Brewery, Watford. *Noted Breweries of Great Britain and Northern Ireland*, Vol. 4, London, 1891, pp.28–50.

Cornell, M. Benskin's of Watford, *Brewery History Society Journal*, 1987, No. 51, pp.10–19.

Hertfordshire Archives and Local Studies. a. Tithe Map of Watford, 1844, b. Acc. 3883, Box 1 Details of Benskin's tied estate in Beds, Bucks, Cambs and London bought or leased, c. D/E Be/T1 (Smith's), d. Acc. 3883, Box 25 Sedgwick estate in Herts, Beds, Bucks and London (includes summary of purchase of Colne Valley Brewery, Uxbridge), e. Acc. 3883, Box 24 Property registers for London and Watford (include Sedgwick's and Wells') also Sedgwick's Brewery Tenants Register 1910–20, 1921–23, f. Acc. 3883, Box 4 Details of Wells' Brewery and estate, g. Acc. 3883, Box 12 Volumes of *Pennant* (Benskin's magazine), h. Acc.3883, Box 13 Conveyance of Speedy's Brewery to Sedgwick.

Investors' Guardian, 25 December 1920. Article about Benskin's.

Petty Sessions Licensing Records for Hertfordshire, Bedfordshire, Buckinghamshire, Cambridgeshire and west Essex.

Poole, H. *Here for the Beer*, Watford Museum, 1984, pp. 53–9.

Richmond, L. and Turton, A. (eds.) *The Brewing Industry: A Guide to Historical Records*, Manchester University Press, 1990, pp.65–6 (Benskin).

Smith, K.A. The Popes and the Dysons. Five generations of Watford brewers. *Hertfordshire's Past*, 1988, Vol. 25, pp.2–7.

CHAPTER THIRTY

Welwyn

Welwyn Brewery was established in the 1800s in a small two-storey building in School Lane by the bridge over the River Mimram. There was also an off-licence next to the brewery where local people could take jugs to buy small quantities of beer. Between 1839 and 1897 there were a number of owners and leaseholders.

In 1839 the brewery was owned by George Cass, who was a brewer, a maltster, a corn merchant and a coal merchant. By 1851, James Deards was a cooper at the brewery and later became the brewery owner. His son John Deards bought the *Fox* at Woolmer Green from Benjamin Young of Hertford in 1860. This was the only tied house the brewery ever owned. In 1860 Samuel Gentle of Kimpton initially leased the brewery for five years. The lease was taken over by Samuel Kidd in 1881, who expanded the product range – by 1886 brewing six draught beers, stout and porter and also manufacturing lemonade and ginger beer. Six years later John Deards assigned the lease to the Mew family from the Isle of Wight when there were six staff and three horses and carts for deliveries.

Alfred Hawden took over the lease in 1895 but in 1897 he sold the remainder of the lease for the brewery, the off-licence and the *Fox* to McMullen's of Hertford for £245. McMullen's later bought the *Fox*, which they still own, and the off-licence, which they kept until 1954 when the licence was transferred to the *Tavern* on the other side of the High Street. However McMullen's did not buy the brewery. This building was used later for various purposes including wartime research and as a tyre company store before it was pulled down.

References

Poole, H. *Here for the Beer*, Watford Museum, 1984, p.60.

Rook, T. *Of Local Interest: A book of Welwyn pubs*, 1986.

Welwyn and Hatfield Times, 29 June 1979, Looking at an age when small beer was 'ale and 'earty.

CHAPTER THIRTY-ONE

Wheathampstead

The *Bull* by the River Lea, the *Tin Pot* at Gustard Wood and the *Bell* and the *Swan* near the village church were all licensed inns by 1706. All probably had their own brewhouses on the premises. In 1743 the *Swan* had a malting, malt lofts, a barn, stables, outhouses, an orchard and 12 acres of land. There were also maltings at the *Bell* and the *Bull*. By 1753, Isaac House of Grove Farm had bought

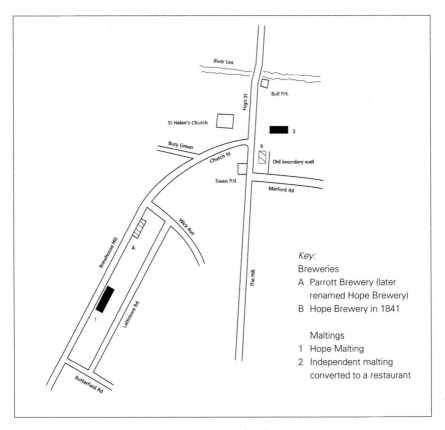

Figure 31.1 Brewery and malting sites

the *Swan* and associated property and later sold the whole property to James Wilkins I, who was already an established brewer before 1781.

Parrott Brewery

Historically the road leading from Wheathampstead Church to Amwell was known as Hamwell Hill. In 1781, Westminster Abbey granted 'James Wilkins I of Whethamsted ... Brewer a piece of land being part of the Chalk Delves containing about three rods ... in length ... and in breadth two poles and an half' (Workers' Educational Association, 1974). A brewery was built on this land and became known as the Parrott Brewery and the road eventually became known as Brewhouse Hill. James Wilkins died in 1787 and was succeeded by his son James Wilkins II who later bought the *Gibraltar Castle* in Batford before 1799. The Wilkins family had stopped brewing before 1834 at the Parrott Brewery (Pigot, 1834).

The *Swan* was sold to James Isaac House in 1836 but he was not recorded as a brewer in Wheathampstead between 1834 and 1839. In the meantime the House family had established a brewery in Harpenden. It would appear that the Parrott Brewery was unused for some time, unless the Sutton family who were also brewing in the village had taken over the building. Unfortunately their place of work in 1838 and 1839 is not recorded (Pigot, 1838, 1839). There is no evidence on the 1841 tithe map to indicate there was any active brewery on Brewhouse Hill or attached to the *Swan*. However George Sutton did own a house and cottages on tithe plot 15 on Brewhouse Hill which would appear to have been the Parrott Brewery site.

Hope Brewery

The 1841 tithe map does record a small brewery was on tithe plot 33 on the corner of the High Street and Marford Road opposite the church. This was called the Hope Brewery and was owned by the Lattimore family who lived next door on tithe plot 34 (Pigot 1838, 1839). All traces of this brewery have now been destroyed by later developments except for a possible stretch of brick and flint boundary wall. In the 1820s William Digby Lattimore had mortgaged the *Three Oaks* with a brewhouse at the hamlet of Amwell from Joseph Simpson. However this property may not have been actually licensed until the 1830s.

After 1841 the Lattimores moved to the much bigger ex-Parrott Brewery

Figure 31.2 Hope Brewery and tunnel

building on Brewhouse Hill and renamed it as the Hope Brewery. It is a very distinctive building over a tunnel going into the hillside. The tunnel and the house above it are thought to date from the early 1780s, as a messuage or tenement is mentioned at the Court Baron in 1787, recorded after James Wilkins I had died (Workers' Educational Association, 1974). It is evident that no part of the building on tithe plot 15 was being used as a brewery in 1841. A twenty quarter malting was built near the brewery together with stables and other buildings. The family stopped using the original brewery opposite the *Swan*.

The Lattimore family bought the *Green Man* and a malting in Sandridge in 1846 and then steadily increased their tied estate within the locality until the late 1880s. Their most distant purchases were in North Mymms, Hemel Hempstead, Luton and Welwyn.

In 1897 they initially released the leases, and later in 1904 sold a number of licensed properties to Pryor, Reid & Co. of Hatfield. In the same year Woolridge

Figure 31.3 Hope Brewery and Brewery house

Figure 31.4 Hope Brewery malting

Hill bought the brewery and took over the remainder of the tied estate that consisted of the leases of six beer houses, one public house and an off-licence. Some of these properties had previously been leased to William Hill-Archer who had owned the brewery in Whitwell.

When the brewery was put up for sale again in 1902, the sales literature stated that the property included a grinding room, a mash room, cooling and

Table 31.1 Lattimore's tied estate which had been sold or leased before or during 1897

Herts			
Amwell	*Red Cow* 1866*	St Albans	*Duke of Marlborough* 1868*
Codicote	*Globe* 1881		*Garibaldi* BH 1869
Harpenden	*Engineer* 1868	Sandridge	*Green Man* 1846*
	Queen's Head 1866	Welwyn	*Black Horse* L.
Hatfield	*Black Bull* LH to 1878 **		*Queen's Head*
	Butcher's Arms 1855*		*Steamer* 1881*
	Prince of Wales	Wheathampstead	*Cherry Trees* 1869
Hemel Hempstead	*White Lion* 1876 #		*Railway Hotel* 1869*
Lemsford	*Long and Short Arm* L.1876		*Three Oaks* 1820s
North Mymms	*Sibthorp Arms* BH		
Beds			
Caddington	*Rose and Crown* BH 1878	Luton	*Lamb* BH 1972
Luton	*George and Dragon* 1872	World's End	OL 1875

Key: * Leased to Pryor, Reid & Co. of Hatfield in 1897 and bought in 1904
        ** At Puttocks Oak
        # At Water End

Table 31.2 Hope Brewery tied estate in 1902 (all leasehold)

Herts			
Bendish	*White Hart* BH	Whiteway Bottom	*Green Man* BH
Codicote	*Queen's Head* BH	Whitwell	*Lamb* BH
Diamond End	*Woodman* BH*		*Maidenhead* FL
Kimpton	*Black Horse* BH		
Beds			
Luton	OL High Town Rd		

Key: * Leased from the Earl of Strathmore

fermenting rooms, a tun room and a furnace room with a five quarter steam plant. There was also a very large brick cellar with access by a large distinctive tunnel, a yard, a dray shed, two cask sheds and other buildings. The stabling had five stalls and a loose box. There was also an attached brewery house. In 1902 Chambers & Co bought the brewery and took over the leases of the leasehold properties holding them until 1904 when the brewery finally closed.

The twenty quarter malting further up Brewhouse Hill had a twenty quarter couch, three cement growing floors and two ten quarter kilns, each with wire floors and a furnace plus malt stores. This malting was also sold to Pryor, Reid & Co. who continued to own it until at least 1910.

Much later the brewery was acquired by Collins Antiques of Wheathampstead and used as an additional showroom. In 1938 the local district council issued an order to demolish the building which was fortunately withdrawn, a preservation order finally being made in 1971. More recently parts of the building became surplus to requirements and were let as an art gallery in 1996. The building is at present let as a beauty salon. Meanwhile the malting has been converted into office accommodation.

References

Petty Sessions Licensing Records for Hertfordshire and Bedfordshire.

Pigot's Directory of Hertfordshire for 1834, 1838, 1839.

Poole, H. *Here for the Beer*, Watford Museum, 1984, p.60.

Workers' Education Association (Harpenden and St Albans Branches). *About Wheathampstead*, 1974, p.10.

Workers' Education Association (Harpenden and St Albans Branches). *Wheathampstead and Harpenden IV: The Age of Independence*, Harpenden, The History Publishing Society, 1978.

CHAPTER THIRTY-TWO

Whitwell

During the 1800s a small brewery was established on the northern side of Whitwell High Street which was owned by the Archer and Hill families. In 1839 John Hill was described as a brewer and maltster. He was succeeded in 1846 by Rob Hill who went into partnership with a Mr Archer from 1850 to 1859 or slightly later. In 1862 Frederick Hill-Archer took over the brewery and was followed by William Hill-Archer in 1878.

The known tied estate of this brewery was extremely local in North Hertfordshire. It consisted of the *White Hart* BH in Bendish, the *Woodman* BH at Diamond End near King's Walden, the *Green Man* BH at Whiteway Bottom near St Paul's Walden and the *Lamb* BH and the *Maidenhead* FL in Whitwell. The *Woodman* was leased from the Earl of Strathmore of St Paul's Walden. The tied estate was leased to the Hope Brewery in Wheathampstead after the brewery closed. The brewery and brewer's house still exist but they now have been converted to a private dwelling.

References

Petty Sessions Licensing Records for Hertfordshire.
Poole, H. *Here for the Beer*, Watford Museum, 1984, pp.61–2.

Out-of-county breweries

Out-of-county breweries

Being an inland county Hertfordshire shares boundaries with Buckinghamshire, Bedfordshire, Cambridgeshire, Essex and Greater London. It is already evident from the first part of this book that the tied estates of many of the breweries extended into adjoining counties. A few of the breweries made take-overs of breweries outside the county. The 1902 survey (Table 1.2b) shows that thirty-five breweries owned a few properties in Hertfordshire and six owned more than ten. These breweries will now be considered in this final part of the book working in a clockwise direction beginning with Buckinghamshire.

Weller's of Amersham had a significant presence in the west part of the county before being taken over by Benskin's in 1930. The Chesham Brewery was active in a similar area as well as making take-overs of the Anchor Brewery in Hemel Hempstead in 1891 and the Swan Brewery in Berkhamsted in 1898. Roberts & Wilson of Ivinghoe had established themselves in the north west of the county before also being taken over by Benskin's in 1927. Bennett's of Dunstable bought properties in the western half of the county, leased Glover's brewery in Harpenden in 1874 and leased the Redbourn Brewery in 1879. For a few years they had a Hertfordshire registered business base in Harpenden before returning to Dunstable. Green's of Luton slowly bought properties in the north and central parts of the county as well as taking over Adey & White of St Albans in 1936, Phillips of Royston in 1949 and Fordham's of Ashwell in 1952. Wells of Bedford historically owned a few properties in Hitchin and nearby villages. Some of them have since been closed. Gradually the brewery has made a few more purchases elsewhere in the county. However it is the only out-of-county brewery that was mentioned in the 1902 survey that is still an independent working brewery that might in the future buy more licensed properties in the county. No brewery in Cambridgeshire ever had any significant presence in the county. The Anchor Brewery of Saffron Walden owned a small number of properties in and near Bishop's Stortford but most of the tied estate was in

Essex. This brewery was then bought by Taylor's of Bishop's Stortford to become Hertfordshire-owned (1839–97), sold to Reid & Co (later Watney, Coombe & Reid) and this particular tied estate was sold to Benskin's of Watford (1919–57). At the time of the 1902 survey the Hertfordshire component of the ex-Anchor Brewery estate made up most of the total for Watney & Co. Clutterbuck's of Stanmore had established a large part of their tied estate in the west and central part of the county for over a hundred years until they were taken over by the Cannon Brewery in 1923. Although Holt's Marine Brewery of East London bought a few properties in Ware this brewery was only active in Hertfordshire for a very short while before a take-over by the Cannon Brewery in 1912. This one brewery will not be dealt with in this last part of the book.

CHAPTER THIRTY-THREE

Amersham, Buckinghamshire

Amersham Brewery

William Weller is reputed to have started the brewery in Church Street in Amersham Old Town in 1771. Eventually he bequeathed the business to his son William who died in 1857. The second William was succeeded by a third William Weller.

The brewery by the River Misburn opposite the town church became the major source of employment in the town. On the opposite side of Church Street

Table 33.1 Weller's tied estate taken over by Benskin's in 1930

Herts			
Berkhampsted	*Queen's Arms* FL	King's Langley	*Red Lion*, Waterside
Bovingdon	*Bell*		*Saracen's Head* FL
	Bricklayer's Arms BH	Leverstock Green	*Leather Bottle* FL
Boxmoor	*Railway Tavern*		*Red Lion* FL
Chipperfield	*Windmill* BH	Markyate	*Sun*
Chorley Wood	*Rose and Crown*	Rickmansworth	*King's Arms* FL
Hemel Hempstead	*Bricklayer's Arms* BH		*Prince of Wales*
	Papermakers' Arms BH	Sarratt	*Wheatsheaf*
	Queen's Head FL	Tring	*Swan* BH
	Red Lion, Nash Mills	Watford	*White Lion*, Nascot
	Saracen's Head FL		

Bucks			
Amersham	*Boot and Slipper* FL	Great Missenden	*Barley Mow*
	Chequers FL		*Crown* FL
	Crown FL		*Nag's Head*
	Eagle FL		*Swan*
	King's Arms FL		*White Horse* FL
	Lord Nelson BH		*White Lion* FL
	Old Griffin FL	Haddenham	*Waggon and Horses*
	Old Plough BH	Hambledon	*Pheasant* BH
	Queen's Head FL	Hawridge	*Rose and Crown*
	Red Lion FL, Common	Hedgerley	*Brickmould* FL
	Red Lion FL, High St	High Wycombe	*Angel* FL
	Saracen's Head FL		*Cross Keys* FL
	Station (*Iron Horse*)		*Gate* FL

	Wheatsheaf BH		*Golden Fleece* FL
	White Horse FL		*Jolly Butchers* BH
	White Lion FL		*Nag's Head* BH
Asheridge	*Blue Ball*		*New Inn* FL
Askett	*Three Crowns*		*Van Inn* FL
Aylesbury	*Green Man* FL		*White Horse*
	Red Lion	Holmer Green	*Bat and Ball*
Beaconsfield	*Railway Hotel*		*Earl Howe*
Bellingdon	*Bull*	Horton	*Halfway House*
Bledlow	*Barley Corn* BH	Hughendon	*Pole Cat* FL
Bourne End	*Railway Hotel* FL		*Red Lion* BH
Bradenham	*Red Lion* BH	Knotty Green	*Red Lion*
Burnham	*Red Lion* BH	Little Hampden	*Rising Sun* FL
Cadsden	*Plough*	Little Kingshill	*Full Moon*
Chalfont St Giles	*Merlin's Cave* FL	Little Marlow	*Queen's Head* BH
	Pheasant FL	Little Missenden	*Red Lion*
	Rose and Crown FL	Marlow	*Bank of England*
Chalfont St Peter	*Jolly Farmer*		*Verney Arms* BH
	Rose and Crown	Penn	*Red Lion* FL
	Uncle Tom's Cabin BH	Penn Street	*Squirrel* BH
Chartridge	*Bell*	Prestwood	*Chequers*
Chenies	*Red Lion* BH		*Pole Cat* FL
Chesham	*Black Horse,* Vale	Princes Risborough	*Bell* FL
	Black Horse, Waterside		*Crown* FL
	Blue Ball FL		*George and Dragon*
	Elephant and Castle BH		*Pink and Lily* FL
	Golden Ball	St Leonards	*White Lion* FL
	Pheasant BH	Stoke Mandeville	*Bull* FL
	Queen's Head FL	Stokenchurch	*Four Horseshoes* BH
	Red Lion FL	Taplow	*Feathers* FL
Coleshill	*Fleur de Lis* FL	The Lee	*Gate* FL
	Magpies FL	Tylers Green	*Horse and Jockey* BH
	Queen's Head FL	Wendover	*King and Queen*
	Red Lion FL		*Leather Bottle* FL
Denham	*Waggon and Horses* BH		*Nag's Head*
Dinton	*White Horse* FL		*Rose and Crown*
Edesborough	*Traveller's Rest*		*Station Hotel* FL
Farnham Royal	*Stag and Hounds* BH	Wendover Dean	*Halfway House*
Frith Hill	*Black Horse*	Wooburn	*Chequers*
Gerrards Cross	*French Horn* FL		*Compasses* FL
	Pack Horse BH		*Harrow* BH
Gold Hill	*Jolly Farmer*		*Queen and Albert* FL
Great Kimble	*Bernard Arms*		*Railway Inn* FL
Great Kingshill	*Red Lion*		*Red Lion* FL

Greater London

Cranford	*Stag and Hounds*	Uxbridge	*Eagle*
Harefield	*Cricketers* FL		*Rose and Crown*

Oxon

Chinnor	*Wheatsheaf*	Thame	*Two Brewers*
Cowley	*Royal Oak*	Watlington	*Royal Oak*

Berks

Cookham	*Royal Exchange*	Cookham Dean	*Uncle Tom's Cabin*

Table 33.2 Weller's disposals before 1930

Herts

Abbot's Langley	*Farrier's Arms*	Hemel Hempstead	*Salmon* BH
	George	Rickmansworth	*Cross Keys*
	Red Lion		*Dove*
Berkhampsted	*King Edward VI* BH		*Four Horseshoes* BH
	Sawyers' Arms		*George and Dragon*
Bovingdon	*Red Lion*		*Railway*
Hemel Hempstead	*Half Moon* FL		*Spotted Dog* BH
	Railway Tavern FL		

Bucks

Amersham	*Black Horse* FL	High Wycombe	*One Star*
	Fleur de Lys BH		*Three Cups*
	Magpie FL	Hitcham	*Maypole* BH
	Potter's Arms BH, L.	Hughenden	*Gate*
	Squirrel BH		*King's Head*
Aston Clinton	*White Lion* FL		*Wheel* FL
Aylesbury	*Plume of Feathers* BH	Hunton	*Farriers*
Beaconsfield	*Farrier's Arms* FL	Hyde Heath	*Red Cow*
	Rose and Crown BH	Lacey Green	*Crown*
	White Hart L.	Lane End	*Old Arm Chair* BH
Bledlow	*Seven Stars* FL	Langley Marsh	*Two Yew Trees* BH
Bourne End	*Walnut Tree* BH	Lee Common	*Red Lion*
Buckland	*White Lion*		*Swan*
Burnham	*Alma*	Little Missenden	*Nag's Head* BH
Chalfont St Peter	*Pack Horse* FL		*Royal Oak*
Chesham	*Green Man* FL	Loosely Row	*Salmon*
	Huntsman	Loudwater	*New Inn*
	One Bell BH	Marlow	*Bricklayer's Arms* BH
	Red Cow BH		*Saddlers' Arms*
	Seven Stars FL		*Traveller's Friend* BH
	Star and Garter BH	Monks Risborough	*Plough*
			Shoulder of Mutton
Corner Hall	*Queen's Head*		*Three Crows* BH
Denham	*Queen's Head* FL, L.	Oakley	*Wheatsheaf*
Frogmore	*Bell*	Penn	*Victoria*
Fulmer	*Bell* FL	Princes Risborough	*Railway Tavern* BH
	French Horn FL	Quainton	*White Lion*
Gerrards Cross	*Fox and Hounds*	Seer Green	*Yew Trees*
Granford	*Stag and Hounds*	Stoke Poges	*Stag*
Hempstead	*Half Moon*	Three Households	*Uncle Tom's Cabin*
High Wycombe	*George*	Tylers Hill	*Five Bells*
	Horse and Groom BH	Wooburn Moor	*Farriers*
	Horse and Jockey		

Greater London

Harlington	*Wheatsheaf*	Uxbridge	*Great Western*
Pinner	*Hand in Hand*		

Beds		Berks	
Caddington *Sun*		Cookham Dean	*Heaven*

were the stables. Further away at the corner of Church Street and School Lane was a tithe barn that was used by the brewery for storage and has now been converted into a house called Three Gables. A malting complex and extra stabling were built in 1829 in Barn Meadows off School Lane. These extensive buildings are still in use for light industry and craft workshops.

Most of the tied estate was in Buckinghamshire with a strong presence in Amersham, Chesham and High Wycombe. In 1903 the brewery owned or leased twenty-nine full-licence properties and beer houses in Hertfordshire in the Petty Sessions licensing districts of Hemel Hempstead and Watford. In 1929 the brewery had approximately 150 licensed properties in Buckinghamshire, Hertfordshire, Middlesex and Oxfordshire. At this time the owners, William and George Weller, decided to sell the brewery. However there were legal difficulties and the brewery was auctioned to overcome the problems. Benskin's of Watford were the successful bidders and purchased the brewery and 132 properties of the tied estate, including eighteen in Hertfordshire on 1 April 1930 (Table 33.1). The known earlier disposals in Hertfordshire and other counties are given in Table 33.2.

At Benskin's annual general meeting in December 1929, the chairman had stated that many of Weller's public houses were within their own Watford brewery delivery area. The remainder of the properties in new and developing districts, mainly on the outskirts of London, could be reached easily by brewery delivery lorries.

After Benskin's takeover the disused Amersham brewery site was sold to Goya International Beauty Products. This company became a major local employer. Recently the buildings have been converted into an office complex called Badminton Court. Because Amersham Old Town has a policy to keep and preserve old buildings it is still possible to walk round the conservation area to appreciate the size of the brewery and associated buildings needed for a tied estate of approximately 150 public houses.

References

Allied Archives. Benskin's Annual General Meeting 1929.

Amersham Society. *Amersham. A walk around the old town*, 1998, revised 2nd edition.

Buckinghamshire County Record Office. a. AR 96/2002 Weller's ledger for 1925, Notebooks *c.*1907.

Hertfordshire Archives and Local Studies. a. Acc. 3883. Box 25. Property registers; All

Counties 1919–47, Chesham Area 1937–78, Herts and Bucks 1969–84 (these registers normally record the original brewery owner), b. Acc. 3883. Box 12. *Pennant* magazine – for Weller's estate bought by Benskin's.

Petty Sessions Licensing Records for Hertfordshire, Bedfordshire and Buckinghamshire.

CHAPTER THIRTY-FOUR

Chesham, Buckinghamshire

T. & J. Nash Ltd, Chesham Brewery

Thomas and James Nash opened Chesham Brewery in the High Street in 1841. Because the brewery was so near to the western Hertfordshire border it was logical to buy licensed properties in Berkhamsted, Bovingdon, Boxmoor, Hemel Hempstead, Northchurch and some of the neighbouring villages and other towns. Their first brewery take-over in Hertfordshire was the Anchor Brewery in Hemel Hempstead as well as a tied estate of twenty-four licensed properties in 1891. Most of these properties were beer houses. Later the company bought the small Victoria Brewery in St Albans Road, Watford plus an off-licence in 1896. During 1898 they bought Fosters' Swan Brewery in Berkhamsted and fourteen licensed properties. Details of their own original tied estate and those from other breweries in Hertfordshire are given in Table 34.1.

In 1898 they also bought the rival brewery of Mrs Sarah How & Sons of Chesham. Much later in 1946 they merged with Hopcroft & Norris of Brackley, Northamptonshire with a tied estate of seventy-nine properties and became established as the Chesham & Brackley Breweries Ltd. Details of the properties in Hertfordshire that became part of the merged estate in 1946 are given in the first part of Table 34.1 and disposals or closures before 1946 are given in the second part of this table. Ten years later this new company was taken over by Taylor Walker & Co. Ltd of London. Subsequently Taylor Walker became part of Ind Coope Ltd. In 1962 the licensed properties were transferred to Benskin's Watford Brewery Ltd which previously had been taken over by Ind Coope in 1957.

Table 34.1 T. & J. Nash's tied estate in Hertfordshire

a) Became part of the merger of the Chesham and Brackley Brewery in 1946

Berkhamsted	*Black Horse* BH*	Hemel Hempstead	*Royal Oak* BH*
	Brownlow Arms FL**		*Shah* BH*
	Compasses BH		*Spotted Cow* BH*
	George FL**		*Swan and Trout* BH*
	Railway Tavern FL		*Three Horseshoes* BH*
	OL Charles St 1**		*Whip and Collar* BH*
	OL Charles St 2		*White Lion* BH
Bovingdon	*Halfway House* FL	Markyate	*Star and Garter* BH
Chipperfield	*Boot* BH*	Northchurch	*Compasses* BH
Great Gaddesden	*Fox* BH*		*Rose and Crown* BH
Hemel Hempstead	*Anchor* BH*	Potters Crouch	*Holly Bush* FL
	Bell FL*	Redbourn	*Greyhound* BH
	Brewer's Arms BH*		*Jolly Gardeners* BH
	Fishery FL		*Tom in Bedlam* FL
	Green Man BH	Tring	*Black Horse* BH*
	Midland Hotel FL	Watford	*Railway Arms* FL
	Oddfellows' Arms BH*		*Verulam Arms* FL
	Prince's Arms BH		

b) Sold or closed before 1946

Berkhamsted	*Rose and Crown*	Hemel Hempstead	*Green Man* BH
	Swan FL**		*Nag's Head* BH*
	OL George St**		*Papermakers' Arms* BH
	OL High St		*Post Office Arms* BH*
	OL Kittsbury**		*Queen's Arms* BH*
Bovingdon	*Friend at Hand* BH		*Rose and Crown* FL
	Hope and Anchor BH**		*Three Crows* BH
	Rose and Crown FL		OL Anchor Brewery*
Bushey	*Rose and Crown*	King's Langley	*Griffin* BH
Chidwick Green #	*One Bell* BH		*Jolly Miller* BH*
Hemel Hempstead	*Artichoke* BH*		*Swan* BH
	Drayman BH*	Northchurch	*Fox and Hounds* BH*
	Foundry Arms BH		*Pheasant* BH
	Fox and Hounds BH*		*Rose and Crown* BH
	Friend at Hand BH		OL

Key: * Originally tied estate of Anchor Brewery, Hemel Hempstead
        ** Originally tied estate of Foster's Swan Brewery, Berkhamsted
        # Chidwick Green is on the Chidwickbury estate north of St Albans

References

Petty Sessions Licensing Records for Hertfordshire.

Poole, H. *Here for the Beer,* Watford Museum, 1984, p.12 (Anchor Brewery).

Richmond, L. and Poole, A. (eds.) *The Brewing Industry: A Guide to Historical Records,* 1990, pp.100–1.

CHAPTER THIRTY-FIVE

Ivinghoe, Buckinghamshire

Roberts & Wilson Ltd

Although the village of Ivinghoe is in Buckinghamshire it is very near to the borders of Hertfordshire and Bedfordshire. A brewery was built on the south side of the village church in a lane running between the church and a large house that is now a youth hostel. This brewery was initially owned by the Rackshaw family until 1845, the Meacher family from 1845 to the 1870s and finally by Roberts & Wilson until 1927. Benskin's of Watford bought the brewery and tied estate in 1927 and closed the brewery soon after purchase. Later the site was cleared and the land has been used for building a small housing estate.

When the brewery was originally put up for sale in 1845 it had a tun room, a mill room, stores, stabling for five horses, a ten quarter malting, a fifteen quarter malting plus twenty-eight licensed properties. The tied estate in Bedfordshire, Hertfordshire and Buckinghamshire was increased in size during the 1870s and 1880s under Roberts & Wilson's ownership. They finally sold thirty-eight properties to Benskin's in 1927 and transferred ten leases. This estate consisted of thirteen properties in Hertfordshire, seventeen in Bedfordshire, seventeen in Buckinghamshire and one in Oxfordshire (Table 35.1). Before this sale they had previously disposed of a few other properties mainly in small villages in Bedfordshire and Buckinghamshire that were often selling very low volumes of beer (Table 35.2).

References

Hertfordshire Archives and Local Studies. a. D/Ex 672 (Sale details of 1845), b. Acc. 3883.
  Box 15. Herts and Bucks: Benskin's properties A-Z, original brewery owner.
  c. Acc. 3883. Box 12. *Pennant* magazine. Roberts & Wilson properties owned by
  Benskin's.
Petty Sessions Licensing Records for Hertfordshire, Bedfordshire and Buckinghamshire.

Table 35.1 Ivinghoe Brewery tied estate sold and leases transferred to Benskin's in 1927

Herts

Berkhamsted	*Crystal Palace* 1903	Tring	*Bell* 1845
Boxmoor	*Steam Coach* 1903		*Grand Junction* 1903
Hemel Hempstead	OL Charles St 1903		*Robin Hood* 1845
Kinsbourne Green	*Fox* 1845		OL King St 1903
Long Marston	*White Hart* 1845	Water End, H.H.	*Red Lion* 1845
Markyate	*Plume of Feathers* 1903	Wiggington	*Brew House* 1903
	Red Lion 1845		

Beds

Billington	*Greyhound*	Leighton Buzzard	*Black Horse* L.
Caddington	*Harrow* 1876		*Ram* 1891
Dunstable	*Nag's Head* 1891	Linslade	*Elephant and Castle* L.
Eaton Bray	*Bedford Arms*		*Hare* L.
	Five Bells 1845	Luton	*Stag's Head*
	Plough 1876	Tottenhoe	*Old Farm* 1891 L.
Eggington	*Three Horseshoes* 1845	Whipsnade	*Chequers* 1845
Houghton Regis	*King's Arms* 1845	Wolverton	*Locomotive* L.
Leighton Buzzard	*Bell and Woolpack* L.	Woodside	*Harrow*

Bucks

Aylesbury	*Broad Leys*	Ivinghoe	*Rose and Crown*
	Rockwood 1872	Marsworth	*Queeen's Head* 1872
	Ship Inn	Pitstone	*Bell* 1891
	BH Ardenham St L.		*Chequers* 1903
Buckland	*Boot and Slipper* 1845	Slapton	*Carpenters' Arms* L.
Cheddington	*Roseberry Arms* L.	Stewkley	*Black Swan* L.
	Three Horseshoes		*Carpenters' Arms*
Dagnall	*Red Lion* 1872	Weston Turville	*Chandos Arms*
Ivinghoe	*King's Head*		

Oxon

Water Eaton	*Plough*

Key: H.H. Hemel Hempstead

Table 35.2 Roberts & Wilson's disposals of their tied estate before the sale of the brewery
to Benskin's in 1927

Herts

Kemsworth	BH*

Beds

Billington	*Cock* #	Humbershoe	*Red Lion*
Dunstable	*Rising Sun* #	Leighton Buzzard	*Greyhound* #
	Rose and Crown #	Luton	*Belgium Arms* **
Eaton Bray	*Fountain* #	Potsgrove	*Fox and Hounds* #

Bucks

Aylesbury	*Ship* *	Pightless Thorne	*Chequers* *
Edesborough	*Red Lion* *	Wendover	*Swan* *
Pightless Thorne	*Bell* *		

Key: * After 1872
          ** After 1876
          # After 1903

CHAPTER THIRTY-SIX

Dunstable, Bedfordshire

Bennett's breweries

The history of the Bennett family in relation to brewing is unusual. Initially the family owned a small brewery in Dunstable, Bedfordshire. Later a lease was agreed for the Harpenden Brewery in Harpenden (Curtis, Healey) and another lease for Edward's brewery in Redbourn. At this stage the family were described as Bennett's of Harpenden. This implies that the business base had moved into Hertfordshire. In 1887 Benjamin Bennett II bought the small North Western Brewery in Houghton Regis in Bedfordshire. After the leases finished for the Harpenden and Redbourn breweries, the North Western Brewery became the only brewery site until the business was sold to Mann, Crossman & Paulin in 1938.

Benjamin Bennett I was born in 1810 and described as a brewer and maltster by 1839. He bought the small ale and porter brewery in Chambers Yard, 12–16 High Street North, Dunstable. This brewery was on a plot behind Lloyds Bank, near to the north-east corner of Church Street and West Street. A tied estate was created and it included the *Anchor* (*White Horse*) in Dunstable, the *White Horse* in Eton Bray, the *Crown* and the *Swan* in Houghton Regis, the *King's Arms*, the *Oddfellows' Arms* and the *Three Horseshoes* in Luton and the *Hare* in Toddington.

Benjamin Bennett II inherited his father's business when he was living at Cheveralls Park near Markyate. During 1874 he obtained a leasing agreement of nineteen years for Healey's Harpenden Brewery. Shortly afterwards his business became known as Bennett's of Harpenden in licensing records in both Bedfordshire and Hertfordshire. A little later, from 1882 to 1897, he leased the Redbourn Brewery from the Bowes Lyon family. This Redbourn site was probably used for extra brewing and malting capacity for his growing tied estate. He later bought some of the Redbourn Brewery tied estate from the Bowes Lyon family (see Table 21.1).

Table 36.1 Bennett's known tied estate

Herts

Abbot's Langley	Rose and Crown	High Barnet	White Horse
Apsley	White Lion m.	Hitchin	Old White Horse
Bendish	Woodman	Leverstock Green	Plough m.
Bushey	Forester's Arms m.	London Colney	Bull and Butcher L.*
Flamstead	Chequers m.	Mangrove, Lilley	King William IV OL
	Horse and Groom*	Markyate	Horse and Groom*
	Three Blackbirds m.	Offley	Bull m.
	Waggon and Horses *		OL*
Great Gaddesden	Cock and Bottle m.	Redbourn	Bull L.*
Hadley	White Horse		Saracen's Head m.
Harpenden	Carpenters' Arms m.		Sheep Wash
	Leather Bottle	St Albans	Hope BH
	Marquis of Granby m.		Queen BH
	Old Bell m.		Queen Victoria
	Plough and Harrow		Verulam Arms L.
	White Lion		White Hart
Hatfield	Rising Sun m.		White Hart Tap
Hemel Hempstead	Brickmakers' OL m.		OL Alexandra Rd m.
	Lock House*	St Paul's Walden	Strathmore Arms m.
	Old Bell Gate*	Wheathampstead	Rose and Crown m.
	White Lion m.	Whitwell	Woodmill

Beds

Caddington	Bell	Houghton Regis	Oddfellows' Arms
	Cricketers m.		Pheasant m.
	Horse and Jockey m.		Swan L.
Chalton	Star Inn m.		Wheatsheaf m.
Dunstable	Anchor (White Horse)	Humbershoe	Bull and Butcher OL
	Britannia L.	Kemsworth	Farmer's Boy m.
	Carpenters' Arms		Rose and Crown
	Crown m.	Leighton Buzzard	Wheatsheaf m.
	Eight Bells m.	Limbury	Three Horseshoes L.
	First and Last m.	Luton	Albion # m.
	Greyhound m.		Black Horse m.
	New Inn L.		Blockers' Arms m.
	Nightingale		Blue Lion
	Rifle Volunteer m.		Cock and Magpie m.
	Sportsman's Arms m.		King's Arms ## m.
	Star and Garter m.		Moulder's Arms m.
	Victoria m.		Oddfellows' Arms m.
	Wheelwrights' Arms L.		Sugar Loaf m.
Eaton Bray	Chequers m.		Welcome Stranger m.
	Hope and Anchor m.		BH 3 Boyle St m.
	Victoria Arms		BH 12 Havelock Rd m.
	Volunteer (Rifleman)		BH 48 Midland Rd m.
Eversholt	Pheasant m.		BH address unclear m.
Harlington	Carpenters' Arms m.	Shefford	Swan m.
	Rising Sun	Toddington	Hare
Houghton Regis	Crown m.		Oddfellows' Arms m.
	Five Bells		Pheasant
	Star		

Greater London

Edgware	*Beehive* m.	Harrow Weald	*Alma* m.
	Leather Bottle m.		

Key: * Not after 1903
            # Ebenezer Street
            ## Chapel Hill
            m. Sold to Mann & Co.

During 1887 Benjamin Bennett II acquired Cutler & Henceman's North Western Brewery in Houghton Regis on the north-west corner of High Street North and Chiltern Road. Between 1864 and 1869 it had been owned by Henry Simpson and then by his widow until 1876. The tied estate had included the *Carpenters' Arms* at Harlington, the *Sugar Loaf* at Luton and the *White Hart* at Sundon. Rowland Cutler bought the brewery in 1877. He already was employed as the manager and he also owned the *Hope and Anchor* at Eaton Bray. In 1885 Cutler went into partnership with Henry Henchman. They became the registered owners of the *Borough Arms*, the *Carpenters' Arms*, the *Eight Bells* and the *New Inn*, all in Dunstable. This partnership ceased and Henchman went into partnership with W.S. Green. Unfortunately Green died a few months later and the brewery was again for sale in November when bought by Benjamin Bennett II.

Soon afterwards the ale and porter brewery was converted into a malting and all brewing in Dunstable was transferred to the North Western Brewery. Gradually this site was developed with additions in 1888 and 1893 to increase brewing capacity and also for mineral water manufacture. Bennett built up a tied estate of over fifty properties during the 1890s including three tied houses in Middlesex. In 1905 there was a major fire on the Dunstable site and much of the complex had to be rebuilt. There was another fire in 1908 when the malting on the ale and porter brewery site was damaged.

Bennett II died in 1911 and the brewery was then successfully managed by a group of trustees, but tied houses were registered in Petty Sessions licensing records as belonging to Mrs Louisa Charlotte Susannah Bennett. Extensions were made to the fermenting room at the brewery in 1924 and further extensions were made to the maltings in 1922 and 1936. Small additions to the tied estate included the *Farmer's Boy* at Kensworth and in 1922 the brewery was supplying beer to the *Swan*, a free house at Studham. In June 1938 the brewery and fifty-nine tied houses were sold to Mann, Crossman & Paulin. It has been possible to identify thirty-five in Bedfordshire, seventeen in Hertfordshire and three in Greater London (Table 36.1). The remaining four are thought to have been in

Buckinghamshire and Greater London. Brewing ceased at the North Western Brewery in Dunstable very soon after the sale. Buildings on this site were finally demolished in 1971.

References

Bedfordshire County Record Office. B/DP 1046 (1936 plan of extension to malting in Dunstable). There are also B/DP plans for the brewery and malting in 1888, 1893, 1911, 1922 and 1924.

Hertfordshire Archives and Local Studies. D/Ex 98 Z8 (Rate assessment for public houses in Harpenden and Wheathampstead).

Osbourne, K.W. *Bedfordshire Barrels*, Hampshire Hogsheads, 2005, pp.50–3.

Petty Sessions Licensing Records for Hertfordshire, Bedfordshire and North London.

Richmond, L. and Turton, A. (eds.) *The Brewing Industry: A Guide to Historical Records*, Manchester University Press, 1990, p.65.

Luton, Bedfordshire

Phoenix Brewery

John William Green bought the Phoenix Brewery in Luton from Henry and Frederick Pearman in 1869 when he was only twenty-two, using money from an inheritance. Later in Luton he also acquired the small brewery of Wadsworth & Thaire and the larger brewery belonging to the Sworders with fifty-eight licensed properties. The Phoenix Brewery then became the main site for brewing. Most of the tied estate was in Bedfordshire but a small number of individual purchases were made in North Hertfordshire (Table 37.1).

In 1919, John Green began a long-term major acquisition programme that was later continued by Bernard Dixon. In Hertfordshire it began with Glover & Sons of Harpenden (1919), followed by W.S. Lucas of Hitchin (1923), Adey & White of St Albans (1936), J. & J.E. Phillips of Royston (1949) and finally K.E. Fordham of Ashwell (1952). This gave Green's a major presence in Hertfordshire as well as other tied houses in Cambridgeshire, Essex and Suffolk. Elsewhere there were take-overs of Morris & Co. of Ampthill (1926), W.E. & H. Kelsey of Tunbridge Wells (1948), George Ware & Sons of Frant (1950), Soulby, Sons & Winch of Grantham (1951) and finally Flower & Sons of Stratford on Avon (1954). The business was renamed Flowers Breweries Ltd (formerly J.W. Green Ltd). At this stage it had a tied estate of over 1,500 tied properties with the main brewery sites in Luton and Stratford on Avon. Eight years later the company was itself taken over by Whitbread & Company Ltd.

Table 37.1 Green's independent tied estate in Hertfordshire

Herts			
Baldock	*Victoria* F	Preston	*Red Lion* F
Codicote	*Bell* F	Redbourn	*Lark* BH
Flamstead	*Half Moon* F		*Queen Victoria* BH
Harpenden	*Engineer* BH	St Albans	*Blacksmiths' Arms* BH
	Forester's Arms BH		*Cricketers* F
Hemel Hempstead	*Queen's Head* BH		*Crown* F
Hitchin	*Bedford Arms* BH		*Duke of St Albans* BH
	Prince Albert F		*Jolly Maltster* BH
	Radcliffe Arms BH		*Plough* F
	Sugar Loaf BH		*Rising Sun* BH
Markyate	*Bull & Butcher* OL	St Ippollytts	*Olive Branch* BH
Offley	*Green Man* F, L.	Wheathampstead	*Bull* F
Pirton	*White Horse* F		

References

Petty Sessions Licensing Records for Hertfordshire.

Richmond, L. and Turton, A. (eds.) *The Brewing Industry: A Guide to Historical Records*, Manchester University Press, 1990, pp.144–5.

Smith, S. *Pubs and Pints: The story of Luton's public houses and breweries*, Dunstable, The Book Castle, 1995, pp.13–37.

CHAPTER THIRTY-EIGHT

Bedford, Bedfordshire

Charles Wells Ltd

Charles Wells bought the Horne Lane Brewery in Bedford plus thirty-five licensed properties in 1876 from Joseph Piggott and Henry Wells. The brewery was rebuilt in 1877 and further additions were made in the 1880s and 1890s. The business was increased in size by the takeovers of the Newport Pagnell Brewery in 1919, part of the tied estate of Day & Co. of St Neots in 1920, Jarvis & Co. of Bedford in 1923, Fuller & Son of Bedford in 1935 and Abington Park Brewery of Northampton in 1963. The Horne Lane Brewery was closed in 1976 and brewing was transferred to a new purpose-built brewery in Havelock Street, Bedford.

Charles Wells Ltd has never taken over any breweries in Hertfordshire but gradually bought licensed properties throughout the county from 1872 to the present day (Table 38.1). The original purchases in Hitchin were probably justified because of the advantage of the direct railway link between Bedford and Hitchin over slow delivery by horse and brewery dray. Most other properties were obtained when the management of other major breweries decided to sell individual properties. The Hertfordshire component of the estate is only a small part of the present-day tied estate of approximately 300 properties.

References

Page, K. Personal communication. Historical details of tied estate in Hertfordshire.
Petty Sessions Licensing Records for Hertfordshire.
Richmond, L. and Turton, A. (eds.) *The Brewing Industry: A Guide to Historical Records*, Manchester University Press, 1990, p.358.

Table 38.1 Charles Wells' brewery estate in Hertfordshire

		Notes
Ashwell	*Bushel and Strike*	Bought from Flowers 1964
Borehamwood	*Suffolk Punch*	Bought from Bass 1978, sold 1981
Bushey	*King's Head*	Bought from Allied 1989
	Royal Oak	Bought from Allied 1986
Charlton	*Windmill*	Bought from Flowers 1960
Harpenden	*Silver Cup*	Bought from Flowers 1979
Hemel Hempstead	*Olde King's Arms*	Bought from McMullen 1979
Hitchin	*Bricklayer's Arms*	Bought from Pickering 1895
	Fountain	Opened 1959*, closed 1996
	King William IV	Bought from Pickering 1895, closed 1959*
	Robin Hood	Owned in 1872, closed by early 1900s
	Two Brewers	Bought from Lucas 1885, closed 1921
New Barnet	*Railway Tavern*	Bought from Bass 1991
Pirton	*Cat and Fiddle*	Bought from Pickering 1895
Royston	*Chequers*	Bought from Whitbread 1990
	Old Bull	Bought from Whitbread 1988
St Albans	*Jolly Sailor*	Bought from Allied 1976

Key: * Change of licence

CHAPTER THIRTY-NINE

Saffron Walden, Essex

Anchor Brewery

In the early 1800s, the Gibsons, a Quaker family owned the Anchor Brewery and a malting in the High Street, Saffron Walden. Members of the Gibson family were also partners in a bank in the town. The brewery was bought in 1839 by another Quaker, Joseph Taylor, who was a malt factor and barge owner in Bishop's Stortford. He did a considerable amount of business with Trumans and other big London breweries. Joseph passed on the ownership of the brewery and a malting to his son Henry who was followed by W. & J. Taylor in 1861. They were in turn succeeded by J.W. & J.L. Taylor in 1877. During 1897 the brewery and tied estate of eighty licensed houses was sold to Reid & Co. at the Griffin Brewery, London EC1. The company directors soon decided to stop brewing in Saffron Walden but keep the tied estate. In 1898 Reid & Co. Ltd amalgamated with Watney, Combe & Co. at the Stag Brewery, Pimlico, London SW.

During the First World War, transport and distribution of beer from London to the north-west of Essex became a major logistical problem. In 1919, Watney's East Anglian tied estate (ex-Taylors) of approximately seventy to eighty public houses was therefore put up for sale. Benskin's of Watford purchased these properties on 15 December 1919. Benskin's brewery already was well established in Essex, since it previously had bought Hawkes' Brewery in Bishop's Stortford in 1898, and therefore owned licensed properties in many of the small towns and villages on the western side of Essex. The Hawkes' brewery site was already an established distribution depot in 1919.

Benskin's available records of licensed properties originally belonging to Taylor's lists fifty-seven in Essex, eleven in Cambridgeshire, three in Suffolk and six in Hertfordshire giving a total of seventy-five. Essex Petty Sessions licensing records show that the *Gate* at Chrisall and the *Red Lion* at Withersfield had their licences refused while being owned by Watney's. The combined total of seventy-

Table 39.1 Taylor's tied estate in East Anglia sold to Benskin's

Herts

Bishop's Stortford	Black Lion	Great Amwell	Royal Oak
	Jolly Brewers	Thorley	Coach and Horses
	Plume of Feathers	Ware	Royal Oak

Cambs

Balsham	Bell	Linton	Bell
Brinkley	Red Lion	Sawston	White Lion
Duxford	Three Horseshoes	Shudy Camps	Chequers
Great Chishill	Plough		Three Horseshoes
Horseheath	Red Lion	West Wratting	Waggon and Horses
Ickleton	Duke of Wellington		

Essex

Arkesden	Green Man	Saffron Walden	Castle
Ashdon	Fox		Cross Keys
	Lamb		Eight Bells
Birdbrook	Plough		Fleur de Lys
Bocking	Horse and Groom		George
Debden	Fox		Greyhound
	White Hart		Hoops
Dunmow	Boar's Head		King's Arms
	Star		Railway Arms
Elmdon	King's Head		White Horse
Elsenham	Crown	Sewards End	Butcher's Arms
Great Chesterford	Crown and Thistle		Fox
	White Horse		Green Dragon
Great Sampford	Black Bull	Stansted	Barley Mow
Great Wratting	Red Lion		Bell and Feathers
Hempstead	Rose and Crown	Stebbing	King's Head
Henham	Bell	Steeple Bumpstead	Fox and Hounds
Lindsell	Crown	Thaxted	Bull
Little Chesterford	Bushel and Strike		Star
	Crown	Ugley	White Hart
Little Walden	Crown	Wendens Ambo	Fighting Cocks
Littlebury	Queen's Head		Neville Arms
Newport	Coach and Horses	Widdington	Fleur de Lys
	Hercules	Wimbish	Pudding
	Railway		Star
	Three Tuns		White Hart
Quendon	King's Head	Withersfield	White Horse
Radwinter	Red Lion		

Suffolk

Haverhill	Bull	Haverhill	Rose and Crown
	Ram		

seven known properties suggests that there might have been as many as few as three closures or property sales between 1897 and 1919 (Watney's) or since 1919 (Benskin's, Ind Coope, Allied Breweries, etc.) that have not been identified.

There are also three properties on a Benskin's transfer document to Ind Coope (East Anglia) in 1957 that may have originally belonged to Taylor's. These are an off-licence in Feering, the *Rayleigh Arms* at Terling and the *New Inn* at Waltham Abbey which need further research to establish their original brewery ties.

References

Allied Archives. Benskin's 1957 East Anglian estate.

Hertfordshire Archives and Local Studies. a. Acc. 3883. Box 24 Shelf 50–1. Property registers for Bishop's Stortford and Essex for 1959–73 (Details of ex-Taylor's properties).

Petty Sessions Licensing Records for Hertfordshire, Cambridgeshire and west Essex.

Richmond, L. and Turton, A. (eds) *The Brewing Industry: A Guide to Historical Records*, Manchester University Press, 1990, pp.66, 274.

Stratford, I. Personal communication about ex-Taylor's estate.

CHAPTER FORTY

Stanmore, Greater London

Thomas Clutterbuck & Co.

Clutterbuck's Brewery on the top of Stanmore Hill was established in 1763 by Thomas Clutterbuck in a partnership with Thomas Meadows, a Watford corn dealer. Since 1740 Thomas Clutterbuck had previously held the post of land agent to the Earl of Essex. He married Sarah Thurgood, the daughter of Robert Thurgood a brewer in Baldock. When her father died in 1775 she inherited the

Table 40.1 Clutterbuck's tied estate in Hertfordshire sold to the Cannon Brewery

Herts			
Abbot's Langley	Maltman's Arms	Chipping Barnet	Bull
	Three Tuns		Bull's Head
	Unicorn	Colney Street	George and Dragon
	Waggon and Horses		Red Cow
Aldenham	Red Lion	Croxley Green	Artichoke
	Three Horseshoes	East Barnet	King's Head
	Waggon and Horses		Railway Bell
Arkeley	Gate (Old Bell)	Elstree	Artichoke
Barnet	Bell		Old Holly Bush
	Green Dragon		Plough
	Lord Nelson	Hemel Hempstead	White Hart
Bedmond	Bell	King's Langley	Lamb
Boreham Wood	Crown	Lilley	Red Lion
Bricket Wood	Gate	North Mymms	Old Maypole
Bushey	Bell	Oxhey	Victoria
	Black Boy	Park Street	Red Lion
	Coach and Horses	Potters Bar	Green Man
	Fishmonger's Arms	St Albans	Six Bells
	King's Head	Sarratt	Cart and Horses
	Merry Month of May		Jolly Gardeners
	Railway Tavern	South Mimms	Green Man
	Rifle Volunteer	Watford	Green Man
	Stag		Horns
	Three Crowns		Spread Eagle
Chandlers Cross	Clarendon Arms		Victoria
Chipping Barnet	Black Horse		

Table 40.2 Clutterbuck's disposals from their tied estate in Hertfordshire before the takeover by the Cannon Brewery in 1923

Herts			
Aldenham	Coach and Horses	Park Street	Red Cow
	Jolly Gardeners	Radlett	Jolly Gardeners
Barnet	Three Horseshoes	Redbourn	Saracen's Head
Berkhamsted	Red Lion	Rickmansworth	Forester's Arms
Bricket Wood	Old Fox		Queen's Arms
Bushey	Crown and Sceptre		Red Lion
Chipping Barnet	Lord Nelson	St Albans	Peacock L. c.1780
Colney Street	Black Horse	Shenley	BH
Flamstead	Three Blackbirds	Watford	Crystal Palace
Hemel Hempstead	Swan Bourne End		Gander
Lilley	Lilley Arms L.		Rifle Volunteer
	Silver Lion L.		Three Horseshoes
London Colney	White Horse	Watford Heath	Royal Oak
Park Street	Green Dragon		

Mansion House, a brewery and a malting in Baldock High Street, and a small tied estate. Their son, Robert Clutterbuck, inherited the Baldock brewery and estate in 1788. However his grandfather, Robert Thurgood, had put certain constraints in his will. It was necessary to obtain a private act of parliament before Robert could legally sell the Baldock bequest to the Pryor family in 1799. It is likely that the money obtained from the Baldock sale was invested in the expansion of the Stanmore brewery when Robert succeeded his father Thomas and began buying inns and beer houses to form a tied estate.

This policy was continued for the next hundred years until the tied estate extended to Norwood Green, Greater London to the south and as far north as Redbourn and Lilley in Hertfordshire. There were originally eight tied houses in Stanmore including the *Vine* (Brewery Tap), *Crown, May Tree* and *Royal Oak*. In Harrow Weald there was the *Seven Bells* and in Pinner the *Queen's Head*. However the major part of the estate was in the south west of Hertfordshire where there were originally eleven tied houses in Bushey and ten in Barnet (including Chipping and East Barnet). This widespread estate must have made delivery by horse and dray a major undertaking before the widespread use of motorised transport.

Other members of the Clutterbuck family owned large farms in Bushey and Sarratt near Watford. Hops were grown on the Warren House estate. Malting barley may have been grown to supply the Clutterbuck malting in Sopwell Lane, St Albans and two other maltings in Watford and Langleybury (sites unknown).

The brewery never bottled its own beers. Instead supplies of both bottled and other draught beers were obtained from Bass & Co. of Burton on Trent. Brewing was stopped at Stanmore in 1916 and the site was only used for storage and as a depot. All beers were subsequently bought from Bass. When the brewery was finally sold in 1923 to the Cannon Brewery of Clerkenwell, London, the estate consisted of eighty-three properties, of which forty-seven were in Hertfordshire and another twenty-six in Hertfordshire had been closed, sold or leases terminated (Table 40.1 and 40.2).

From the late 1920s until the 1980s, the brewery buildings were used by a company that made garden and sports equipment. Afterwards most of the site was cleared for a small housing development. Now only the clock tower, the coach house and the head brewer's house remain.

References

Dines, D. Thomas Clutterbuck's Stanmore Brewery, *Brewery History*, 1994, No. 77, pp.33–40.

Petty Sessions Licensing Records for Hertfordshire.

General Index

271

Places Index

Public House Index